The Astrology
of
Awakening

Volume 2:
Chart Application and Counseling

Eric Meyers, M.A.

The Astrology of Awakening
Volume 2: Chart Application & Counseling

Published by Astrology Sight Publishing
Sacramento, California

ISBN Number: 978-0-9747766-2-0

Printed in the United States of America

For more info about Eric and his astrology services, books, or newsletter, please visit the website:

www.SoulVisionConsulting.com

email: eric@soulvisionconsulting.com

Cover image is a Crab Nebula taken from the Hubble Telescope, it appears courtesy of NASA

Graphic design and interior figures by Bill Streett
Back cover photograph taken by Kathy Brodie

Dedicated to all of the clients I've had the privilege to serve.
Thank you for generously entrusting me with your souls.

Also by the author:

The Astrology of Awakening Volume 1:
Eclipse of the Ego
(2012)

Elements & Evolution:
The Spiritual Landscape of Astrology
(2010)

Uranus: The Constant of Change
(2008)

Between Past & Presence:
A Spiritual View of the Moon & Sun
(2006)

The Arrow's Ascent:
Astrology & The Quest for Meaning
(2004)

"There are two basic motivating forces: fear and love. When we are afraid, we pull back from life. When we are in love, we open to all that life has to offer with passion, excitement, and acceptance. We need to learn to love ourselves first, in all our glory and our imperfections. If we cannot love ourselves, we cannot fully open to our ability to love others or our potential to create. Evolution and all hopes for a better world rest in the fearlessness and open-hearted vision of people who embrace life."
~John Lennon

"We are made of Light. We are children of Light. We are sons and daughters of the Sun." ~Thich Nhat Hanh

"In order to come into our full potential and to embody the truth and radiance of what we are, we must come vitally alive; we must lean once again into presence; we must pour ourselves forth into life, instead of trying to escape life and avoid its challenges. Then our lives themselves become expressions of love, of overflow, because we have compassionately given ourselves to life, to our incarnation, as a means to redeem it—to bring everything home, back to its source, to the eternal radiance within each and every one of us." ~Adyashanti

"The nature of awakening is not transcendence. It is not detachment. It is not leaving our bodies. It is not dismissing our shadow. It is not bashing our story. It is not feigned positivity. It is not new age mysticism. It is not pseudo non-duality. The nature of awakening is inclusivity. It is connectiveness. It is shadow and light. It is enheartened presence. And presence is not to be found on the skyways of self-avoidance. Presence is to be found right down here, in our body temples, sole to soul on mother earth. Awakening requires that we show up for all of it. The great in-wakening. The wholly holy." ~Jeff Brown

Contents

Part 2 — Counseling

Introduction

"Love is the bridge between you and everything." ~Rumi

The heart is a divine muscle—as it develops, so does the world. As we deepen into the self, we strengthen our core spiritual foundation. Love is joyously radiated out into all of life and shapes our existence. What was once an uncertain (and sometimes threatening) world transforms into a haven of grace. Sounds simple, but it is a process that can take a *very* long time to develop.

It's useful to have a guide for the journey. The aim of this book is to clarify how each person's astrology chart depicts a unique path of awakening. The roots of our spiritual condition are clarified as a foundation to flower into the creativity of our souls. We extend outwards to make conscious connection with all of life. It turns out that the life force that envelops us is an organization of unfathomable intelligence.

And here we are, the individual in relationship with the enormity of nature. The individual seems to be limited, finite, gloriously imperfect and human, while nature operates in exquisite eternal perfection. However, we might bridge these worlds and bring "heaven" down to "earth" and create a partnership. We accomplish this by securing a loving foundation and resolving the issues and blockages that obscure the light of our souls. Then we become a clear vessel of physicality to distribute spiritual creativity.

C.S. Lewis is quoted as saying, "You do not have a soul. You are a soul. You have a body." Astrology can help us remember who we *really* are, essentially a temporary physical vessel for an eternal soul. Many of us have forgotten our inherent genius, our energetic spiritual power. The Sun's light illuminates everything, and its heat sustains all of existence. Spaceship Earth orbits around the Sun, which holds it in place through gravity. The Sun is our star, the source of life for us all. We are *children of the Sun*, occupying our beautiful and precious humanness to ground this creative energy in tangible expressions for our evolution.

As children of the universe, we naturally start out less mature in the evolutionary curriculum and advance as we go. We attend to the requirements of being human, mainly to survive and attain happiness. Initially, we forget that we're the pervasive light of divinity that shines through everything.

Glinda the Good Witch tells Dorothy at the conclusion of the *Wizard of Oz* that she has always had the power within her to go home. The Scarecrow asks Glinda why she didn't tell Dorothy earlier. Glinda responds that Dorothy wouldn't have believed her—*she had to learn it for herself.* Likewise, we each go through many lessons as we learn of our inherent divinity, a homecoming into our spiritual selves.

From a spiritual perspective, the Sun is the radiance of soul realization—we have access to the boundless, multidimensional creativity of being the life force itself. Our task is to realize this in physical form (Moon) as separate beings, as the children of the Sun. Now is the crucial time frame in which we're being challenged to become adults. Much of this is to accept our spiritual lessons with openness, responsibility and joy, rather than to jockey for only positive experiences at the personality level. This book aims to structure a new approach to astrology with that goal.

Spiritual Counseling

The Astrology of Awakening approach is a form of *spiritual counseling*, which can be loaded with connotations. There is absolutely no religiosity to our use of this word; the meaning is far broader. Eckhart Tolle says, "You are the universe expressing itself as a human for a little while." The aim of this approach is simple: to mature the human part of us so we can identify and connect with the broader universe. We are waking up from identifying solely as an "I," then using the "I" in greater partnership with the intelligence that envelops us.

Some are cautious, skeptical or resistant to bringing any spirituality into astrology. To this author, this is inconsistent with the nature of what astrology points to. Anyone who studies astrology can clearly see that there is an intelligence operating that is beyond us. Humans did not design the Solar System and starry heavens.

The question is not whether we should acknowledge spirituality in our astrological approach, but how we choose to do so. As will be discussed in the opening chapter, this approach is based on universal principles of spiritual evolution that have the broadest possible consensus. The *Perennial Philosophy* forms the foundation—the basic idea that Oneness operates within separation and can be realized consciously. Therefore, as Tolle mentions, we are awakening an awareness that there is more to us than we realize—a lot more!

I believe we are at a new frontier with our use of astrology. Relatively speaking, there is not much written about astrological counseling. The overwhelming focus is on "reading" charts for clients to provide them with information, to tell them of their energetic composition and what the universe has in store for them. Instead of supporting spiritual maturation, the terms of the discussion are largely to provide the self-knowledge to understand our "fate." Now we are poised to move forward—to *consult* with clients about strengthening a *partnership* with this intelligent cosmos.

On Reform

I write this book between 2012 and 2015, during the climax of the Uranus–Pluto square. There is evidence everywhere of this frictional dynamic between opening to progressive new visions and the resistance to change and entrenchment in the past. With Uranus in Aries, each individual is learning to summon the personal courage to reinvent the self, and together we change the world. With Pluto in Capricorn, we ideally sift through what we've inherited, preserving and strengthening what survives the test of time. The integration occurs when we bring a new vision (Uranus in Aries) to a durable foundation.

Too often people think in competitive ways, as if one way emerges as victorious and everything else is misguided. Instead, I invite you to look at this approach as building from the foundation already in place. Just as the planets orbit in concentric circles around the Sun, there are layers around layers of consciousness. When we discover a new layer, it doesn't render the previous as erroneous but rather complements and builds on it. This is the spirit of evolution and is found in all fields. Plugging in guitars to make them electrified is an innovation, not a statement that acoustic guitars are wrong. Adding new technologies to our automobiles enhances them, most people use computers now instead of typewriters, and advancements in science assist the medical industry in treating patients through MRI and the like. The view here is that astrology can be *like all other fields* that adapt and modernize with the times.

The approach spelled out in this book renews and honors the universal, time-tested basics of the astrological system (planets, signs, houses, aspects, elements, and modalities). Astrology developed with Saturn as the furthest known orbiting planet, and we previously thought the Earth was at the center of the universe. The field developed the only way it could: within a

Saturnian and egocentric mindset and value system. This is relevant to one perspective, but there are others. We will explore astrology by integrating a trans-Saturnian perspective. After all, we are looking at a *metaphysical* system. The *Awakening* approach integrates with consciousness beyond Saturn and is based on today's understanding of the composition of our Solar System.

The Path Ahead

This book is split into two main parts. Chart Application comprises the first nine chapters, while Counseling (and Discussion) forms the remainder. The first part mainly discusses how to understand charts from the perspective described in brief above. Though many people interested in astrology do not come to be professional counseling astrologers, I believe all readers will find the second part to be of interest. In fact, much of the material in that section would be useful for anyone interested in spiritual growth.

Chapter 1 reviews the basis of this approach, and provides a condensed account of some main points from Volume 1 of this series and my earlier works. In particular, it lays out the model of evolutionary levels of consciousness, with which the reader should become familiar.

Chapter 2 addresses fundamental building blocks of astrology: planets, signs, houses, aspects, elements and modalities. All of these will be introduced and discussed from a spiritual perspective.

The Moon, the Nodes of the Moon, and the Sun form the crux of this approach. They are addressed in Chapters 3 through 6. Analogous to the seed (Moon), the gardening (Nodes of the Moon), and the flower (Sun), they detail the process of spiritual awakening from initial egoic identification (Moon), the habits and patterns which stem from this (Nodes), and the blossoming into the soul self (Sun).

In addition to these factors, Pluto is the final piece that completes what I term the *chart skeleton.* Chapter 7 will explore the Plutonian shadow and its relation to the awakening process. The chart skeleton is the basic structure of evolutionary motion in this approach, and chart examples will bring it to life.

Chapter 8 focuses on charts: factors concerning set-up, organization and how to approach what we see. How do we make meaning of the various pieces and connect them? This chapter touches on various topics such as retrogrades and declination, as well as the process of chart synthesis.

Chapter 9 explores the collective scope of Jupiter and Saturn, and the transpersonal scope of Uranus and Neptune as represented in charts.

The second part of the book addresses counseling. Chapter 10 is a discussion of the role of the astrological counselor. What are we really doing? What is involved? A conversation about logistical issues and counseling is offered.

Chapter 11 provides in-depth commentary on how a session is conducted. There are four major segments: Introduction, Deepening, Emergence and Conclusion. We will go through a session from beginning to end, illustrating the art of astrological counseling using the *Awakening* approach.

The next two chapters introduce many counseling strategies and techniques that can be brought in. I explain and share many of the counseling "tools" I have used in actual sessions. Chapter 12 mainly addresses how to work with the issues that keep people unconsciously perpetuating their patterns. Chapter 13 is organized to address the four levels of experience (physical, emotional, mental, soul) in a counseling context, and suggestions to work with each of these realms.

Chapter 14 is a discussion of issues which tend to emerge with clients: how to address frequently asked questions, giving advice, personal sharing, perceptions of astrology, addressing darkness, professional boundaries and more.

Finally, Chapter 15 is a discussion and summation of the main points, clarifying the message and vision of this approach. I share a bit of my process in writing this book and end with some brief acknowledgements.

Part 1 — Chart Application

Chapter 1
Overview of the Awakening Approach

Volume 1 of this series was philosophical, while this book is dedicated to chart application. It would be redundant to spend a lot of time explaining the underpinnings of this approach; the reader is encouraged to refer to the previous work. However, it may be of service to provide a brief outline of some of the main points to orient the reader and to serve as a handy reference resource. Also, this approach is new to most, so some reinforcement of the key points can be helpful. (There is some intentional repetition of major points in this book as we are learning to view life through a different construct.) This chapter is a review of the basis of the approach, covering the overarching motion of evolutionary growth, levels of consciousness, and the two main levels of reality (the transpersonal and the relative).

Evolutionary Growth

The concept of spiritual evolution is central to this approach. Though controversial to some, a belief in reincarnation enjoys increasing popularity worldwide, including in the United States. To me, in an endlessly intelligent, multi-dimensional and meaningful universe in which energy is never created or destroyed, it would actually be surprising if we didn't grow in the way implied through reincarnation. Nature portrays the cycles of the seasons, the regeneration of life in the spring after the decay in winter. To be forthright, it's difficult for me to understand the birth chart without this framework. Why would there be particular tendencies, unresolved needs and ingrained patterns if we were blank slates at birth? It's beyond the scope of this book to debate the legitimacy of the phenomenon thoroughly. I assume that if you're reading this, you have, at least, some openness to it.

Human development, the growth from infant to child to adult, is obvious and universal. We can look at this as a parallel to spiritual growth. We all begin in states of less maturation, learn through experience, and attain greater wisdom as we go. It is helpful in our development to live out the ways in which we are not yet spiritually mature and conscious to increase awareness of what we need to work on. In this approach, we look to the Moon like a baby human seed that is spiritually flowering.

There have been countless models of spiritual evolution put forth, in a myriad of historical periods and cultures. The table below is based on the cross-cultural and integrative work of transpersonal philosopher Ken Wilber. He strived to clarify a universal process of spiritual development, which enjoys the broadest possible consensus. The reader is encouraged to become familiar with these stages, as they will be referred to throughout the book. Each stage has a number and a name, as well as a particular developmental process. To translate the stages into astrological terms, I have included associations with the planets.

Our Model of Spiritual Development

Stage	Name	Planet(s)	Developmental Process
1	Physical Self	Earth Venus and Mercury	Identification as a body: foundation, senses, embodiment, physical orientation
2	Emotional Self	Moon, Mars	Identification with emotions: survival, protection, instinct

3	Conceptual Self	Air Venus and Mercury	Identification with the mind: perception, understanding and connection with the surrounding world
4	Role Self	Asteroids, Jupiter, Saturn	Identification as a social self: establishment of roles, viability and achievement, ethical standards
5	Mature Ego	Jupiter, Saturn	Identification as part of the collective: social interdependence, worldcentric view
6	Centaur	Chiron	Integration of body/mind system, healing and wholeness, resolution of separation
7	Psychic – Nature Mysticism	Uranus	Awakening to identify as nature: experience of self beyond separation, connected to "divine GPS"
8	Subtle – Deity Mysticism	Neptune, Pluto	Engagement with transpersonal experiences: mystical union, reconciliation of the shadow, conscious navigation of the dream space
9	Causal – Formless Mysticism	Sun	Identification as Source: abidance of consciousness in the emptiness of pure awareness and creative presence; enlightenment

The first three levels are basic and almost universally achieved in early child development. We all establish a relationship to body, heart, and mind quite naturally. The main point to take away is the building from physical (earth) to emotional (water) to mental (air), which we will review in the *elemental levels* later on. Central to this astrological approach is how the seed (Moon) develops into a flower (Sun). We see here that the first level (physical, earth) is analogous to the soil. After a foundation is attained (Level 1), our spiritual process begins with our emotional need for survival and happiness (2) as we grow to understand the surrounding world (3).

An individual enters the broader social milieu. It is necessary to get basic needs met (food, shelter, support, procreation), so there is a competitive outlook. We tend to evaluate quality of life in terms of how well these needs are met. The Conceptual Self (3) is trying to figure things out in the wider world (4) and uses dualistic pairings (good/bad, male/female) to help organize and understand life. People have roles based on these pairings, such as the traditional model of men going out in the world and women staying in the home.

At Level 4, the fabric of society becomes organized to *maintain stability*, and conformity is extremely important. Social order helps society advance. A workable social contract is attained—ideally people relax the egoic need for survival because resources are successfully allocated. However, the price to pay is adherence to the hierarchal structures put in place by those who have elbowed their way to the top.

Within Western culture in the modern era, men have unquestionably controlled the levers of power and have inserted a set of values and conditions that furthers their aims. This Patriarchal Value System (PVS) is thoroughly reviewed in the first volume of this series, and the reader is directed to that text for more information. The point is not that patriarchy should be seen as "bad" or "wrong." Rather, it has been an evolutionary step that can be understood at Level 4 of this model. The issue is whether we renew life at this level or keep progressing. The astrology at the time of this writing (Uranus–Pluto square) is precisely about this issue.

As the collective consciousness was necessarily operating at this developmental level, its values and perspectives enter and influence all of life, including astrology. It simply cannot be another way — in fact, our knowledge of the universe at the dawn of astrology precisely reflects this level. Saturn was known as the outermost planet, signifying that separation consciousness contained the collective experience. The Earth was understood as flat, indicative of *leveling distinctions of depth and height*. This is what we'll refer to as "flatland astrology," the negation of consciousness as an interactive variable. The planets were thought to revolve around the Earth, reflecting the egocentricity of conventional astrology. The Sun and Moon *appeared* to be the same size, and both were thought to produce light (called "the luminaries"). There is a *relative* truth to this view of the Sun and Moon, but we can all agree that it's not fully accurate or complete. It is the view from ego, which projects its most immediate experience (dualism, gender) onto life. (Today we know that 64 million Moons would fit inside the Sun. The Moon orbits around the Sun while reflecting its light.)

When astrology was developing, monarchies were the accepted government and economic structure, and technology was relatively primitive (compared to today). It was hundreds of years until the Copernican revolution or the pervasiveness of evolution as a concept. There was virtually no understanding of the complexities of consciousness as the field of psychology proliferated in the 20th Century. The last century also brought us greater synthesis between physics and consciousness, revealing the co-creative relationship between our minds and reality. We no longer can say that there's an objective world that operates like a machine. The modern concept is more akin to a dream laboratory drenched in subjectivity and conscious participation.

The planet Uranus was discovered in the 18th Century and correlated with the rise of democracy and major scientific advances. Astrology increasingly became estranged from mainstream institutions and was seen as occult and delegitimized. Meanwhile, Level 5 consciousness (Mature Ego) was gathering momentum. This worldcentric view of interdependence (instead of the domination and self-gain that typifies Level 4) accelerated evolution through a more democratic and collaborative mindset.

In the 19th Century, Neptune was discovered, and further exploration into consciousness (hypnosis, the beginnings of psychology, the Romantic Movement, mysticism) became more widespread. Pluto was discovered in 1930—the Neptunian "heights" of consciousness became more balanced by the Plutonian "depths" (shadow, sexuality, the specter of nuclear war, the Holocaust, etc.). The 20th Century saw a collective struggle of evolving consciousness from Levels 4 to 5—and the inevitable resistance. This reached a climax in the 1960s, which brought a marked increase in progressive and humanitarian consciousness (Level 5) petitioning the more domination ideology (Level 4) to reform.

Astrology enjoyed a resurgence of popularity at the Uranus–Pluto conjunction in the 1960s. A new, more humanistic and psychological wave flourished, which reflects Level 5 consciousness. The division of traditional and modern astrology created a polarization, one that still largely defines the field. The Uranus–Pluto conjunction launched a new epic of evolution, which has unfolded rapidly. Since the 1960s, technology has dramatically advanced, and our understanding of our Solar System, and the universe itself, has exponentially increased. Civil rights and feminism made great strides in opening the grip of patriarchy.

The advancement to Level 6 consciousness (Centaur) began to accelerate with the discovery of Chiron (a Centaur) in 1977 in synchronous fashion. There was an incredible proliferation of healing modalities that became widespread and available (Reiki, acupuncture, aromatherapy, chakra work, etc.). People began striving for maximal health and well-being as a central part of emotional and spiritual development. The human condition can now be seen as an *energy system* in need of balance, integration and attunement. This is vastly different from the materialistic focus of Saturn, with its characteristic cause-and-effect simplicity and mundane concerns.

We arrive at the Uranus–Pluto square in the 21st Century, the dominant astrological alignment of these times. The next step is the integration of the transpersonal. Level 7 consciousness (Nature Mysticism) opens to a thrilling and expansive connection with the universe. Ideally, the body–mind system is healed, integrated and aligned (Level 6), so the proverbial ship is ready to sail into the unknown. Just as each level has a different orientation to the world, *the world itself appears different at these levels*. At Level 4, it's a place to conquer, whereas Level 5 conveys a social contract to collectively advance. Level 6 sees the need to heal and transcend the issues that divide, both in the self and the world. The gargantuan movement to Level 7 is the awareness that the world is the self!

The Transpersonal

The Sun is radiant, shining its energy onto everything. Similarly, we project who we are onto life. We interact with our perception of the world, which originates in our thoughts, feelings and biases. Everything external to an individual is simply matter and energy; we create the stories about it all and experience the resulting drama. Similar to the content within dreams while asleep, waking life is an interaction with self. Each of us has a version of the world that is completely unique. This is the "ego dream" from which we are awakening.

Accepting that the external world is the self is quite perplexing, even threatening, at earlier developmental states. For many, it sounds like complete nonsense. The transpersonal is easily ignored, and society tends to condition us to do so. "Ideas of reference" is a phrase used by modern psychology as a diagnostic measurement of mental illness. It is "the notion that everything one perceives in the world relates to one's own destiny." Also called "delusions of reference," the implication is that seeing oneself in what is external is pathological. Certainly, the world can be misconstrued by disorganized thinking, and mental illness exists. However, this is the darker end of the spectrum, while the brighter side is mysticism. Instead of making this important distinction, society has thrown out the mystical baby with the dirty bath water of pathology. There is a tacit collective agreement to stay "sane" within separation consciousness, which may turn out to be completely backwards and contraindicative to spiritual health.

The myth of Saturn and Uranus portrays the removal (castration) of the transpersonal from everyday consciousness. Ouranos (Uranus) was seen as detached, tyrannical and inflexible. His wife Gaia was displeased by his lack of affection and did not care for his despotic rule over the children. Chronos (Saturn) took his scythe and castrated his father. This act portrays the state of separation in the manifest world (Saturn, Gaia) "severed" from the broader metaphysical realm of interconnectedness (Uranus). In the state of separation, we may become preoccupied with ensuring our survival. Saturn devoured his children in fear of being usurped himself. As physical beings, survival is necessary, but an over-attachment to this requirement inhibits our development, and we may end up harming others with our self-preoccupation!

We may be at the time in history when we heal the mythic castration. In fact, Level 6 is about healing and body–mind integration. Since Chiron's discovery, there has been a marked increase in developing maximal well-being and enhanced health—a surge of awareness about what we put into our bodies and how to maintain their integrity. All of this is preparation for the awakening into the transpersonal and its inclusion into culture, society, and the everyday world (Saturn). If we are sick, low-energy, off-kilter or battling ailments in some way, it's more of a challenge to experience a clarity of awareness and to be present to all of life.

At Level 7, the mystical viewpoint is being affirmed by modern science, particularly quantum physics, which pro-liferated in the last century. The universe can be understood as a phenomenal neural matrix in which all things are interconnected. Matter is a temporary crystallization of energy, just a slower vibration. All energy is in a state of uncertainty, continually in flux. Instead of solidity or objectivity, there are *tendencies to exist*. These tendencies can be understood as probability fields, and *the interaction of consciousness co-creates our perception and experience of the world.* It is now accepted that "the observer impacts the object of observation," an admission that our consciousness is not contained within the human system. Physicists remove themselves from observing their own experiments because their consciousness is an influencing variable.

Uranus (and its associated sign Aquarius) concerns the vast mental organization of nature. Astrology itself is a part of its scope. The connections between an individual and the greater universe operate *metaphysically* (through energy, awareness), not purely through physical connections such as cables or wires. The parallel we are seeing with technology ("cloud" storage, wifi, cell phones, etc.) illustrates that we are rapidly developing beyond dependency on the earth realm. We are incorporating an airy orientation as we move into the much-heralded "Age of Aquarius," gradually learning to see life in non-physical ways. However, the mindset in place for thousands of years places great emphasis on the earth realm and appraises it in terms of potential worth. Most people are highly conditioned to see the external world as separate and remain "down to earth."

Historically and conventionally, awareness is only understood as being contained *within* the parameters of the skin (Saturn). At Level 7, we understand the light of awareness as universal. It is the state of Spirit simply *being* in its eternality. This field of spiritual presence envelops us, continually partnering with us. Spiritual teacher Alan Watts says it this way:

"The source of all light is in the eye. If there were no eyes in this world, the Sun would not be light. You evoke light out of the universe. Every one of us is an aperture in which the whole cosmos looks out. It's as if you had a light covered by a black ball. And in this ball are pinholes, and in each pinhole is an aperture in which the light comes out. *Every one of us is a pinhole in which existence itself looks out.* Only the game we're playing is not noticed. What you call the external world is as much you as your own body. Your skin doesn't separate you from the world. It's a bridge through which the external world flows into you, and you flow into it. What you are basically deep deep down, far far in, is simply the fabric and structure of existence itself and when you find that out you laugh yourself silly."

And here's the catch. Though universal awareness and presence continually operate through our systems, we tend to inject a lot of distortion. Watts mentions a light covered by a black ball. Think of the phenomena of a solar eclipse, which I discuss at length in Volume 1 as the *egoic takeover*. We tend to obscure spiritual realization with our own attachments, identifications, stories, unresolved emotions, judgments, erroneous thinking patterns and the like. In short, the developmental process has us starting out unconscious (Moon: just like a baby), and we have no idea that we are "the fabric and structure of existence itself."

Spiritual awakening (movement beyond Saturn) and enlightenment (increasing wattage of the Sun) is not about learning or attaining anything. It has to do with getting ourselves "out of the way" in order to exist as we truly are, to have the light shine through us without distortion. Awakening is a process of *deconstruction*, the elimination of our egoic blockages.

It is absolutely crucial to understand that the Moon's initial unconscious distortions are <u>not</u> "bad," while the clarity of the Sun's awareness is "good." The Moon is our beautiful imperfect humanness and is to be honored and cherished. Incarnating in separation consciousness (Moon) allows us to have autonomy and jurisdiction on how we navigate, and we all begin at the earliest stages of development typified by unconsciousness. As we proceed through the evolutionary levels, we awaken to our true nature. It's not "bad" to be an infant, developmentally or within the spiritual journey. It's just where we start. Any judgments are completely unnecessary and unhelpful.

We are grounded to the relative realm within linear time (Moon), gradually aging and growing, playing out our historical dramas in the eternal present (Sun). Our soul connection to the world (Sun) assists the evolving ego (Moon) to resolve its past in the glorious invitation of every present moment. Spiritual awareness (Sun) entering the unconscious (Moon) brings consciousness. Spiritual teacher Thich Nhat Hanh says, "Awareness is like the Sun. When it shines on things, they are transformed."

The interaction between awareness (Sun) and the unique conditions of a human biological system (water, depth, Moon) creates what we understand as our *stream of consciousness*, a projection flowing through time. We project our consciousness out and *interact with ourselves* in what is reflected, just as the Moon (relative realm) reflects the Sun (soul, transpersonal).

Spiritual awakening is the recognition of the self in all of nature. At Level 7, we learn to bridge worlds by connecting the separate (relative, Moon) with the universal (transpersonal, Sun). It turns out that calling ourselves "human beings" is quite appropriate—we are a beautiful mixture of a physical foundation in our humanness (Moon), while also existing in a state of simply being (Sun).

Implications of the Transpersonal

A defining characteristic of the transpersonal is freedom. In short, we see through the realm of separation and can learn to approach it in a new way. We don't operate above it all; rather, we connect to life with more awareness. There are two main ways the approach works: from the standpoint of the self, and how we receive other people.

From the position of the self, we realize we are interacting with our own consciousness at all times. We are co-creating our experience of a tree, an authority figure, or a piece of music. Everything is just energy, and our consciousness interprets it in highly subjective ways, all contingent on how our emotional consciousness (Moon) has been developing in the soul journey. The astrology chart depicts the nature of our energetic attunement to life, the structure of our projections. We experience all of life along these lines because it's how our dream is being dreamed. There is a great range to how it might play out, from the darkness of unconsciousness to the brightness of enlightenment, all consistent with the themes and dynamics of the chart.

Through this co-creative relationship with the universe, none of our experiences are random. Everything is energetically summoned to help us awaken. We can either resist what we ourselves are drawing in, or learn to trust life and participate fully. It all comes down to whether we trust the self. Abraham Maslow says, "In any given moment we have two options: to step forward into growth or step back into safety." If we solidify a solid foundation of love (the healed and conscious Moon), then that's what we will experience in the sacred reflections from the world. Without this, we are prone to looking externally for love, support or security, never realizing everything in life is a mirror pointing us back to the self. When we drop the demand that the world meet our needs, we are poised to awaken into our empowerment and create the reality we desire.

As the external world is the self, there are no outside forces that are doing things *to* us. To paraphrase Deepak Chopra: the trees are my lungs, the rivers my circulation, the earth my body. We might add that *the planets are the frequencies of my consciousness.* Just as we wouldn't call an arm "benefic" or a leg "malefic," at this level we see astrology (the planets, signs, etc.) as the self, just like our limbs. Absolutely nothing in the entire system is any better or worse than anything else, for that mindset originates at the Saturnian level. Furthermore, since we are interacting with the self through the world, there is nothing on the astrology chart that can represent anyone else. Though the Moon conventionally is paired with the mother, at this level we understand that the mother is one (of countless) canvasses of projection of lunar issues (a very important one, especially in the early years).

In terms of receiving others, there is a tremendous amount of freedom available. First and foremost, we can never "mess up" for another person! Since all people reside in their own dreams and interpret life contingent with their consciousness, everything that we could possibly do fits into their spiritual lessons. We become characters in their stories. If they experience us as mean, then they are working on dealing with mean people. No matter what we do, it is perfect! We never have to protect people from their spiritual lessons, what they themselves are actually creating for themselves *through* us. The question is whether we are acting in our highest selves, from love. We do not act from love and integrity for their benefit (they may still interpret our actions as mean if that is their agenda); rather, we seek to embody our soul selves.

Another liberating facet is that we don't ever have to take others' behavior personally. Once we see that they are interacting with themselves through us, we can receive them with compassion. If we have an issue with what is occurring with another person, then we know that school is in session for us! There's nothing that we can do that isn't helpful for others' growth. Critics say, "What if you stab a person? How is that good for that person?" The problem with this question is that it does not refer to what is actually being energetically co-created between these souls. This understanding deals with reality, not hypotheticals. A stabbing, and any other crime, is unconscious dreaming gone awry. Usually these events are accompanied by great consequences, such as jail time, which serve as the teaching. Again, everything that actually occurs is grist for learning how to be more awake.

At the transpersonal level *nothing "bad" can ever happen*. This realm of experience is beyond duality; life is not evaluated in such terms. Everything has spiritual value. Instead of judging good or bad (Saturnian level), at Level 7 we see life as the movement from unconsciousness to more enlightened. When an infant cuts herself by playing with a pair of scissors, she is not being "bad" but rather just unconscious—she didn't know better.

Likewise, we can extend this universally. However we "play with scissors" as adults is just how unconsciousness is unfolding—*we know not what we do*. And also, at the Saturnian level, there are crimes and consequences and good and bad, too! *There are two levels going on simultaneously.*

At the relative level, there is separation. You and I are different. We each have autonomy to make our own choices, and we develop a sense of self. The focus is necessarily on surviving in what appears to be an unpredictable world. Eating vegetables is "good" for you, and eating pieces of metal is "bad." We tend to evaluate life in terms of what might serve our aims. In fact, there are carefully constructed hierarchies that help us organize what is most useful. From grades (A through F), to the various ranks in the military or levels of management, to "top shelf" products, to gold medals, every facet of life receives some form of judgment on a spectrum of more to less preferred or advanced.

Time goes by in clockwork precision, the orderly laws of classical physics create a predictable universe (when you strike a billiard ball at a certain angle, it's guaranteed to follow a particular trajectory), and reason prevails. There is pressure to stay in the "real world," to be "down to earth" and cooperate within the agreed upon consensus reality—what is most obvious, apparent and seemingly irrefutable to our immediate experience.

At the transpersonal level, everything dramatically changes. No longer is there any separation; everything is eternally interconnected. At this level of unity, the same energy runs through and connects you and me. Therefore, everything is a reflection of itself. The focus of the soul is evolution and broader connection. Life is not evaluated in terms of potential benefit—the view is towards *learning*. There are no judgments, for *everything is equal as part of the One*.

As the levels of consciousness (depicted in the table presented earlier) portray, we begin our journey by orienting to the earth realm (1), then develop the emotional and intellectual capacities (2 and 3) to become viable (4) in it. After maturation (5) and healing (6), we venture into the air (7). The task is the *integration* of these levels, not to somehow transcend the ego/body/personality system in order to exist as a disembodied soul. We are not leaving the physical realm; rather, we are resolving our issues within it and our attachments to it. Then, we become clear and healthy physical vessels of spiritual creativity.

Clarifying how astrology operates at Level 7 is crucial for evolution to continue, but it's not an endpoint. It potentially provides the framework for further development: deeper journeying through consciousness for visioning and shadow work (8) and fuller mindfulness and presence (9). These last two levels are *experiential* (8–water–Neptune and Pluto; and 9–fire–Sun) rather than conceptual, so our focus is to clarify an astrological approach at Level 7 (air–Uranus), which has to do with a transpersonal organization.

Elemental Levels

The levels of consciousness discussed above can be brought to a simpler, four-step framework of spiritual growth that focuses on the elements. We find a connection with the elements at Levels 1 (physical–earth), 2 (emotional–water), 3 (mental–air) and 9 (soul–fire). We have a rather quick orientation and development of body, heart and mind for the far longer journey to consciously realize soul. These "intermediate" levels (4–8) are the "playing field" for our evolutionary situation, where we spend the most time. The work largely involves evolving one's attachment and identification from mind to the broader expanse of soul.

Within this structure we see the motion from earth to water to air to fire, and that is exactly the procession of evolution through "elemental levels" that I have been putting forth in my previous works. A summary of this is included here, as it does inform the spiritual philosophy on which this approach rests. This concept seamlessly connects with the *Perennial Philosophy*, the universal understanding of the interplay between Oneness and separation. To quote Aldous Huxley, "Rudiments of the perennial philosophy may be found among the traditional lore of primitive peoples in every region of the world, and in its fully developed forms it has a place in every one of the higher religions."

The basic idea is that evolution involves an epic exchange between energy (transpersonal) and matter (relative). As separate selves, we begin on the earth and grow upwards, just like flowers reaching towards the Sun that sustains them. In the other direction, Spirit descends from its unity to separate into matter and dualism, residing in tangibility on the Earth. We will call these two complementary channels liberation and manifestation, each of them resembling a pyramid (as depicted below).

The liberating channel concerns *growth*. Earth is the great foundation, the broadest and most mundane level. Life (water) emerges in the form of autonomous organisms, which appropriately require water for sustenance. Next is the development of intellectual and communicative (air) skills, with an accompanying form of nervous system. The mental level is more advanced and exclusive than the water level, which is more sophisticated than the earth level. For instance, intelligent animals are more advanced than vegetables, which are more advanced than matter that doesn't grow, such as a piece of coal. Carrots require water; they are living and grow into their fullness. Humans are at the air level; we eat carrots (and many other things), which supports our evolution. Carrots, of course, originate from the ground (earth level).

Each level builds upon the previous, while also moving beyond it. At the apex is spiritual realization (fire), which is more exclusive than the previous levels, though universally attainable should we evolve.

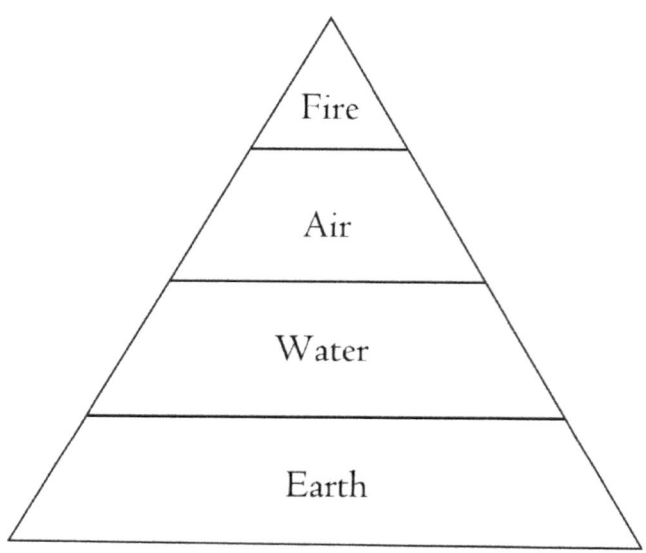

The Liberating Pyramid

The fire level (soul) connects the evolving self with all of life. The top of the pyramid is a singular point, Oneness, the full illumination of Spirit or enlightenment (fire). Spirit is not a "level" itself, as it envelops everything! Soul realization at the fire level can be understood in the liberating channel as the pinnacle of our personal growth.

Higher levels are not better than lower ones, just more developed; similar to the way an adult is not better than an infant. This evolutionary procession is best understood as the development from the physical to the nonphysical. When we evolve, we don't leave the denser (or lower) levels behind. Rather, the point is integration. As we psychologically mature, our inner child remains inside and requires the maintenance of love. However, one's *identification* shifts to the more mature level.

The manifesting channel illustrates the motion of spiritual unity (fire/energy) descending into separate form (earth/matter). At the fire level, energy begins the process of separation. Note how a large flame can have individual candles lit from it. The fire of individual souls are separate, while they also maintain a connection to the oneness of Spirit.

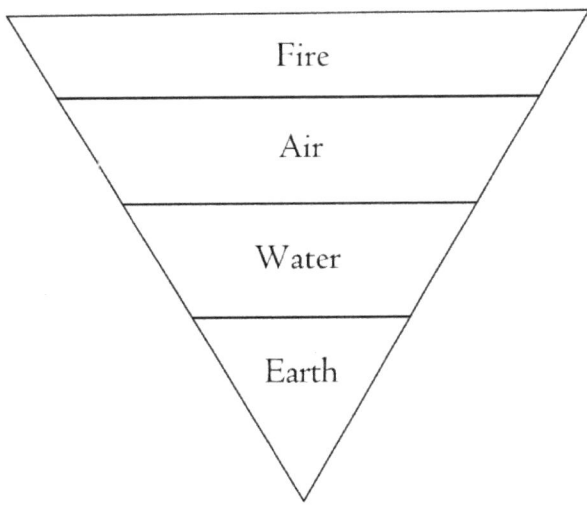

The Manifesting Pyramid

The manifesting channel narrows through the "elemental levels" to arrive on Earth. Descending from the fire level is air, the conceptual level, which holds many possibilities. Astrology is at this level, and the natal chart depicts the soul's intentions for an incarnation. Next, embodied life is actualized at the water (biological) level—a fetus is incubated in the waters of the womb. Upon birth, we arrive on the Earth as autonomous beings, and the earth level is engaged.

We exist in the middle of two complementary channels of evolution—simultaneously learning to grow (liberation) and also to ground spiritual intent in the now, to simply *be* (manifestation). From the orientation of separation consciousness, our most immediate experience tends to focus on growth in the relative world. We notice that everything alive changes every day, potentially developing. However, everything is also abiding in the eternal present in a state of being (manifestation). Our task is to bridge these worlds, and the Sun and Moon play the central roles in this process.

The Sun & Moon

Through a spiritual lens, the Moon relates to our connection with the relative realm and the Sun to the transpersonal. The Moon is physical, resides within the separating energy of Saturn, and equates to our smaller, egoic selves, which want to survive and be happy. Similar to a child maturing into an adult, the Moon relates to the spiritual childhood we all must go through on the way to broader spiritual realization.

The Sun is energetic and sustains all living things. The separating force of Saturn orbits around the Sun, illustrating how *the relative realm is dependent on the transpersonal*. Also, the Moon reflects the light of the Sun, showing how the physical, separate self (Moon) reflects our divinity—or to phrase it another way, "We are made in the image of God" and are "children of the Sun." 64 million Moons would fit inside the Sun, so the Sun is understood as our larger soul self—*with absolutely no judgment whatsoever* that the Sun is "better" than the Moon. Sun and Moon relate to energy and matter, soul connection and human separation.

The astrological Sun is the mediator between the eternal, unified energy of Spirit and an individual's life force. This fiery spiritual connection illuminates and sustains our physicality in separation consciousness (Moon). On average, we exist at 98.6

degrees Fahrenheit. The Moon grounds us to the conditions of incarnated life, the necessity to eat, sleep and exercise. We *absorb* (Moon/water) all of our experiences, and as with food, we must digest what we take in. We are *energy processing systems*, and whatever material stays in our systems influences our attachments and identifications. We reincarnate to resolve and process this material. It becomes projected out through our energy field (Sun) to shape our reality for us to address. This is how soul (Sun) assists the ego (Moon) in its development through the liberating channel.

Initially we tend to have a more immediate orientation with the physical (relative) level. Egoic needs (survival, happiness) tend to be more urgent than developing spiritual realization. We initially develop a healthy sense of "I." As a result, the astrological Sun (our life energy) is conventionally seen in egoic and personality ways. We don't yet realize that we are distributing Spirit, that we are *borrowing* energy from the universe. In the *Awakening* approach, we understand the Sun's role in liberating from ego—it's not the ego itself.

At this time, we are collectively learning to evolve our identification from mind to soul and organize life in accordance. The Copernican Revolution made us rethink our conception of the Solar System, and that reconceiving has parallels to this shift. Prior the 16th Century, we erroneously believed that the Sun, Moon and planets orbited around the Earth. The *apparent* reality was that the Sun and Moon were of equal size and that both were sources of light—they are termed "the luminaries." Perceiving the world from the dualistic lens of ego, the similar sizes of these celestial orbs became a natural fit for the two genders. Rooted in our humanness, we see the world as a reflection of self.

The conventional paradigm has a relative truth and is perfectly valid. *We rightly see the Sun as yang (masculine) and the Moon as yin (feminine), from the dualistic perspective of ego.* This perception of Sun/Moon equality has become a fixture in our collective consciousness, and though it is scientifically inaccurate, we tend to live in accordance with the illusion. We speak of the Sun rising or setting (instead of the Earth turning) and of moonlight (instead of reflected sunlight). If you ask the person on the street if the Sun and Moon are the same size, he or she is likely to reflexively say yes—or pause and think before providing the correct answer. In my research, very few people are aware of the actual size differential. Observable reality is that convincing.

The transpersonal perspective is not wedded to the vantage point of the Earth's surface. It brings an *additional* lens of perception, not a replacement. If we don't acknowledge the transpersonal perspective, we have quite a problem because science has moved us forward. The conventional paradigm makes sense only in a pre-Copernican world. There is a broader reality, the transpersonal (Uranus) orbits beyond the relative (Saturn). The conventional view of the Moon and Sun (complementary pair, yin/yang) is contained *within* the transpersonal view.

In the state of separation, we take on roles (Level 4), and life is full of stories. The Sun and Moon—and all of the planets— form a fantastic theater of characters for us to identify with and play out. The Sun can be the ruling monarch, and the Moon becomes his nurturing wife who takes his name (reflects his light). Ram Dass once said, "In most of our human relationships, we spend much of our time reassuring one another that our costumes of identity are on straight." Gender is a costume, not our ultimate reality. We are all made from the same light of divinity that runs through everything. At the transpersonal level, we are the eternal life force of the Sun temporarily illuminating and sustaining a physical vessel (Moon).

The Spiritual Vision

In some way, and at some time, we all have to address the eternal question, "Why are we here?" Whether or not we are conscious of it, our belief systems guide our lives, including our astrological approaches. It is helpful to be clear and upfront about the foundations of our viewpoints.

A very basic spiritual vision guides this work. Some spiritual teachers have compared life to a colossal game of hide and seek—the dance of unity and duality. Spirit separates, and sentient beings with autonomy gradually put the pieces back together and realize the Oneness that was actually there all along. Then the game is played again. With all of eternity, what else is Spirit going to do? We have these epic phases of evolution in which the "game" plays out. Right now, we are entering the much-heralded Age of Aquarius (Level 7, realization of our connectedness). If, for whatever reason, the scattered pieces within separation are unable to consciously unite, energy recycles for another try. At the transpersonal level, there is no urgency or endpoint or any judgment on our ability. The process of figuring it out is analogous to school. We need to learn the necessary lessons to realize we are One and act accordingly.

What's needed first is an actual school. Spirit creates planets that support life, and here we are on our host planet Earth—potentially one of many different "schools" in this unending universe. With billions of galaxies filled with billions of stars out there, the existence of numerous schools is extremely likely. With this basic layout of the game, let's look more closely at our unique school in this beautiful Solar System.

Encircling our home is our Moon. Instead of seeing the Moon as a planet (which it's not, though it has that designation in conventional astrology), we can understand it as our satellite, the Earth's partner. As discussed in Volume 1, the relationship between Earth and Moon is an energetic *system*, a unit. Astrologically, the Moon is considered a water energy (the Moon does have water at its poles). Water is the element of biology—the prerequisite for life. It adds the component of depth and is related to both emotion and consciousness, which have many *levels*. The Moon conveys our fundamental *humanness*.

We start out interpreting life from the reference point of Earth, ensconced in human unconsciousness, learning as we go. The Earth appears to be flat, with everything revolving around it. The Sun and Moon appear to be the same size, and Saturn is the last visible planet—initially understood as the perimeter of the Solar System. Astrologically, Saturn (an earth energy) is a separating force that sets up the conditions of the relative world, including time and form. Within those confines orbit Jupiter (life philosophy, belief systems), Mars (drive, action), Venus (socialization, aesthetics), and Mercury (cognition, communication). As each of these energies resides within Saturn, they function dualistically. We understand a "right" or "wrong" way to govern our life with Jupiter. We move towards or away from something with Mars. We like or dislike things with Venus, and we tend to view life itself dualistically (good/bad, male/female) with Mercury.

Initially, the Sun, too, would be seen as orbiting within Saturn. With the dualistic perspective, masculine (Sun) and feminine (Moon) are naturally assigned to these energies. As the game continues, new perspectives gradually emerge. Eventually, a more informed orientation is achieved. Instead of the Sun orbiting around the Earth and being contained within Saturn, now we understand that Saturn (and everything else) is completely *dependent on the Sun*. This signals the necessity to shift perspectives, as well as alerting us to the sobering reality that we are prone to living under false pretenses and illusions.

As evolution unfolds, more of the Solar System (and beyond) is discovered. The transpersonal planets Uranus, Neptune and Pluto were discovered in the 18th, 19th and 20th centuries, respectively. Over the last few hundred years, we have been more consciously grappling with these perplexing energies. Uranus is an organizational intelligence, a vast matrix of energy. Everything is instantly and synchronously connected, like the neural workings of a brain. Neptune conveys the dreaming process, how consciousness permeates this matrix to design our lives. Pluto ensures that we must own and integrate our dream material, to fiercely confront the shadow of unconscious dreaming.

We find there is no limit to expansion. Many objects beyond Pluto are discovered; we progressively learn more of the structure of the broader universe and gradually unlock its secrets. We see that life only within the confines of Saturn is a miniscule slice of reality, and one filled with distortion at that. We see that the Sun is a *star* that energetically connects us beyond our home to a starry pantheon of lights. We awaken to the reality that we are made and sustained by the creative life force of our Sun, our spiritual life source.

The world within duality is legitimate and a necessary starting point, but it's far from the only dimension of experience. The vessel of the separate self learns to engage the mystery of what is beyond the familiar. What is eventually discovered and experienced is that the eternal light of the universe was the self all along! The game of hide-and-seek ends with a celebratory laugh; the cosmic joke is revealed. There wasn't ever any separation — the relative and transpersonal worlds are *consciously* bridged. We use the vessel of our physicality (Moon) to channel spiritual creativity (Sun).

The major theme, and potential contribution, of *The Astrology of Awakening* series is that we can explore the Sun and

Moon from a spiritual viewpoint. This approach comes alive with chart application, and that is where we turn our focus.

Chapter 2
Astrological Building Blocks

In this chapter, the various planets, signs, houses, aspects, elements and modalities will be introduced. We will orient to the astrology chart from *The Astrology of Awakening* perspective. Volume 1 of the series has detailed information about the evolutionary cycle—how the motion through the signs and houses is a template for our spiritual growth. *Elements & Evolution* has extensive information about the elements from a spiritual viewpoint and the evolutionary significance of every aspect. There is a voluminous amount of information in beginner textbooks about the facets of the system. The intention here is a brief introduction from this spiritual perspective.

Conventional astrology tends to be geared towards egoic concerns of potential benefit (Saturn: Patriarchal Value System, Level 4), while the *Awakening* approach is an attempt to clarify how to partner with the system for spiritual growth (Uranus: Level 7). Therefore, absolutely nothing in the system is seen as "good" or "bad." *Everything has spiritual significance*. There are no preferable sign or house placements or aspects, nor are there any judgments about a person's chart. Instead, we look at it as we would a person's body. Every person has the perfect genetic composition at the physical level, as well as the ideal energetic make-up at the metaphysical level, for his or her unique spiritual curriculum.

It is the consciousness of the chart owner that inhabits the energetic dynamics the chart portrays. In the usual approach (flatland astrology), depth of consciousness is excluded in favor of various rankings and judgments about chart factors. In the *Awakening* approach, consciousness is the crucial and central variable in how the chart is managed. There's a continuum between the darkness of unconsciousness and the brightness of a more enlightened way.

A usual criticism of a transpersonal approach is that it's disconnected from the "real world" in favor of "pie in the sky" abstractions. As you will see, this is not what is promoted here. We maintain complete awareness of, and integration with, the Saturnian realm and its centrality in a person's life. The most immediate experience is of separation, and this is not to be ignored! *It's simply brought into a broader context.*

At Level 4, we initially see life in terms of roles—for instance, men are from Mars, and women from Venus. Traditionally, men have taken on greater leadership roles, while women have emphasized relationship and domesticity. Life used to be more organized in this dichotomous manner, but continuing to put forth *only* this view inhibits advancement to other levels. Also, many modern people reject these stereotypes. At the transpersonal level, we retract these relative projections and see Venus and Mars (and everything else) within the context of the chart owner's consciousness. Everyone relates to others and the world (Venus) and exercises behavior choices (Mars).

We will explore how the facets of astrology are understood at both the relative and transpersonal perspectives.

Planets

Sun: The life force; a person's energy, which radiates out and connects with all of life. When we are not awake, we erroneously believe that the composition of our essential nature is egoic, and this is the predominant view of the Sun in conventional astrology. The "egoic takeover" is seeing our life energy in strictly personality-based, rather than spiritual, ways. Sun sign astrology is the clearest, and most pervasive, example of this phenomenon.

From the relative perspective (ego, dualism), the Sun is seen in terms of being "yang" energy and is associated with the masculine. As a person moves along the spectrum of consciousness, the identification and experience of being Source energy itself ultimately becomes one's reality (Level 9). The Sun is not Spirit itself, for it is just one star out of billions. However, it has to do with spiritual realization or enlightenment, *our soul connection with all of life*—like one candle of billions lit from Spirit's eternal flame. How brightly we radiate Spirit is analogous to a light on a dimmer switch: there is endless "wattage." As "divine humans," the Sun is the divine part.

Moon: Our fundamental humanness—the physical vessel of the separate self, which operates at the biological level in the relative world. Watery in nature, the Moon is how we *absorb* the impact of life. Absorption of experience creates familiarity, attachments, identifications and a rootedness in the personal story. When we don't energetically process our experience, the material hardens and keeps us tethered to the past. Enrolled in a process of growth, the Moon continually changes, just as we notice various lunar phases in the sky. As we mature, we develop physically, emotionally, psychologically, intellectually and spiritually. In fact, everything at the biological level (plants, animals) evolves. At the role level, the Moon is understood as yin energy and is conventionally paired with the feminine. As "divine humans," the Moon is the human part that allows us to bridge worlds.

Mercury: The energy of knowledge, analysis, reason, and communication—phenomena associated with the left brain. We develop cognitively and learn to excel in school and life. Learning to be intelligent and strategic enables the separate self to understand this existence, take care of the self and earn a living. From a spiritual view, the issue with Mercury is its promotion of importance, which can inhibit motion beyond it. The over-identification with and attachment to one's thoughts and what can be accomplished through intelligence frames and reduces life within these terms. As evolution proceeds, we realize that we are not our thoughts, and the mind becomes a tool, not our identification. Mercury is in many ways a trickster, and up his sleeve is perhaps the secret that the Hermes/Mercury archetype may be broader than the left brain, a complete revolution of how we think. Integrated with the right brain, Mercury becomes an intuitive lightning rod for the transpersonal.

Venus: The orientation to the sensual and social realms— involving artistry and aesthetics, social norms and etiquette. Concerning relationship and beauty, its conventional association is feminine. With Venus, we might play out egoic games (money, status, popularity, reputation, fame, influence, etc.) largely based on the ability to curry favor in financial (earth) and social (air) ways. It's easy for the ego to get seduced by the so-called "benefic" charms of Venus. Alternatively, we can approach the physical and social realms to exchange spiritual *currency*. The conscious Venus creates an optimal social and economic order that is universally agreeable and supportive for all. Venus serves as a sacred mirror. It is our "sister planet," known for its similar size and close proximity. We are connecting with the self through others and also the natural world. After tempering the need for security and gain, we open to the spiritual reflection others, and nature, provide.

Mars: Motivation, drive, the energy that gets you from A to B. Mars is instinctual, how we naturally assert the self to survive. Traditionally considered "malefic," Mars does relate to conflict, strife and personal challenge. At the egoic level, we simply have to deal with the daily grind of life. In a modern context, Mars is the "spiritual warrior," who eagerly embraces life's lessons and taps a wellspring of passionate energy to meet such challenges. The egoic takeover corrects itself behaviorally with Mars. Instead of being our karma creator through acting unconsciously, it becomes a karma resolver through courageous and conscious action. It is helpful to hone our focus and attune our physical system through athletics and all forms of exercise (including martial arts), sexuality, and learning to take risks.

Jupiter: Expansion from personal concerns into broader social/cultural settings. How can we find purpose and meaning, discover a life path stemming from a belief system and sense of morality? Ideally, we make an impact in life as a reflection of our own growth. When we advance confidently, the universe tends to "meet us" by opening doors. However, when the ego is in charge, there is demand for self-gain and favorable outcomes. This has been projected onto Jupiter with the "benefic" designation, as though Jupiter is like Santa Claus, and he should arrive bearing gifts. The unconscious Jupiter may grab power, unnecessarily bolster resources at the expense of others, and demand that others follow its rules. From the spiritual view, we are *learning* to be more successful, to launch new endeavors with spirited action towards our aims. We may learn to expand towards spiritual perspectives that lift our scope from ego only. Then, Jupiter plays a central role in reforming culture and society to be connected with universal metaphysical principles. Our educational, religious and other settings can unite us within the relative realm.

Saturn: An organizational energy that structures ambition into form. As we mature, we become masters and elders who contribute to the development and sturdiness of functional society. Saturn concretizes consciousness at its current level, whatever that may be. We can perpetuate what has already been manifested indefinitely, thereby living in the past, or take the initiative to keep evolution moving. The process of maturation typically requires effort, focus and determination. When we are more youthful in our spiritual curriculum, we may not want to fulfill responsibilities that are tiresome or not pleasurable. Saturn has the reputation of being somewhat of a sourpuss, as the planet certainly can be "malefic" to the ego. From a spiritual perspective, Saturn is valued and appreciated for setting up the conditions (time, space, gravity) for us to engage our spiritual curriculum. The more maturely we walk our paths, the more wisdom and integrity we hold and results we achieve. Saturn is the gateway from the relative to the transpersonal. When we are in full acceptance of the limits of reality, we are able to bring broader spiritual awareness and nourishment to the Saturnian experience.

Chiron: The energy of health and well-being, reaching greater alignment of the body–mind system and making adjustments to be able to venture onward. Chiron has skills in many areas and crafts, all to assist the human condition, which tends to get off-kilter in the state of separation. With the initial focus on survival and maintenance, we often forget we are souls having human experiences. Chiron heals this egoic splintering away from Source. There are a plethora of methodologies to assist us. These are often alternative and progressive, as Chiron orbits beyond Saturn—any metaphysical fair will feature a large selection. Chiron matures to become a mentor and teacher, assisting others in their spiritual health.

Uranus: Residing beyond the consensus reality of Saturn, Uranus initially points to energy that has been unintegrated and problematic in the soul history. As we mature (Saturn), we become ready and able to venture beyond our prior limitations and handle Uranian energy more consciously. Then, we have access to some form of brilliance. Uranus points to extraordinary aptitude in the very areas that previously challenged us. Done consciously, Uranus allows us to teach what we have learned to the collective and thereby reform and modernize culture and society. The darker version surfaces when we unconsciously play out the more devious and anti-establishment side. The planet can be reckless and unnecessarily disruptive. At the transpersonal level, Uranus is the metaphysical structure that organizes the broader intelligence of nature/Spirit. When we engage the awakening process, we have greater access to use this neural "web." We no longer see it as God's mind; it becomes our own. The planets are the frequencies of our consciousness as we design the contours of our lives.

Neptune: The energy of visioning, dreaming, intuition and imagination. The dreamer (Moon) connects with the dream space (Neptune), which is held in place by the organizational energy of Uranus. The dreamer (Moon) radiates out (Sun) its inner psychic material to shape reality according to the inner vision. When less conscious, we are lost in the dream space and fall back into survival mode. As we become more conscious, we direct the dreaming process and have enormous power to further both personal and collective evolution. On the road to being a mystic, Neptune initially points to material that has caused sorrow, disenchantment, loss or some form of resignation about things that didn't work out. As we grow, we learn to see that all of this was the result of previously dreaming less consciously, so we learn to have acceptance, compassion and love for the self. Then we are able to leave the past behind and actively create our visions in the heart.

Pluto: The shadow. The dream material that is most painful and "unacceptable" gets banished to the outer regions of the Solar System. Unlike the well of the unconscious that we will admit is ours in moments of honesty, Plutonian material is severed from our identity. Few admit that Adolph Hitler, a suicidal maniac, or any other pathology, is a personal reflection. At the transpersonal level, each of us *is* the entire universe, so we need to accept all of humanity in order to integrate with this energy. Prior to broader awakening, life becomes heavily influenced by the unconsciousness of our Plutonian material. When we are disconnected from our identification, that material is in charge of us until we recognize it. We unconsciously project it out, which continually gives us the task of identifying it or assigning it to others. Eventually, we learn to embrace all of the self. Then, our "shit" becomes the fertilizer that nourishes our power, and how we might impact the world. At the transpersonal level, Pluto correlates with the regenerative power of nature. It is both the subtle and (at times) overt forces of evolution that catalyze change.

Signs

The signs of the zodiac are well known to any astrology student, so a thorough description of their qualities is not necessary. Instead, below are some brief summations of how they operate at the spiritual level, where they pertain to *lessons*. This is in contrast to much of astrological literature, which discusses the signs in terms of personality characteristics. For instance, the earth signs are practical and resourceful at the personality level, while the spiritual lessons involve the development of self-worth, mastery of craft, or manifestation of intention. Below is a concise explanation of each of the twelve evolutionary programs as seen through the signs.

Aries: The development of courage. The Ram is learning how to use its autonomy to potently put forth its truth and act decisively on its behalf. Leadership is not always connected to popularity or consensus, so a call to bravery is part of the lesson. The conscious Aries uses the separate self as a vehicle to distribute spiritual intention. In contrast to the spiritual warrior, the darker possibility is aggression and brashness, i.e., being a "jerk."

Taurus: The development of self-sufficiency. The Bull is learning to settle into its naturalness as a physical being and find comfort and worth in itself. Becoming more solid and self-aligned brings greater endurance. The conscious Taurus is committed to itself, whereas the unconscious version loses itself in comforts and other forms of gluttony and placation. Working effectively with the tangible world creates beautiful expressions of Spirit. Taurus is learning to rise above materialism and "be in the world, but not of it."

Gemini: The development of the intellect and communication of knowledge. The Twins dialogue endlessly, figuring out this fascinating existence. Upon greater maturation, Gemini is the storyteller, teacher, author or messenger. The less conscious Gemini is the eternal student or puer, adrift in speculation and unable to focus. The third sign conveys the evolutionary necessity of upgrading the mind, not becoming trapped in its workings.

Cancer: The development of personal love. The Crab is learning to be more sensitive about our fundamental humanness, to invest emotionally in the self, family, and loved ones. This sign involves the motion out of unconsciousness through unconditional self-love and acceptance of the past. If there are challenges around self-love, then Cancer unconsciously plays this out in ways that reinforce negativity. The Crab can be highly upset, irritable and "crabby." How can we strengthen the heart to withstand the tumult of this earth-walk?

Leo: The development of character. The Lion is learning to be more present and self-aware—to use the personality creatively for self-expression and jubilation. Those awakening to this promise learn to rise above egoic distortion. The darker version is all about egoic bombast and self-preoccupation, becoming an attention hog, which stems from insecurity. Often misunderstood, Leo fashions the world as a spiritual playground where we can radiate our purity and innocence. This is made possible, and done authentically, when the inner child paradoxically matures.

Virgo: The development of expertise. The Virgin is learning to invest in the mastering of skills, creating works and personally improving. The careful and precise eye is able to smooth out rough edges and assist others in similarly growing. Whereas the bright version is the specialist, practitioner or craftsman, the dark side involves self-abusive tendencies that limit effectiveness and promote neurosis. This evolutionary program is about engaging the projects and programs that support evolution itself.

Libra: The development of the social self. The Scales seek balance and equilibrium, harmoniously connecting the self with others and the world. Libra brings civility, peace and grace into how we relate. The shadow is the creation of artificial and unsatisfying ways to connect. The unconscious Libra is prone to giving its power away. The more awake version perceives the landscape of our social milieu as a phenomenal hall of mirrors of self, endlessly reflecting love.

Scorpio: The development of intimacy and power. The Scorpion is learning greater fluency of the psychological dynamics between self and other. Also, this sign is learning to be unflinching around darkness in general. As Scorpio concerns the shadow, it may easily get caught in it! The entire buffet table of pathology is available. Dealing with psychological extremity, including a variety of uncomfortable feeling states, Scorpio achieves deep wisdom about the human condition upon successful navigation. The conscious management of this curriculum results in making a profound impact on others and potentially our collective evolution, too.

Sagittarius: The development of broader purpose and spiritual understanding. The Archer aims to develop a mission that serves as a compass to direct the pathway through life. This spirited sign involves direction and inspires others to similarly "go for it." As a life philosophy is being worked out, Sagittarius may harden its convictions prematurely. Then it becomes misguided, even dangerous with its zeal. Ultimately, the Archer evolves into the wise scholar or adventurer who has a breadth of life experience to draw from.

Capricorn: The development of professional stature. The Goat is learning to influence collective evolution from positions of authority. Through hands-on management and making tough decisions, this leadership-oriented sign gets the job done. Along the way, Capricorn can lose a spark for life or separate from others in pursuit of ambition. Ideally, its serious side transitions into wisdom and accessibility, like a kind grandparent. Though the darker side is overly traditional and afraid of change, Capricorn is learning to become prominent while also acting with its own sense of integrity.

Aquarius: The development of progressive vision. The Water Bearer is plugged into the net of endless possibilities and has the task of reforming systems and paradigms in accordance with this brilliance. An innovative spark awakens us to the future, but this sign's darker version is unconsciously and unnecessarily destructive and oppositional. As it develops, Aquarius guides evolutionary progress though non-attachment and advocating conscious interconnectedness. The realization of a world family is the promise of the eleventh sign.

Pisces: The development of unconditional love of humanity. The Fish swims in the currents of compassion and acceptance of life. This gentle sign soothes and nourishes us as we experience the bump and grind of being incarnate. The darker version is lost and gullible, lacking discernment. As Pisces develops, it uses its visionary imagination to inspire and touches us with its grace and gratitude. We see the spiritual poetry and sublime depth that envelops us all.

Houses

The twelve houses follow the same development and rhythm as the twelve signs; they are thematically and archetypally related. The essential difference between houses and signs is one of scope. Signs are evolutionary programs (Aries–courage, Taurus–worth, etc.) and also portray stylistic approaches to life. Houses are the realms of experience where such learning plays out in the world.

Where the Sun rises becomes the Ascendant, and its culmination at its maximal height in the sky becomes the Midheaven. These two positions create the "angles" of the chart and determine the Descendant (opposite Ascendant) and Nadir (opposite Midheaven). The cusps of Houses 1, 4, 7 and 10 are established by sunrise and culmination, while there are several ways to derive the intermediate cusps (more on this later). Houses 2, 5, 8 and 11 are called the "succedent" houses, while 3, 6, 9 and 12 are the "cadent" houses.

We can think of the chart layout as being like a compass, with the angles serving as the four directions. The houses illustrate how we are *oriented* to the world around us. The Ascendant suggests an orientation to the self, how life is approached. The Nadir conveys an orientation to location, home and family. The Descendant is an orientation to others, while the Midheaven is an orientation to public life. The signs on house cusps suggest the nature of this orientation, while the planets that disposit the signs give more information about the energy that drives us in these areas.

It has been stated that the planets are the "what," signs are the "how," and houses are the "where" to astrology. Planets are energy, signs are learning programs, and houses are locations. Houses are simply where life plays out, and the movement of the planets through the houses portrays the temporal motion to the unfolding of our lives. The Ascendant is of new beginnings, while the twelfth house involves endings. In between, we proceed through a universal template of evolutionary movement.

To further distinguish planets, signs and houses, let's look at a couple of examples. Mercury is the cognitive energy you hear inside your head, the ongoing chatter that makes evaluations and decisions. Gemini is the developmental program of learning. The third house points to *areas* of learning, spending time writing or thinking, and our perception of the immediate environment. This house indicates how intellectual matters connect with the world. The Moon is the energy you feel inside your heart. Cancer is the developmental program of self-love, nurturing and the creation of family. The fourth house is where we are rooted to life—our home base, family system and inward orientation.

Below are brief descriptions of the twelve houses.

House 1: Self-orientation, personal approach to the world, style, instinctual tendencies, persona and display of personality characteristics

House 2: Resources such as money and materials, as well as inner resources such as confidence, inner strength, personal value and worth

House 3: Areas of learning, involvement with intellectual and communicative pursuits, perception of the immediate environment

House 4: Location, home, roots, genealogical connection, internal self-orientation

House 5: Extension of social self outwards, recreation, playful and romantic areas, creative pursuits, the exercising of talents

House 6: Areas of service and skill development, orientation to social hierarchies, training and instruction, health practices and guidance, work space

House 7: Orientation to others and social dynamics, personal friendships, romantic partners, commerce and business associations

House 8: Interpersonal psychological dynamics, sexuality, contracts and agendas with others, shared resources, inheritance and other matters regarding death

House 9: Global expansion, outreach, areas of travel and adventure, political realms, higher learning, publishing, religious settings

House 10: Orientation to public life and identity, profession and vocation, "what we do" and "how we're seen"

House 11: Membership in communities and groups, networks, allies and acquaintances, humanitarian involvement, movements and causes

House 12: Areas of retreat, removal, exploration of nature, consciousness and dreams, prisons and other institutions, spiritual practice

One way this approach differs from more conventional forms of astrology is how to comprehend and work with the Ascendant. Recall that houses are about the "where," *how we locate the self in the world*. However, it is quite common to hear the Ascendant discussed as if it were a planet, a part of consciousness. Someone might proclaim, "I'm a double Capricorn," if he or she has the Sun and Ascendant in that sign. The first house cusp is given major significance. (I have even heard some astrologers say that 80 percent of the chart's importance is found through the Ascendant!) The *Awakening* approach does not conflate the Ascendant with consciousness (planets) but rather sees the Ascendant in terms of *orientation*.

The Ascendant orients us to the eastern horizon, where the Sun rises. Just as the Sun's emergence in the morning declares the start of a day, the Ascendant is the gate between inspiration and action. When we are walking east (Ascendant), who we are (consciousness) is not literally east; we're moving towards a particular evolutionary program. In the same way, the sign of the Ascendant conveys how we move, like the car we drive or the clothes we wear. The Ascendant has to do with stylistic and personality characteristics, *how we partner with a certain evolutionary program in how we approach the world.*

One reason the Ascendant has received so much attention is the historical focus on the personal self. Thematically associated with Aries and Mars, the first house is uncompromisingly self-aligned and necessarily about "me." With a less egoic focus, we can step back and look at the layout of twelve houses and appreciate that each has equal validity, just as Pisces, Libra and Gemini are not less important than Aries.

An alternative to assigning the four angles greater importance is to simply think of them as *more immediate in our experience.* Self-orientation (1), family (4), relationships (7) and career (10) play central roles for most. In daily conversation, we might ask someone we meet, "How are you?" (1), "Where are you from?" (4), "Are you married?" (7), or "What do you do for a living?" (10). Rarely do we initially hear, "How's your mind?" (3), "What are you seeking to develop?" (6), "What is your mission in life?" (9), or "How is your spiritual practice?" (12). These issues may come up upon deepening the exchange—similar to the cadent houses coming after the angular in the unfolding of the cycle.

For that matter, north, south, east and west are not more *important* than northwest or south/southeast—all these points establish direction. Self, home/family, relationships and career do serve as the four reference points to our surroundings. As we cease assigning judgments on the various facets of astrology, we are better able to value the importance of everything in the system. I want make this point abundantly clear: in this approach, *the Ascendant is important*—we explore it for what it is, a house cusp—and all of the houses portray how we navigate the world.

Aspects

Aspects connect planets together in a variety of geometric patterns. They create "dialogues," or ways to collaborate and unify. Since consciousness is not understood as the determining variable in much of the astrology we've inherited, aspects have a legacy of being seen as influencing factors. Conventionally, there are "good" and "bad" aspects, which are used to forecast outcomes. In the approach presented in this book, we see an aspect as a bridge. How matters play out is up to the consciousness of the chart owner. Aspects *set up the lines of communication.*

Aspects concern spatial relations. There are geometrical patterns that exist between the planets. All aspectual interchanges have different degrees of strength depending on two factors, one constant, and the other changeable. The constant is the tightness of the orbs (degrees of separation). The changeable factor is, over time, how much the aspect is developed.

The tighter the orb, the more central the aspectual interchange is in the chart. For an analogy, the lines of communication can be thought of as threads, cords or cables. Two planets that are opposed with an orb of ten degrees have a connecting thread—they are in a dialogue—but the strength may be overshadowed by other exchanges that are tighter. A closer orb (say, a five-degree opposition) is like a cord, more durable, while an exact aspect is a cable, incredibly strong and very difficult to separate.

Although the orbs between natal planets never change, the second factor, development, influences how aspects actually play out.

62

Let's say a man has Mars in the sixth house in Taurus trine Saturn in the tenth house in Virgo. He decides to spend nine hours a day working at a gym, putting plenty of time into building his own body. These energies are going to be more bolstered than his twelfth house Mercury conjunct Neptune in Scorpio. Though intuitive development is available, he would need to pump some energy into that possibility to make it come alive. Too often in astrology, the variable of our co-creation is left out, and the chart is seen as static instead of continually changing.

The conjunction is a different kind of aspect because it is not connecting energies from different locations. Threads, cords and cables are insufficient descriptors here. Degrees of intensity would be more accurate. A wide conjunction has less intensity than a tighter orb. The wider a conjunction, the less fusion takes place. The respective parts retain more autonomy.

It is not necessarily *better* to have many tight aspects (in this approach, everything has evolutionary value). Planets that have few or no aspects have more room for autonomy. This is helpful for more specialized work. For instance, a person with an unaspected Mercury in Virgo can focus intelligence without the chatter from the other planets. The struggle is to then integrate what the Mercury discovers elsewhere. A person with many aspects does function more holistically, which may or may not be advantageous. Sometimes it is helpful to be apart from others and focus, like a meditator on a spiritual retreat.

Next, we'll review the major aspects.

Conjunction

Conjunctions indicate the fusion of two energies to make a new entity. For instance, hydrogen and oxygen merge to create water, and sodium and chlorine become salt. Think of Lennon and McCartney singing a melody together; something new emerges through the unification of their voices. There is debate as to how much orb is necessary for fusion to occur. Certainly the tighter the better, but even loose conjunctions in the same astrology sign are working with the same evolutionary process. In fact, there is whole sign logic. Let's say a person has Mercury at 0 degrees Leo and Uranus at 29 degrees Leo. Though these planets are not technically in conjunction, they are working on the same evolutionary curriculum and, therefore, must have a relationship. Again, the tighter the aspect, the more central the relationship. Conjunctions separated by sign are also relevant. If Uranus at 29 degrees Leo is next to Venus at 0 degrees Virgo, they're connected — just picture it visually, and it becomes clear. The properties of each planet join together, and something entirely new emerges.

Opposition

An opposition (180 degrees) portrays the evolutionary lesson of coming together or coming apart. The opposition implies tension because the planets share the same modality (cardinal–management, fixed–solidification, mutable–dispersal) and, therefore, have competing agendas, illustrated as a tug of war. Oppositions often play out with other people in this antagonistic fashion. If we identify more with one side, the other gets projected. We tend to tango with the projection externally until we learn to integrate it within. Opposite signs are counterparts, like male and female or left and right. Despite any evident differences, there is common ground, identification with the other. Consider the yin/yang symbol, which has a black dot in the white section and vice versa. The opposition portrays the eternal dynamic of connecting in separation to realize Oneness — to recognize self in others and the world.

Trine

The trine is an aspect of flow. Connecting different modalities of the same element, this aspect indicates a complementary and supportive relationship. However, the element in question can be bolstered in unconscious ways, such as workaholism (earth) or bombast (fire). The harmony of the trine is seen through the elegance of the equilateral triangle, which portrays shared power. Though we can classify this aspect as soft, in no way will it ever *modify* the consciousness of the planets it connects. Having an excellent phone line will not repair the relationship of two people in need of honest communication. The evolutionary importance of the trine is to bring us opportunities to work through issues in supportive ways. It is helpful for us to connect with allies along similar lines in open channels.

Square

A square always positions a yin sign (water, earth) with a yang sign (air, fire) of the same modality, resulting in friction and the negotiation of different aims. A handy illustration is perpendicular lines, such as those in a traffic intersection. Without the rules of the road, the cars going in the horizontal direction are bound to collide with the cars traveling on the vertical route. Squares apply pressure to grow—quite useful for those who accept life's challenges. There are times when we need to have surgery, or face unpleasant truths, or bear down and really produce to avoid unseemly consequences. If we refuse to accept these realities, we may blame squares and consider them "bad." Those that have matured beyond egoic jockeying for ease and gain may harness the evolutionary potential of squares in magnificent and productive ways. Squares are a powerhouse aspect that churns the evolutionary wheels forward.

Sextile

The sextile positions a fire sign with air, or a water sign with earth (of a different modality). The complementary elements build off of each other and connect in exciting ways. The 60-degree sextile is exactly half of a trine. Sextiles can therefore be thought of as supporting harmony, but more peripheral in nature. The sides of a hexagon, such as a stop sign, serve as a good visualization of the sextile pattern. In Stephen Arroyo's *Astrology Karma & Transformation,* he writes, "In electrical wiring, a three-phase current at 60-degree spacing is the least stressful way of conducting energy through wires. This corresponds to the sextile (60 degrees) and trine (2 x 60 degrees) aspects in astrology. 90- or 180-degree wiring is very stressful and heats up the wire since there are peaks of too much voltage at times and none at other times." The shadow of the sextile is missed opportunities. Instead of enthusiasm, there can be some degree of activated disappointment. This teaches us to "get with it" next time. Like bees buzzing about, sextiles connect energies in stimulating ways. Indeed, the honeycomb is another example of this aspect found in nature.

What about Five?

Above, we discussed the Ptolemaic, or "major," aspects, but something is missing. A circle divides into two (opposition), three (trine), four (square), and six (sextile) to form the major aspects. What about five? The quintile aspect is 72 degrees: 360 degrees divided by 5. The quintile naturally fits into this sequence and provides numerical precision and completion, yet it's almost completely absent in astrology literature and discourse. Why?

It's somewhat laborious to identify aspects of 72 degrees. The "major" aspects end in 0, so working with them is easier. The quintile challenges our need for order and simplicity, inviting us to stretch. Indeed, the quintile can be thought of as Uranian. It points to novel, inspired and creative possibilities that may or may not manifest in the mundane realm. In this way, it's rightly not included in the major pantheon because, to some degree, it's "optional" to grow in such a way.

Today, bringing in the aspect of potential brilliance is timely and necessary. Working with the quintile enables us to create civilization a bit closer to Aquarian ideals, the promise of this time. The quintile's connection with brilliance should be qualified. Too often, we construe brilliance only as something mental, but leadership, art, mentoring, emotional intelligence or interpersonal skills can convey brilliance. Any area can be complemented by innovative sparks.

We notice the quintile formation (pentagram) in the "Venus Star" pattern, how five conjunctions of Venus with the Sun over every eight-year period forms this pattern. Nature displays the aesthetic precision and perfection of the five-pointed star in a variety of ways, from apple seeds to plants to crystals to galaxies. The mathematics of the segments that form the pentagram reveal the "golden mean," which permeates nature in a host of ways including musical patterns, numerical sequences and brain waves. The quintile connects with the Fibonocci sequence, which unfolds as a spiral. To learn more about this topic, see Arielle Guttman's *Venus Star Rising*. When we work our quintiles, we have access to extraordinary aptitude that reveals a divine intelligence.

The Quincunx

Another aspect that merits discussion is the quincunx. I have affectionately called the quincunx the "star" of my previous work, *Elements & Evolution*, as the aspect revealed itself as one of profound evolutionary importance and, like the quintile, in advanced ways. In the *Elements* work, I came up with a keyword for each of the twelve different quincunxes, which describe the synthesis of the sign's evolutionary lessons. Among them are Leo–Pisces: *Spiritual Awakening*, Virgo–Aquarius: *Technology*, and Cancer–Sagittarius: *Self-Discovery*. These are all challenging programs to develop, more sophisticated than basic survival and happiness requirements. As we create a more advanced global spiritual village, these programs are absolutely necessary. I encourage the reader to consult the *Elements* text to further investigate this topic.

Like the quintile, the quincunx is an aspect that plays a role in geometric completion using basic astrological logic. To illustrate this, think of the twelve phases of astrology, using the language of the signs and their accompanying numbers. We'll use Aries (1) as our reference: It connects to Libra (7) with the opposition, Leo (5) and Sagittarius (9) with the trine, Cancer (4) and Capricorn (10) with the square, and Gemini (3) and Aquarius (11) with the sextile. It's also connected to Pisces (12) and Taurus (2) by being adjacent to them. Signs reveal an evolutionary relationship with their predecessors as they build from each other as the evolutionary cycle unfolds. What's missing here is 6 and 8, i.e., the relationship between Aries (1) and Virgo (6) and Scorpio (8)—the two signs in quincunx. With the inclusion of the quincunx, *every evolutionary stage has a connection with every other stage.* Without the quincunx, every stage has a connection to all but two other stages. Which makes more sense?

The quincunx is an aspect of complexity, and the word "adjustment" is often used with it. The aspect is 150 degrees, or one sign away from an opposition, oblique or skewed—the feeling that you "didn't see it coming." The quincunx has us reconciling *seemingly* incompatible evolutionary programs to create something that is not only progressive but also incredibly useful. Whereas the quintile brings us into more lofty realms of innovation, the quincunx is more worldly, tidying matters up to bring completion and results.

Below is a brief summary of the major aspects, including the quintile and quincunx, used in the *Awakening* approach. The minor aspects are valuable and relevant; however, a thorough discussion and inclusion of them would be somewhat laborious and complicated. I urge the reader to explore them and bring them into practice as experience dictates.

Conjunction (0 degrees separation): Fusion, sharing identification
Sextile (60): Stimulation, upsurge of energy
Quintile (72): Brilliance, novelty
Square (90): Conflict, crisis point, friction
Trine (120): Flow, harmony
Quincunx (150): Adjustment, complexity
Opposition (180): Tension, polarity, coming together

More regarding orbs (degrees of separation): When is something in aspect? How close does it have to be? I have found that standard orbs are a nice guide, but only a guide. The standard orbs are 10 degrees for the conjunction and opposition, 8 degrees for the trine and square, and about 5 for the sextile, quintile and quincunx. However, it's essential not to be too rigid with these guidelines. First of all, using intuition is important—the aim is to always feel the chart at a holistic level. Second, aspects do not turn on and off like light switches when the degrees of separation are passed. Finally, everything in the chart is meaningfully connected to everything else; it's a matter of degree. The tighter an orb, the "hotter" the energetic dialogue; the more central and pressing the planetary communication becomes. With looser orbs, the dialogues are more removed.

Furthermore, as mentioned above, there is whole sign logic. Any two planets in the same sign are working on the same evolutionary curriculum. This can also be extended to the other aspects — any planet in Leo is square Scorpio by sign and therefore at cross-purposes.

Our discussion addresses the natural aspects, for instance, Virgo trine Capricorn in earth signs. Many times, aspects occur "out of sign." A planet in late Virgo can be trine another in early Aquarius. There is still the harmony of the trine; this is not overridden by the difference in elements. As with all aspects, there is a potential gift and challenge.

Elements

Physical (body) – Emotional (heart) – Mental (mind) – Spiritual (soul); a universal template for understanding our humanity. This correlates with the four astrological elements of earth, water, air and fire. Because of the marginalization of the transpersonal, fire is often discussed in personal/egoic, rather than spiritual, ways. Just as the Sun and Moon are most frequently seen at the "role" level, so too have the elements been mostly framed in terms of personality traits and psychological characteristics. This is valid, but a spiritual view is available too. Below are some central points about the elements, seen in terms of growth. The following descriptions are modified from my work *Elements & Evolution*. Please see that book for more about this subject. Both that work and Volume 1 of *The Astrology of Awakening* include discussion of the classification of neutral and charged. The basic idea is that neutral is left brain (content) and charged is right brain (process).

Earth

Elemental Level: Physical
Classification: Yin, neutral
Evolutionary Contribution: Resources, sensuality, substance, structure, foundation, manifestation
Planets: Venus, Mercury, Saturn
Signs: Taurus, Virgo, Capricorn
Houses: 2, 6, 10

Earth is the *matter* or *substance* of life—sensual, tangible, and obvious. As a base or container, earth is *stable and solid.* Earth has the quality of *stillness,* sitting idly until it's utilized. Since it is receptive in this regard, earth is considered a yin element. Earth provides natural resources: shelter, clothing, and food. Nature has provided us with everything we need to live life comfortably and sustainably. Since resources play this valuable role in maintaining a comfortable society, earth assumes *worth.* Houses, vehicles and other possessions are valuable commodities.

Earth is the foundation for our evolutionary circumstance. Matter is the basis for the long evolutionary motion back towards realizing the unity of Spirit. Without membership on the physical level, there is no way to tangibly experience soul lessons. Since matter is a temporary crystallization of energy, the forms that earth takes are fleeting. From a spiritual perspective, the body is seen as a vessel for the soul. Everything physical is *borrowed* and must eventually return to intangibility.

Earth structures our consensus reality, a physical landscape on which we rely. The objects that surround us give us a sense of home and help us maintain our orientation to life. Likewise, earthy people are dependable and grounded in common sense and simplicity. Their priority is maintaining what already works, as opposed to engaging in the speculative.

However, a challenge is oversimplifying things or preserving the status quo at the cost of progress. An overemphasis on earth can also lead to materialism, workaholism, and gluttony. The physical world is abundant with gifts. The pitfall is to forget or neglect that we are also made from the stars.

Water

Elemental Level: Emotional
Classification: Yin, charged
Evolutionary Contribution: Depth of consciousness, emotion, autonomy to life forms, reproduction
Planets: Moon, Pluto, Neptune
Signs: Cancer, Scorpio, Pisces
Houses: 4, 8, 12

Water is a yin element, seeking and then settling at its own level. It's shapeless and fluid, malleable in relation to the solid structure of earth. This lack of definition illustrates how water concerns *process* rather than content. Water can assume solid (ice), liquid, or gaseous (vapor) forms, depending on the temperature. It eludes constancy; water is always in a process of change. Water is *sensitive to its environment, continuously adapting* to its surroundings. Water has various *levels of depth*. From superficial surface layers all the way down to the farthest depths, water acts as the metaphor for levels of *consciousness*.

Water correlates to *emotion,* which is energy in motion. In contrast with the inertia of earth, water is perpetually in a *state of flow.* We see the connection between water and emotion in many bodily fluids. Sadness or great joy generates tears; fear produces sweat; anger triggers adrenaline. Water is a *charged* element, which means it has levels of intensity—from deep upset, hurt feelings and heartache…to love, empathy and a reverence for life.

An evolutionary purpose of water is the establishment of autonomous life. This element thereby provides access to the great drama of biology—survival, reproduction, and the formation of ecosystems. Water concerns the well of the unconscious—the depth of the separate self that is evolving towards greater completeness and awareness.

Watery people tend to be soulful, deep, and in touch with both the strength and vulnerability of the human condition. They are filled with an innate capacity to feel, connect, empathize and nurture both the self and others. Like the other elements, however, water's energy can be out of balance. Water can rage out of control in the form of tirades and acts of fury, or collapse inward into depression and apathy. Watery people can be excessively needy, intrusive, or self-absorbed—or conversely, lacking sensitivity and concern for others.

Air

Elemental Level: Mental
Classification: Yang, neutral
Evolutionary Contribution: The spiritual "nervous system," intellect, communication, socialization
Planets: Mercury, Venus, Uranus
Signs: Gemini, Libra, Aquarius
Houses: 3, 7, 11

The air element is a massive openness that contains all experience. Another word for air is *space*. Air allows us to get distance and, thereby, *perspective*. The air holds innumerable *connections and networks*. At the quantum level, the "empty" space is endlessly busy beyond our usual comprehension. At the spiritual level, air is the nervous system of the cosmos, a gigantic mind.

Air is orderly and rational. Systems of language, mathematics, and logic are part of its scope. Whereas the earth element categorizes the physical realm, the air element categorizes facts and figures. Air is classified as a *neutral* element because of its cool, non-attached, irrefutable reason. Like a list of statistics, a dictionary, or a phone book, air is *informational*. Air is considered a *yang* element because of its expansive nature, as opposed to earth's inertia or water's settling. Absent the friction and gravity of earth, movement proceeds through space without resistance. The ungrounded quality of air lends itself to the concept of *freedom*.

Air brings us out of the limitations of animal consciousness into the complexity and opportunities of advanced intellect. There is an appreciation of aesthetics, beauty and refinement. Air provides the content for schools, universities, and all forms of learning. The mental realm allows for human ingenuity and the resulting technology created. Air relates to perception. There is clarity in the air, a sharpness of vision when views are unobstructed. The neutrality of air allows us to develop an agreed-upon reality.

Air draws us out of instinct and into infinite possibilities. There is a risk here of losing the human touch, of prioritizing freedom to the extent that relational bonds are undervalued and destabilized. An insistence on rationality may lead to a robotic disposition and a tendency to unwittingly harm others through the trappings of cold logic. Air types may endlessly ponder possibilities without committing to a plan. Some become ivory tower intellectuals who lose sight of the "real" world.

Fire

Elemental Level: Spiritual
Classification: Yang, charged
Evolutionary Contribution: The life force, energy, awareness, creativity, intuition, soul realization
Planets: Mars, Sun, Jupiter
Signs: Aries, Leo, Sagittarius
Houses: 1, 5, 9

The fire element contains *light* and *heat*. Its light illuminates the darkness, bringing the potential for awareness and clarity. Heat equates to *vitality*, the sustaining energy of the life force. Heat radiates outward, ready and eager to spread its lively energy. Fire concerns *presence*—it brings us out of the cold and lights and warms our way.

Both light and heat have various *levels of intensity.* As we notice at sunrise and sunset or when adjusting a dimmer switch, there are innumerable shades of brightness. Fire is a *charged* element, rising and falling in levels of intensity. Our passions awaken and diminish depending on a multitude of factors. Anger, lust, motivation or attention-seeking can be aroused, or these passions can subside if the fire is not fed.

Fire is *metaphysical.* As we see with flames, it can shape-shift in a dazzling way. Fire is the energetic vibrating movement within all material, the continual buzzing at the atomic level. It is potent and crackling with *creativity*. Fire is *active and lightning fast.* It is the quickest of the elements. Like a lightning bolt, it can seem to come out of nowhere to awaken us, to suddenly gift us with a "Eureka!" moment of insight. Fire pertains to *intuition* and *awakening,* related to the spiritual level of life—our soul connection to Oneness.

Full of desire and passion, fire can be highly motivated and often urgent. It burns with conviction to attain its goals, seeking fulfillment and intensity. Fire's yang quality is seen in its instigating, restless, energetic disposition. When emphasized in a person, it manifests as extraversion. The element can also be oppressive or invasive and overrun all sense of restraint or reason. Fire can be macho or abusive when out of balance.

Modalities

The modalities concern movement through phases. Any event or process has a beginning, middle, and an end...which leads to another beginning. Spiritual teacher Deepak Chopra has said that if GOD were an acronym, it would stand for "Generation, Organization, and Distribution."

Cardinal comes first, establishing direction and declaring intent. This modality challenges us to figure out how to proceed and get momentum. The cardinal signs of the zodiac are initiatory—setting up the basic structure in which we move. As mentioned in the discussion of houses, the cardinal areas are not more important, just more immediate or central to have established. Aries, Cancer, Libra, and Capricorn are the cardinal signs; respectively, these pertain to autonomy, family, partnerships, and career. These areas provide a base of power from which to operate.

The fixed modality concentrates and solidifies; energy is deepened and given more focus. The initiatory momentum is tempered, allowing for the cultivation of greater strength. Taurus, Leo, Scorpio, and Aquarius are the fixed signs, correlating with personal resources, creative self-expression, interpersonal intimacy and shared resources, and a systemic collective vision. These areas require investment and persistence to create a sturdy center and maximize our potential impact in the world. This leads to the inevitable energetic dispersal in the mutable phase.

The mutable modality expands and reaches, builds bridges and actively engages in learning experiences. What was begun in the cardinal phase ideally reaches completion. There are unlimited possibilities here—acceleration from the fixed phase into greater diversity. Gemini, Virgo, Sagittarius, and Pisces are the mutable signs. They represent the endless realm of ideas, the varieties of earthly manifestation of these ideas, the movement toward meaning and purpose, and the return to sources of spiritual nourishment by integrating understanding into consciousness.

Chapter 3
The Moon

Recall that the Moon is the satellite of Earth, traveling with us through space. Rather than seeing the Moon as a "planet" out there, we can see the Earth and Moon as a *unit*, an energetic system between two celestial bodies. The Moon orbits the Earth, parallel to how we are ensconced in unconsciousness when we are less developed and vulnerable. The Moon is our initial ground of experience; we all begin as infants in the womb. Our focus begins with the Moon because it conveys the origins of each person's journey as a separate self in the process of spiritual maturation.

A handy way to conceptualize the Moon is to think of a child in elementary school. The Moon is the part of us that wants to learn and grow, cope with the realities around us, fit in and have safety and security. We all survey our surroundings, figure out a strategy and do the best we can. There is a fundamental insecurity with the Moon; the human experience is full of hazards and unpredictability.

The core issue is a love of self, which has nothing to do with personality or egoic bolstering—in fact, it's quite the opposite. Self-love is internal. It's what we feel with our hands on our heart, caring and investing in one's fragile humanness. It's accepting weakness and vulnerability, willing to be blown open by the glorious pain of life. Self-love has absolutely nothing to do with anyone else; it's a return to our emotionally naked innocence.

In my counseling practice, I have become acutely aware of how much people are not connected to themselves. Much of the healing of the Moon involves securing a deep and solid internal foundation of unconditional self-love. Then we are better able to trust life and navigate with greater assurance. Most, if not all, of us have been working towards achieving deeper self-love for a long, long time.

From a spiritual view, the Moon is the basin of absorbed experiences in the soul history, what has been concretized as a durable sense of self. As we move from lifetime to lifetime, most of our collected experience is unconscious. The key to remember is that all of it was gathered when we were even less mature than we are today! We move from infant to child to adolescent to adult in a process of maturation; the same dynamic applies in our broader spiritual development. *The Moon is a window into what remains unresolved from our spiritual childhood.*

In this approach, the Moon is equated to the *ego dream* — the organization of an identity as a "me" (ego), which then projects this subjectivity (dream) onto the world. What remains from the past tends to lack resolution. Walking down the street when nothing in particular happens is far less memorable than looking up and seeing planes fly into skyscrapers. The Moon conveys an emotionally charged memory bank. Like the proverbial onion, we progressively venture deeper into the unconscious and release all of what we've been holding on to; then we are better able to abide in the creative presence that underlies life.

As the motor that drives our egoic and personality functioning, the Moon is our connection to the relative world. It evaluates the outside world as being threatening or not, something to move towards or away from. It plays out its issues in separation consciousness—others (and the world itself) are seen as initially responsible for the Moon's pain, struggles, wounds, etc. It starts out completely unaware that it's interacting with itself through the world. Until we awake to this reality, we are prone to deepen a protective (and usually painful) connection with life.

The quote below captures the spirit of the Moon; let it accompany us as we delve deeper into its mysteries:

The moon is a loyal companion. It never leaves. It's always there, watching, steadfast, knowing us in our light and dark moments, changing forever just as we do. Every day it's a different version of itself. Sometimes weak and wan, sometimes strong and full of light. The moon understands what it means to be human. Uncertain. Alone. Cratered by imperfections. ~ Tahereh Mafi

The Depth of the Moon

The Moon is generally not discussed in terms of past lives in conventional astrology or, much of the time, in the various forms of "evolutionary astrology" either. The South Node of the Moon tends to be viewed as the window to the past, and the Sun and Moon are often seen only in the conventional format. In the *Awakening* approach, we will be looking at the Moon as indicative of the past in a variety of ways:

1) Conditioning: As the Moon is contained within the Saturnian realm, it has been influenced and conditioned to be a certain way to operate in consensus reality. It contains remnants of the false self, socially conditioned strategies that were developed in times of less maturation to adapt. Much of the accumulated energy we carry forth illustrates who we've been, but not necessarily who we want to become. Therefore, it's essential to become conscious of our conditioning and to release what is no longer necessary for further development.

2) Identifications and attachments: Everyone has an identity. "I'm _____." This is "me," and outside of my skin are things that are "not me." Such identifications include "nice,"

"smart," "fun," "sexy," "crazy," "dumb," or "lazy." A sense of self hardens (Moon) and becomes our familiar way of operating. We become attached—to particular activities or tendencies, such as working, socializing, cleaning, recreation, sexuality or self-development. In the extreme, these attachments turn into addictions. When less urgent, they are patterns the separate self has developed to have familiarity with life and, therefore, some degree of continuity and contentment. Identifications and attachments keep us tethered to the personal story and a limited way of operating. To expand and awaken, we need to broaden our identifications and release the attachments that restrain us.

3) Temperament and defense mechanisms: We each have a familiar way of approaching the world, our temperament when we're coasting on "autopilot." The Moon conveys the natural rhythms at the biological level, i.e., how we assimilate, process energy and take care of the self. Also, we have instincts and react to what is perceived as threatening stimulation. Some choose to fight, some flee, some grab a bowl of ice cream and others over-analyze everything. Defense is important in (what is perceived by the Moon as) an unpredictable and even threatening world. However, these mechanisms can harden into more globalized regressive tendencies that are completely irrelevant to what is actually occurring.

4) Unfinished business: The Moon suggests what we are holding onto for "better" outcomes. Someone may refuse to let go of a need for greater equality, a solid career, a loving family, community involvement or social acceptance. In early stages of development, we are prone to initially play out these needs in ways that are unconscious, thereby replaying the historical lack of fulfillment in these areas so that they can be addressed. Upon greater awakening and development, we satisfy the outstanding need.

5) Unprocessed emotion: The lunar profile reveals the emotional energy that is not resolved. This is a remnant of operating within separation consciousness, holding onto the feeling that one has been wronged in some way by others or the world itself. The ego doesn't want to let go of this energy because it demands accountability from these external sources. When we awaken, we forgive others because we realize they were mirroring the self. It is very helpful to take measures in processing this energy through the system in order to be in the present. However, this emotional material has been avoided, buried and guarded against — so many times it takes a great catalyst to bring it up.

6) Nurturance/love patterns: The Moon portrays the dynamics of love and care that play out first in the family system and subsequently influence all relationships. The relationship with the mother is found through the Moon, as is (more broadly) the connection with the energetic dynamics of the early family system (see below). How we love, what we find as loving, and what we need to feel love is lunar. *All of this is generated by the historical patterning of self-love in prior lives.* As the dynamics of love are played out in the present life, the opportunity to renew, or work through, the underlying self-love pattern is presented.

The Moon and Mom

As mentioned above, the Moon relates to our *biological* connection with life. All living beings require water for sustenance, and it makes up about 70 percent of the body's composition. (Interestingly, the Earth parallels this by being about the same percentage.) Biology includes (but is certainly not limited to) reproduction. From the reproductive angle, women have a monthly menstrual cycle, paralleling the duration of the lunar cycle. (The use of the phrase "Moon Time" is gaining in popularity.) The womb incubates a developing fetus, and a woman's abdomen rounds out in the shape of the full Moon. All of this is made possible through the transmission of fluid (water) from a man. Not only are men essential for reproduction, they also take part in families, have emotions, form attachments and participate in loving bonds. In fact, reproduction and parenting is a partnership, so men are involved with the Moon as much as women. Reproduction and biology are part of being *human*, which of course includes both genders.

Consistent with the movement towards greater gender equilibrium, men's role in nurturing is becoming increasingly more respected and supported—just as women in the workforce are enjoying greater parity. In the 21st Century, traditional gender stereotypes are decreasing in relevance. Astrology can reflect this development. *Certainly the Moon has relevance to the mother*, as she often plays the central role in nurturing issues, especially in the early years. However, it's timely to now see the Moon from a spiritual perspective.

Whose job is it to nurture us? The more we develop, the more each of us has the job to feed, wash, change ourselves and go to bed at a reasonable time. We are all in charge of a human biological system. Part of maturing is to grow out of seeing this as mom's job. We learn to take care of, and especially love, the self. From a spiritual perspective, we have all been "mothering" an evolving ego for eons: the self. The awakening process involves the retraction of projections, to secure love within.

The Moon in the Chart

Before we attain wholeness within, the natural course of evolution tends to play out love and nurturing issues. The Moon describes a person's emotional unconscious, which is extremely personal and subjective. Applying language can only point at the territory. Ideally, we sink into the Moon being portrayed in the two-dimensional chart with intuition and empathy. There is always a left-brain (analytical) gathering of information, but the right-brain (intuitive) is where we experience its depth.

Planets in Aspect to the Moon

Though many astrologers focus on sign placement as the primary variable in planetary placements, this approach sees energy (planets, frequencies of consciousness) as the principle ingredient of our spiritual composure. Signs *modify* our energy into particular evolutionary programs and styles. Therefore, we first explore the Moon's inherent energy as influenced through planetary aspects.

Planets in aspect to the Moon are *partners*. They illustrate how emotional patterns are played out and indicate the habitual behaviors that are geared to provide sustenance. They also point to what forces have historically caused problems in this regard and ways to work on them.

Smooth aspects (trine, sextile, quintile) to the Moon show emotional strengths—how the person naturally gets needs met and how that person instinctually behaves. These aspects tend to indicate attachment patterns that are not resistant. For example, Moon trine Saturn is agreeable to authority and emotionally attached to complying with the conditioned program to feel loved. Challenging aspects (square, quincunx, opposition) indicate blockages, frustrations and reactive patterns that stem from past emotional difficulty. Moon square Saturn has a strong need to have the greater security and structure that Saturn provides, but has issues around how that has played out. Any planet in conjunction with the Moon is an intimate part of the soul's emotional memory, shaping the unconscious and manifesting strongly. There is identification with the energy—for better or worse, depending on how awake the person is.

The following paragraphs posit some examples of how the various planets in (major) aspect to the Moon might influence it. They convey the general emotional dynamics and must be modified by additional information (the type of aspect, sign and house placement). These possibilities are intended not to be all-inclusive but to give a taste of what the pairing could be like. The focus here is on *why* such an aspect could be represented in a chart, rather than just a description of *how* it plays out.

In general, as is the case with all lunar variables, there is something unresolved or unfinished. The evolving ego has gotten itself involved with particular energies and is in the process of being more conscious with their management.

Moon/Mercury

The Moon in aspect to Mercury connects the unconscious emotional needs to the intellect and communicative function. This combination is learning to master the art of emotional intelligence. Mercury's busyness and chatter has likely been used as a defensive measure. There is an unconscious pull to use the mind at the expense of sinking into the heart. The need to prove one's intellectual skills, the rationalization of emotions, or feeling youthful or naïve are some reasons this aspect may appear.

This combination could manifest as a tendency to speak impulsively—the person who blurts out and then covers the mouth. Conversely, there also may be a tendency to keep one's ideas (Mercury) under wraps (Moon). The Moon colors the otherwise rational intellectual function in highly subjective ways. Attaining precision and clarity of thought could be a challenge. The gift is the ability to speak from the heart and to balance and consider thought processes in relation to their emotional implications. The unresolved work is to connect heart and mind.

Moon/Venus

This combination portrays a strong connection between urgent emotional "needs" (Moon) with the more casual "wants" (Venus). What we want, including gifts, popularity, peace or comfort, can be exaggerated. To feel secure, the person *requires* cooperation from other people, the accumulation of possessions, or leisure time. There are strong attachments to having things run smoothly, and if they don't, there is potential upset.

It is healthy and necessary to connect with others. Moon/Venus people are resolving patterns in their soul histories in which connections did not completely provide the love they desired. As others are a sacred mirror of the self, the work is to befriend and love the self more deeply. Then others (Venus) will ultimately reflect that love back. If greater self-love isn't secured, whatever neuroses, issues or challenges that exist in the emotional unconscious are perpetually played out with others. The conscious version has innate diplomacy skills and a harmonious connection with the sensual world.

Moon/Mars

Mars concerns autonomy, being aligned with one's own power and venturing through life boldly. The Moon in aspect to Mars suggests an incompletion with this prerogative and some frustration, if not anger, about attaining it. There is some issue between attachments (Moon) and independence (Mars) that can make the person edgy or irritable as he or she learns to claim sovereignty.

The management of anger/frustration is necessary. Ideally, this pent-up energy is channeled into efforts that bring about the autonomy being sought. Clear, direct and efficient dispersal of intention is most helpful. Working out, martial arts and exercise promotes personal strength and also helps resolve what is left over from the past. Also, sexual passion and intensity are often areas through which greater fulfillment is sought. Maturation moves towards increasing levels of leadership and empowerment. The person finally becomes unapologetic about being him or herself.

Moon/Jupiter

This combination shows an emotional need to influence culture and society—to do something purposeful that shapes the collective. The evolving ego is actually learning to see and appreciate the self in more meaningful ways, and externalization into the world is a reflection. The spiritual quest is a journey inward towards self-discovery, and ultimately the Moon/Jupiter person behaves with the knowledge that the outside world *is* the self.

In the soul history, this quest for self may have been misguided by previous teachings. Many with this combination have been emotionally indoctrinated into religion, education or belief systems that have been less than fully awake. The vestiges of these patterns require dismantlement and purgation. It can be very painful (Moon) to see, never mind admit, that the principles that have been directing one's life have been erroneous, or only partially true. Moon/Jupiter people develop by questioning everything and arriving at the truth that resonates with the heart. Functioning maturely, there is a loving engagement with the game of life without the need to take it so seriously.

Moon/Saturn

There is an emotional connection with authority, mainstream consciousness or the value system that promotes structure, protection and security. There may be harmony or tension with such themes, but a lack of resolution exists regardless. The root here is some struggle maturing, and that struggle is projected. The Moon/Saturn person is finding greater authority within. Then any unresolved need to hold positions of stature can be achieved.

Along the way there may be patterns of negativity, self-doubt, sometimes even depression. There is emotional material in the well of the unconscious that is stuck. The proverbial lid needs to come off to move that material out, and this requires the ability to feel what was previously repressed. The person may simply be afraid of embracing this, which leads to being afraid of the world. The self-fulfilling prophecy brings hardship and other sobering realities, which can reinforce the mindset that the world is not a loving place. Evolution involves embracing and loving all of the human condition, not just the "positive" dimensions. The gifts are wisdom and the subsequent attainment of greater stature.

Moon/Chiron

This aspect portrays issues around health and well-being. Unloving dynamics towards the self can lead to a lack of nourishment or self-care. Some people are "sick" of themselves, others, or the world. The fracturing away from Sprit's unconditional love has sculpted the ego's journey in emotionally painful ways.

The work is to now take responsibility in loving the self through healthier routines (diet, nutrition, exercise, sleep, meditation, etc.). Often, there are health issues to negotiate. The spiritual stakes are raised. If the prior self-harmful patterns perpetuate, there are greater issues to address. If they are transformed, then a clear and healthy sense of self emerges. Moon/Chiron matures to model and nurture self-care with a particular sensitivity to the vulnerable, sick or with children.

Moon/Uranus

The evolving ego urgently wants to break through to a new level of awareness, experience and metaphysical connection. At early stages of development, there is cluelessness about how to attain this awareness, and this combination can be anxious. Unstable patterns, or a disconnection from what is occurring in the present, are likely. In writing my *Uranus* book, I was struck by how often Moon/Uranus people had challenging nurturing issues in the family of origin or early environment: absentee parents, divorce, being uprooted, homeland in strife, etc. This is all a reflection of the internal distancing from self. There is an underlying anxiety that the "other shoe is going to drop," because in the soul history, it already has!

The work is to accept the prior instability and turmoil, but the ego often tries to secure a better future (Uranus). The key to the future is, paradoxically, being with the past. By breaking through (Uranus) into the heart (Moon), one can move energy through. Releasing anxiety and tension allows the biological system (Moon) to catch up to the present moment. The development of Moon/Uranus is emotional liberation, and people with these aspects become adept at supporting such freedom in others.

Moon/Neptune

The emotional need is for the return to unconditional love. Initially, there can be grief or alienation from the world. Some cling to idealism or transcendence, which may distance the self from its more basic and primal needs. Others cope through escapist tendencies, lose a sense of self, and are ghosts to their own existence. Instead of trying to ease pain, the way through is to love and accept our emotions.

This combination may point to some degree of emotional confusion about what would constitute nurturing and/or deprivation of nurturing. People with these aspects may try to be incredibly loving and compassionate to others, not realizing that they want this for themselves. There's often a pronounced need to make contact with something redemptive and uplifting. Of course, the redemption is the return to self. As the Moon conveys unprocessed emotion, there may be sadness or dejection to release. With greater maturation, heightened intuition, psychic abilities and right-brain creativity are discovered. There can be a fuller embrace of nature and an evolution into the mystic.

Moon/Pluto

The unresolved need is to make profound contact with life, to feel deeply and potently what it means to be alive. In early stages of spiritual development, this need did not play out consciously and subsequently led to wounding. As a result, there is an enflamed well of wounded emotion that needs to be dealt with. The severity of the condition is in equal measure to the powerful potential available upon successful healing and resolution.

Emotional breakdown into the unconscious well is fuel for a breakthrough. Upon deeper bonding with self, the person connects powerfully with others and the world. With greater maturation, there is no longer a need to play out pain. In contrast, life becomes an ongoing experience of ecstasy. Pluto deals with extremes, and the conscious end of the spectrum has the most passionate embrace of life imaginable. Moon/Pluto individuals have likely been affected by extreme circumstances in their soul histories. Prior lives have left an enduring mark, and now is the time to take full responsibility for that unconscious dreaming. By so doing, deep, life-altering intimacy—and even the ability to shake and stir our collective evolution—is attainable.

Moon in the Signs

Astrology signs convey evolutionary curricula; for instance, Aries is learning about courage, and Capricorn, stature. Signs are also stylistic and play out in very personal ways with the Moon. Taurus can be stubborn, Leo showy and Libra charming. There is a wide range to these programs and styles, and all of us start out at the unconscious end of the spectrum.

Aries Moon

The cardinal fire Moon wants to achieve greater autonomy and assertion, to do things "my way." There is likely some degree of frustration or anger around prior treatment, intensity inside that wants to declare its independence. Exercise, venting or directing passion purposely into projects is helpful to release the charge. Without such actions, the Aries Moon is prone to creating conflict with others, even releasing a rampage. The most anti-social and brash behaviors are found in its darkness. What the Aries Moon person actually wants is to behave in bold and courageous ways, as there is interest in becoming a leader. Attached to its passion and identified with its fire, Aries can stay confined in a very lonely soul cage of "me against the world." Further steps of awakening inevitably bring the reality that Aries has been arguing, and in conflict, with only the self. With greater self-love, the conscious Aries is able to assertively use the vehicle of the separate self as an instrument for change.

Taurus Moon

The fixed earth quality suggests some degree of being stuck, a resistance to change or pronounced need for comfort and stability. Taurus may be conditioned to be reliable, a "rock" for others. It may over-identify and become attached to the body, pleasures, money, the physical realm and keeping things simple. There are often unresolved issues with the sensual—healing occurs through touch, massage or self-care. Taurus is learning greater self-alignment, inner peace and strength. Protective measures tend to focus on soothing, such as eating comfort foods or gathering possessions. The unconscious Taurus struggles with self-doubt and self-worth issues. From this insecure base of operations, Taurus may limit social connection in preference of safety, or enter connections requiring others to be his or her "rock." When a stronger foundation of self-love is developed, Taurus achieves the self-alignment and conscious determination it truly desires. Spiritual creativity is given form—the Taurus Moon is capable of distributing beauty and artistry generously, without any fear of scarcity or limitation.

Gemini Moon

Mutable air can be restless, scattered or immature. There's a deep-seated curiosity about life, the need to be intelligent and versatile. There may be an attachment to dualistic thinking or elaborate mental excursions that keep one stuck in thoughts. The mode of defense is analyzing situations instead of dropping down into the heart and body to actually feel. As a result, there can be coldness or aloofness to the plight of others, as this is a reflection of self. Development of greater emotional (Moon) intelligence (Gemini) allows the person's message to resonate more deeply with others. When a deeper foundation of self-love is secured, Gemini Moons become delightful and irresistible. Their fascinating and articulate take on everything is boosted by an emotional investment in creating a healthier world. They become our great storytellers, communicators and teachers of all stripes. In particular, they might be great at teaching youth, as they are reaching out to the youth inside themselves, who wants more love.

Cancer Moon

This is a most sensitive placement—the Cancer Moon has been willing to feel. However, what has historically been felt was gathered in less developed states of consciousness. Therefore, Cancer Moons are filled with the remnants of experiences that carry unresolved emotion and have possibly internalized negative stories about the self. They can be lonely, protective, defensive and hurt—hiding from what is seen as a cruel world. This moodiness is rectified through deeper self-love. It is spiritual practice for the Cancer Moon to go down memory lane and to accept and love the past. With the view that we are interacting with the self through others, the blame game is unraveled. The Cancer Moon is then able to emerge from its shell and satisfy the unresolved need to bond. This may play out with a new, more conscious relationship with family—either the system of origin, as a parent, or both. More broadly, aware Cancer Moons join with the broader world in ways that strengthen the emotional "glue" among us. They are natural counselors, using the broadest definition.

Leo Moon

The Leo Moon has a history of seeking validation from others and accepting how things are with a sunny disposition. A defense mechanism is to minimize emotion, keep it light, and put on a happy face. Underneath, they actually want more joy, and the way to get it is to actually feel what they are avoiding. There is unfinished business around being appreciated, and this is resolved by appreciating more deeply who they are. If they avoid this, then they unconsciously petition the outer world to provide that recognition. They act in attention-seeking ways that may lead to the same rejection they are actually playing out within themselves. When the inner life is more loved and secure, Leo Moons are able to become more authentically colorful, charismatic and entertaining. Other people are warmed by their spirit, and they attain the popularity and inclusion that they seek. They invite others to accept their emotions and join in affirmative ways to celebrate our humanness.

Virgo Moon

The conditioning of the Virgo Moon is to be a part of the flock—obedience, compliance, and doing the necessary tasks to keep everyone content. I like to joke that they are "full of should." I *should* be helpful, and I *shouldn't* complain. All of this keeps unprocessed emotion at bay. They tend to judge themselves, and these evaluations may inhibit joy and being present. Their default tendency is to seek to be better. The externalized need to perform and be seen as competent is actually a reflection of the need for inner work. Virgo can be analytical, critical, anxious and self-flagellating. Like every other Moon placement, these darker facets become brightened by self-love. With a more secure and loving inner foundation, they become more adept at developing whatever contribution they want to offer. Virgo Moons potentially become our experts, master craftsmen, specialists and instructors. With self-satisfaction, they assist others in similarly reaching greater health and effectiveness in navigating life. They are devoted to making the human project functional and prosperous, reflecting how they now feel inside.

Libra Moon

All of us cooperate with social norms to some degree, but Libra is particularly prone to selling out to the directives of others, and society as a whole. The underlying need for connection is a subtle form of self-abandonment. Libra Moons are really seeking greater inner peace, and the externalization of this need potentially creates co-dependence or a lack of authenticity. They can be fawning and slick, trying to charm others in order to have everything seem okay. When asked how they are, Libra Moons tend to say "fine." With greater realism and acceptance of all emotions, Libra finally befriends the self. Then the sacred reflection from others mirrors this bond, and they attain happy relationships. Adept at socialization, conscious Libra Moons are excellent in a variety of roles in culture and society. They are liberated to share their artistry, bringing touches of grace and beauty that enhance life. Through a deeper trust and bond with the self, they discover that everything actually is fine, and they make the world a finer place.

Scorpio Moon

The unconscious Scorpio refuses to accept the "negative" things that occur. The controlling of one's emotions then becomes externalized as a need to control situations and others. All the while, the intensity of the emotion that is being avoided creates drama and conflict. What Scorpio really desires is powerful connections, to really feel invested and passionate about life. On the road to experiencing this, Scorpio Moons may test the world to provoke reactions. If they can't experience positive intimacy, then negative intimacy (manipulation, harshness, brooding, etc.) is substituted. This ups the stakes for the eventual climactic embrace of the self. When the Scorpio Moon changes tactics and discovers connection within, the power of the internal world becomes a foundation for a powerful impact in whatever Scorpio chooses to do. Scorpio Moons are purposeful and determined, able to get to the heart of the matter and be true agents of growth. They achieve what they always needed, to see the world (a reflection of the self) evolve and thrive.

Sagittarius Moon

Sagittarius is driven by what is understood as "right" action. Emotions can get in the way of purposeful action, so a Sagittarius Moon is initially avoidant. This pattern tends to harden into dogmatic or arrogant "I know best" behaviors. If challenged, the fiery defense mechanism potentially turns harmful. An Archer fires an arrow, a metaphor of meaningful motion, but the darker version is a weapon. When Sagittarius deepens into the self, he or she is more able to satisfy the unmet need for answers. Instead of empty opinions and theories, conscious Sagittarius Moons have the wisdom and depth found through greater self-connection. Then they develop authentic life philosophies stemming from the heart. They do things that make a difference in the world and join with others in uplifting and adventurous ways. Sagittarius Moons are inspirational and learn to champion the emotional expansion of an awakened view.

Capricorn Moon

As with the other earth signs, Capricorn has been conditioned to be pragmatic and comply with the dictates of conventional society. With an emotional need to align with the status quo, Capricorn Moons are prone to initially trust tradition and dominant power structures. There is an unmet need to have more stature, authority or impact—to excel in society. Oftentimes, this pursuit leads to the mismanagement of their emotions, as these are seen as distractions. Dark Capricorn Moons become shut down, even cold, wintry. The way they develop greater management skills is through greater self-management of love and acceptance. If they skip this vital step, then they occupy positions in dictatorial ways. This leads to problems with others, further triggering the necessity to work out issues and more fully humanize their experiences. From a more emotionally sensitive inner foundation, they excel in positions in which they control the levers of power. They are now motivated by love instead of fear, and invite others to similarly mature into their spiritual authority.

Aquarius Moon

With this placement comes an underlying identification as being different. Inside, there has historically been a need (at times, quite unconscious) to individuate from social and cultural conditioning. There may have been reluctance to act in accordance with the true self, as the risks involved were too challenging. Aquarius Moons have a future orientation, the hope for a more fulfilling existence tomorrow. They may be detached or disconnected from emotions in the present. Some with this placement have shock or trauma, which also creates a disconnection if not worked through. The more Aquarius Moons affirm the inner foundation of love, the more willing they are to reach out and bring their brilliance into form. They no longer have fear or trepidation because they see that the world is their own reflection. Then they claim the freedom they've been longing for and do exactly as they please. By so doing, they are at the forefront of evolution—establishing communities, investing in progressive causes and sparking the youth to rise into their creative power.

Pisces Moon

Often there's a well of unprocessed grief or sadness with the Pisces Moon. Those with this placement have been let down by life, wishing that events played out in more fulfilling ways. They have coped by imagining what could be and are yearning to see that realized. In some cases, there is identity confusion or the lack of a healthy ego structure. Pisces Moons may be invisible, ghosts in their lives, escaping in some way. When they embrace their sensitivity and develop greater compassion for themselves, they arise anew with fresh intentions. They relish the prospect of what they can manifest with their visionary outlook and become artists, poets, mystics or metaphysicians who help all of humanity bring Spirit into form. Since they realize that life is but a dream, they help us navigate through the various layers as we awaken.

Moon in the Houses

If signs are the "how" of life playing out, houses are the "where." Houses show a strong attachment to particular areas of life, a fluency of experience. There is familiarity in this realm, but also something unfinished in the affairs there. The house placement of the Moon conveys some historical immaturity in that area, and further awakening will help bring resolution and, ultimately, something meaningful to share. The soul instinctually operates from that realm of life and unconsciously patterns behavior with the house gestalt as a reference.

House 1: It's natural for someone with this placement to act in lunar ways. Many times this indicates caretaking or an innate proclivity for hospitality. Classically emotional, the person can have a heightened sense of caring and sweetness, or defensiveness and reactivity. Prone to acting unconsciously, the first-house Moon may have no idea how he or she is coming across. What is sought is greater empowerment through following the heart.

House 2: There is a marked insecurity in this placement, questions about safety, survival and worth—a need for greater poise or solace. Learning self-sufficiency, earning money, and feeling more secure in the body are helpful. The fundamental question "Am I good enough?" is being reconciled. Upon doing so, second-house Moons have a solid base of operations to be resourceful and effective in their aims.

House 3: Often there is an identification with, and attachment to, the workings of the mind and being seen as intelligent. Some tend to be conditioned to think and say certain things, and they are learning to release this to find greater depth in their own ideas. Sometimes this placement shows an emotional naiveté or a soul lacking wisdom, so the goal is to further the accumulation of experience. As third-house Moons develop, greater respect for their insights is fulfilled, and sharing through writings or teachings is an extension of the heart.

House 4: This placement is indicative of a soul with deep connections to its roots and lineage. There is often a strong need to nest or maintain ties to family members because the conditioning from family systems has been so strong. Sometimes there is a reluctance to be out in the world, a preference for privacy and hiding out. As the inner life strengthens, there is a durable foundation to springboard out into the world and follow the heart.

House 5: The Moon here shows the desire to more fully share oneself, to engage and connect earnestly with life. There can be childlike innocence, an unresolved need to have more playfulness or fun. There also can be issues around having children. The Moon in the fifth house is learning to find more joy within the self, to cease externalizing this need. Then those with this placement can more maturely develop their creativity and offer unique expressions of their talents.

House 6: The Moon here often suggests a soul striving for something, one who feels weak in comparison to others or a legacy of identifying with underdog or downtrodden positions. The emotional nature is organized in a somewhat fragile or insecure manner. There is an inner need to perform tasks to receive love or nurturing from others. Sixth-house Moons have a need to be of assistance to others. Upon development, they love what they do and become very adept at it.

House 7: A pronounced need for others to love and support is quite likely here. There may be little or no awareness that love comes from within and is reflected back. By petitioning others to provide it, seventh-house Moons have agreed to orbit around others and even identify as secondary to them. However, the natives actually seek equality and mutuality. This is achieved by retracting the petition and arriving at greater autonomy. Then relationship becomes optional and enhancing, instead of perpetuating unresolved needs.

House 8: This placement portrays an initial dependency on others for support, emotional, financial or otherwise. What began as an innocent need (Moon) for deep connection leads to the giving away of power. Now the task is to cultivate inner strength and reengage in meaningful connections in a more awake way. Being able to work through prior upset and conflict in new contexts heals the past. There is a pull toward drama and excess as the Moon is becoming more aware of itself. An eighth-house Moon is learning to confront subterranean dynamics in the self and manage how those dynamics play out with others.

House 9: The spiritual quest is unfinished and likely had some navigation error through prior unconsciousness. Some possibilities include the absorption of inaccurate or misguided teachings, or the inability to live life completely on one's own terms. Further steps along a conscious path are next. Ultimately, a sound life philosophy that motives a clear mission is discovered. The attachment to exploration may be stimulating, but the unpredictability of adventure leads to an emotional nature that is unsettled. Ninth-house Moons are finding greater meaning within.

House 10: This placement suggests a need to be seen, to have the public receive one's contribution. A soul with this Moon position feels, or has a strong need to be, important in some way. Emotional energy is bound up with unfinished aspirations. An organized and effective dispersal of this energy into vocational matters brings resolution. Giving a gift to the world that originates from the heart is the intention. Those with the Moon here tend to display their temperament openly. Wearing the heart on the sleeve *does* invite connection—but also turmoil.

House 11: There is a strong need for affiliation here. Cultural/social conditioning from communities, congregations or other group settings has had great influence. Growth involves making a worldly impact in truly progressive ways instead of being shaped by group processes (often unconsciously). Taking part in movements, causes or collective endeavors that make the

102

world more conscious brings integration. When love is found within, the eleventh-house Moon can truly join with a broader web of allies.

House 12: At a personality level, this placement portrays some reticence or shyness, a tendency to stay on the sidelines. At a deeper level, there is an unresolved need to make more contemplative contact with the universe—to feel nourished and revitalized by nature/Spirit. Growth is furthered by trusting life more, feeling inspired and loved and being able to act directly from this source. A twelfth-house Moon may grapple with loss, or the refusal or inability to detach from something dear to the heart. Oftentimes, the emotional nature is lost, excessively private, or drowning in unresolved grief. The promise is redemption through compassion.

Chapter 4
The Nodes of the Moon

The lunar nodes play a major role in just about any form of evolutionary or spiritual astrology, and rightfully so. They are indispensable, clarifying much of the spiritual work an evolving ego takes on in a particular lifetime. We can understand them within the context of awakening detailed in this approach. Simply stated, the Moon is the "seed," the Nodes the "gardening," and the Sun the "flower." In these next two chapters, we will explore the nodes in-depth—but first, let's establish some perspective.

What exactly are the nodes? They are the points of intersection of the Moon with the ecliptic, the revolutionary path of the Earth around the Sun. As the Moon orbits the Earth, the South Node is the point where the Moon travels from above to below the Earth's ecliptic, and the North Node is where the Moon ascends from below to above. Note the theme of reaching down, as in retrieving from the past, to rising up into new and innovative uses.

The nodes indicate the points of intersection—how the emotional basin of the past (Moon) connects with the present reality (Sun) as we travel through life in manifest form. *The Moon's nodes pertain to the resolution of the Moon itself.* From the deep well of absorbed experience, particular spiritual work is taken on for greater attendance. We highlight this crucial connection, which is not found in much of the available astrological literature. The reason for this is the perpetuation of the conventional approach to the Sun and Moon (complementary pair), which undercuts the Moon's depth (as well as the Sun's reach). By integrating a spiritual perspective, our understanding of the nodes broadens significantly.

As we mature, the evolving ego (Moon) chooses various interests or areas as part of its curriculum. We "major" in the South Node, becoming interested in certain themes, dynamics or spiritual work. Some want to become artists, others philosophers, businessmen or humanitarians. The astrology system conveys twelve broad archetypal fields in which to learn. Since the Moon starts out in unconsciousness, it has not received an "A" in the curriculum (portrayed by the South Node) yet. In fact, most of us have injected a good deal of egoic distortion, which makes sense because we all start out as spiritual children.

And here's the pivotal issue: Should we "move away" from this established focus, or learn to do it more consciously? The great departure of the *Awakening* approach, as compared to some other types of evolutionary astrology, is to *assertively advocate the more awakened potentials of the South Node*. The tendency to want to move away from our unconsciousness is yet another strategy of avoidance. Certainly, there may be a desire to abandon what is familiar to move on to new vistas; but to promote greater spiritual maturity, we must finish the work we started, earn an "A," and graduate.

The South Node conveys habitual behavior patterns, while the Moon is internal. Let's say that a person is severely hurt by emotionally trying events, as indicated by an eighth-house Cancer Moon square Pluto. As a protective measure, that person might *choose* to live life as a hermit. The South Node, perhaps in Capricorn in the first house, would reveal that *behavior choice*. The South Node points to biographical tendencies, how we've previously navigated in the world. The Moon is who we really are inside, the ongoing impact from life on an emotional level, which has sculpted the nature of the ego dream.

Since the South Node developed from some degree of unconsciousness, it has remnants of the darker or shadow components of its sign (and attendant factors). The missing

106

elements are provided by the North Node, as it is coming from the polar opposite place. Development of the North Node balances the tendencies and proclivities of the South. Think of a seesaw. We initially sit on one side (South Node) and can get bogged down there. We develop the other (North Node) and attain balance. To maintain equilibrium, we don't sit on the new side and weigh that down. Rather, we have both sides of the seesaw reach a state of harmony. Therefore, it's crucial to keep on developing the South.

The North Node not only helps the South Node get the "A" but also brings to it an entirely new dimension! This is where the magic happens. Unbeknownst to the evolving ego, a concerted effort to develop the North Node will provide unforeseen skills and attributes that will take the South Node further than what was previously imagined. However, achieving that is a challenge, for we truly have to grow. Not only do we have to do the challenging work of gardening (nodal work), we also need to engage the flowering of the awakening process into the promise of the Sun (which we'll address in the next chapter). All of this will be explained with the chart examples that follow.

Lessons

I find a handy way to construe the nodes is to think of them as our spiritual lessons. Though we can explore them in terms of particular biographical situations and karmic stories (and past life regression work may confirm this), the approach here is to deeply understand what we are actually *learning*.

The South Node portrays a very familiar pattern that tends to be universally recognizable. I have yet to see any chart in which this is not the case. The South Node replicates so vividly in the present life because its habits began from unconsciousness. As we start out as children in any lifetime, we reflexively and instinctually act out our unconscious behavior patterns. Some may see this as fate, and in some ways that is right. The way to break out of the soul cage of endless fated repetition is to wake up. Spiritual growth brings freedom.

Who wants to mindlessly do the same thing over and over, do the same thing over and over, do the same thing over and over? Yet that is exactly what most of us have done! We are prone to being on the merry-go-round, the cycles of samsara, until we mature. We can engage the vertical dimension of developing consciousness and address the terrain from new vantage points. At a more advanced level (a higher turn of the spiral), we do the South Node more consciously and thereby resolve the work. Suggesting that we should "move away" from the South Node may actually limit spiritual growth.

In the Vedic tradition, the Nodes are called Rahu (North) and Ketu (South), the dragon's head and tail. We lead with the head (North Node) and advance with great enthusiasm because learning those lessons is the soul's intention. However, we may initially start out quite naïve. Proceeding consciously or not, what we energetically "eat" becomes part of our system and assimilated with what came before (South). As we proceed through life, we attain more experiences and further digest what is still in process.

Out the tail we excrete the "waste" of the South Node. In this sense, we are ridding ourselves of the distortions and missteps from our unconscious prior behaviors. If we have learned and grown through the North Node attributes, our waste becomes excellent fertilizer. There is a gift we give the world through the process of assimilating the poles of the nodal axis. The contribution becomes more advanced and conscious, no longer stumbling or erring in a particular direction, but whole and solid and unmistakably potent. If we don't grow in novel ways, then we perpetually replay our "shit."

The Nodal Analysis

As is the case in other areas of astrology, there has been an overemphasis on sign placement with the nodes. In fact, entire books are written that address only this one factor. In the *Awakening* approach, we consider all pertinent variables: the sign and house placement, the planets in aspect to the nodes, and those that serve as the dispositors. To thoroughly address all possible combinations would be too much to address. Instead, this chapter and the next will outline how to approach the analysis and the major points of synthesis.

Signs convey the evolutionary curriculums in which we have interest, while house placement gives crucial information about the *context* of the soul lessons being addressed. The twelve houses will color the nodal profile in specific areas, (i.e., there are twelve different versions of any of the basic nodal characteristics.) The nodes' dispositors play key roles in describing how the lessons conveyed by the nodes are *energetically* carried out.

The Nodes in the Signs

The nodal axis always bridges one of the six polarities. Opposing signs are in a most dynamic situation because they complement while also stretching each other. They are counterparts—opposites like male and female but, in a way, duplicates too. As seen in the yin/yang symbol, there is a piece of each in the other. The synthesis of these polarities produces wholeness.

The Moon resides in the relative world (within Saturn) and plays out in separation consciousness. There is an identification with being in a certain place, and the external world plays the role of the other. Likewise, the attributes of the Moon's

South Node show an initial familiarity and set of experiences, while the North Node is the other. Recall that the nodes relate directly to the Moon—they indicate how the past has been *navigated* at the level of separation. Resolving the lessons of the nodes (spiritual gardening) helps get us to unity consciousness as we integrate what has been projected.

Below are some thoughts on each of the six polarities. We will address the nature of the familiar curriculum (South), the qualities that complement and bring wholeness (North), and what the synthesis promises.

Aries/Libra

This polarity concerns the lessons of "I–Thou" relating dynamics. It's a delicate balance between the self and others at the personality level. Those with the nodes here are addressing how independence and togetherness fit together.

Aries South Node: This signature shows development towards greater self-alignment and leadership. It is not always the case that the person in question has been a solitary lone wolf who is learning how to socially connect (though that is a possibility). I have noticed time and again that people with this placement would like to be more confident leaders and are challenged about rising to that stature. House placement and planets involved fill in more of the picture; however, an Aries South Node does suggest that the curriculum of personal power is unfinished and needs more conscious navigation. Natives are learning to hold this power more soundly in order to enter interpersonal scenarios (Libra North Node) with strength and directness (Aries) and experience more satisfying and passionate relations.

Libra South Node: This placement suggests that relationship dynamics are an area that the evolving ego is learning about. Unconscious Libran patterns can involve orbiting around others in co-dependency, giving power away to the needs of a partnership, or identifying as part of the relationship instead of as oneself. There is conditioning to be a certain way for others. Also, some with this South Node are simply not so adept at relating yet and are learning greater skills about how to truly connect. They may be completely socialized and inauthentic stemming from a paucity of self-knowledge. The Aries North Node attributes bring greater directness, self-alignment and risk-taking—ingredients necessary for more spirited social engagement. Aries North Nodes are learning healthy selfishness.

Synthesis: At the soul level, others are a reflection of us. The integration of this polarity secures personal strength and autonomous functioning in order to connect with others with this awareness. We are gracious and accepting towards others (Libra) because we provide that to ourselves. We are able to be provocative and daring (Aries) in our social behavior because we are not afraid of who we are.

Taurus/Scorpio

The Taurus/Scorpio tension is between personal security/comfort and dramatic/transformative experiences. How can we balance safety and stability and reach inner calm, while also being open to engaging with life in a bold, unflinching manner?

Taurus South Node: Many with this signature are in the process of developing greater self-worth, deeper inner calm, and more money or security as a result of this growth. On the way towards the promise of the conscious Taurus, they may have been literally stuck. Some are stuck in routine, others in cultural or relationship patterns, and others in simplistic paradigms or materialism. Whatever the case (which the other factors connected with the South Node would reveal), there tends to be

111

resistance to change due to a preference for the status quo. The remedy is nothing short of a complete immersion (Scorpio) into some type of life reinvention. Those with this placement are learning to delve into fear, the source of their resistance, and confront it boldly — and to have a more emotional base of strength on which to proceed. They embody a newfound warrior spirit of empowerment (Scorpio).

Scorpio South Node: There is karma that suggests very edgy or dark scenarios with this placement. In the soul journey, there has been interest in compelling and dramatic experiences, and those experiences have left a mark. The person was not yet fully conscious in this realm, so these encounters ended up being wounding. Now, greater psychological savvy, and a willingness to enter the shadow, equip the person with deeper insight and internal power. He or she reengages with the terrain of intimacy, and the use of power and conflict (Scorpio) from a more centered place, completing the curriculum. All the while, development in the direction of calming pursuits (Taurus North Node) is very supportive. Massage and bodywork, anything to get in touch with the senses, promote greater peace and tranquility. Working with the earth (gardening, art, etc.) brings the psyche in better connection with the here and now.

Synthesis: Bridging this polarity brings soul wisdom (Scorpio) into the body (Taurus). The conscious Scorpio connects us with the evolutionary intelligence of life, which includes the reality of death. This no longer creates fear but rather empowers us to maximize our efficacy in physical form. We cooperate with all of what life brings because we see that it only makes us stronger, both physically (Taurus) and psychologically (Scorpio).

Gemini/Sagittarius

This polarity deals with perceptions and viewpoints — balancing open-ended inquiry (Gemini) and solid convictions (Sagittarius). How can we learn about the world (Gemini) and develop an approach to life (Sagittarius)?

Gemini South Node: Gathering of information is unfinished, and some type of issue needs to be addressed. There may be an overreliance on the left brain, a lack of coherence, extreme receptiveness to others' teachings, or a tendency to identify with and act in youthful or puer patterns. There is interest in becoming more of an intellectual authority, a messenger or communicator of something more advanced. Gemini can be carefree, scattered, ungrounded or immature. Developing greater direction, conviction, or a sense of moral imperative and opinions (Sagittarius North Node) helps bring balance. Then learning areas are informed by a broader philosophy and sense of spiritual investment.

Sagittarius South Node: A life lived with purpose has been central to these souls. However, they weren't yet fully conscious, so the path became rigid or dogmatic to some degree. This signature does correlate with unconsciousness in belief systems and living a life path that was errant in some way. These natives are reengaging with the proverbial quest, which is now complemented by the open-mindedness and curiosity of Gemini. The premature arrival at answers gives way to a refreshed sense of possibility. Then the occupancy of positions that provide life direction (clergy, teacher, coach, etc.) is bolstered by more information and life experience. These people are learning to tell the story (Gemini North Node) of the great quest towards Spirit (Sagittarius).

Synthesis: The mind is limited when it comes to absolute truth while stationed in the relative world. The bridging of this polarity occurs when we deconstruct our thinking patterns altogether and arrive at a whole new level of understanding—that of *becoming* Spirit. The quest reaches a crescendo, we arrive in direct *experience* of the numinous, and we get to teach others all about it.

Cancer/Capricorn

The resolution of this axis is found with emotional (Cancer) maturation (Capricorn). Ideally, we can be both loving and disciplined, putting the heart into our greatest efforts.

Cancer South Node: Family dynamics, self-love and/or emotional security have been issues in the soul history. The evolving ego has entered dynamics in which nurturing patterns have created karma. Often Cancer South Nodes are in caretaking or domestic roles and feel obligated to be a certain way for loved ones (or in some cases, a nurturing family may be absent). The more they mature in themselves, the less entangled they are in love issues with family or others. The Capricorn North Node development includes some degree of toughening up, taking measures to be more grown up and independent. Focusing on vocation, ambitions, and attaining greater personal stature builds greater self-sufficiency. Becoming one's own sense of authority eliminates the need to jockey for love. Then nurturing patterns are healed through this more mature disposition.

Capricorn South Node: This signature shows an allegiance to the dominant value system of the Western world. There is an emphasis on accomplishment, being responsible, grown-up and ambitious. These souls are unfinished in attaining the pinnacle of their aims, so they return to continue the work. Along the way, they may have hardened some restrictive, fearful, repressive or controlled patterns that need greater emotional lubrication (Cancer North Node). Through cooperation with "the system" for many lifetimes, a deeper connection with self is the spiritual work. Then work-related areas, and vocation in general, can be motivated by more loving concerns. Having families or other ways to open the heart is suggested. There is a return to innocence, which nurtures one's contribution.

Synthesis: Eventually we realize that we really do create our own reality through the emotional status operating within. When we *choose* the past, understand the enormous teachings it brought, we arrive at another level of growth. We develop the emotional (Cancer) strength (Capricorn) to understand attachments and are able to gently release them. We lovingly bond (Cancer) with the manifest world (Capricorn) but respect how ephemeral it is. We rely on the self, not the world, to ultimately provide nourishment.

Leo/Aquarius

The resolution of this axis involves using the personal life force in an awakened way. We are bridging the personality (Leo) with the transpersonal (Aquarius).

Leo South Node: The less conscious Leo operates at the personality level and functions with those concerns. There is some issue with being seen, which has a variety of possibilities (depending on related factors). Some have puffed out their chests out of insecurity, while others have been uncomfortable in the limelight and are learning to participate more within it. There is karma around being appreciated or gaining approval. Integration is found with Aquarius. When an evolving ego realizes the nature of the ego dream, it learns to become non-attached from both outcomes and the projections of others. Then there is freedom (Aquarius) to shine one's light (Leo) without concern for approval because others are merely reflectors. When separation consciousness is seen as the illusion it is, Leonian issues may become resolved, and the work is to then contribute to the collective in ways that promote spiritual awakening (Aquarius).

Aquarius South Node: These souls have been involved in broader issues in some way, but there is something unconscious that requires attendance. Sometimes there is a humanitarian, selfless, charitable disposition, and other times there is disconnection and alienation from the world. There are plenty of other options too, and all of them show a reluctance or removal from being personally engaged with life in the fullest way. Further learning of the nature of Aquarius is required. Then those with this placement are able to more fully grasp the meaning of the transpersonal—mainly to realize we can be "in the world but not of it." The Leo North Node is a spiritual instruction to be more in the world! Enjoy the abundance of life, celebrate the human condition, perform and smile and dance—and take absolutely none of it personally (Aquarius).

Synthesis: We can be present and participate (Leo) in connection with the fantastic nervous system of the cosmos (Uranus) that connects everything. By showing up fully, we increase our access to Spirit's intelligence. We learn that the external world (Aquarius) is the self (Leo).

Virgo/Pisces

This axis involves the process of grounding inspiration into works that reflect Spirit. How can we be instruments for this loving universe and create "heaven" on "earth"?

Virgo South Node: Those with this signature have been our worker bees. They have behaved in responsible and dedicated ways, but they have an issue with work. Has it been spiritually meaningful? What has been motivating such efforts? Who have they actually been working for? Most likely the soul has not directed this work. There is very often a participation with the value system that serves authority, organizations or businesses and their aims. An intention is to develop greater contemplative and intuitive awareness to channel into projects and methods. Pisces North Node is an invitation to surrender to spiritual processes, to trust life and this benevolence that envelops us. Then work becomes more uplifting and inspired, which also assists conventional arenas to be more conscious.

Pisces South Node: I have personally seen very few (if any) with this placement claim they are expert meditators, visionaries or mystics. Those with this signature would like to further develop their intuition or creativity, and that is the work they are picking up on. Some are lost or directionless or are ghosts to their own lives. There can be impotence or, in some cases, victim or martyr themes. Virgo characteristics such as dedication, focus, precision and craftsmanship help bring inspiration into form. Natives are selecting specific areas to develop in order to become specialists or experts in their fields. All the while, the greater spiritual awareness being cultivated is brought to such efforts, helping any field or project become a clearer representation of Spirit.

Synthesis: Those with the Virgo/Pisces axis are becoming our practical (Virgo) mystics (Pisces), distributing Spirit in countless ways and forms. They develop deep gratitude for the reverence of life and perform works as a form of meditation. Grounding gifts to the world to assist a collective healing, these souls are our illustrators and agents of compassion.

The Nodes in the Houses

The next piece to address is where the nodes are placed in the chart. Each of the twelve houses provides a context to understand how the issues connected with the sign have played out. Generalizations based on sign placement alone can be ill-informed. For instance, a Capricorn South Node in the tenth house might portray a background of worldly empowerment, but hidden in the twelfth or buried in the fourth, the same node points to a whole different set of issues, perhaps great struggles with making an impact. It is best to think of the South Node in signs in terms of *characteristics*, while houses suggest *realms of experience*.

The key is to apply the spirit of the sign *in* the house. The houses are like rooms, and the signs are like the décor. Beginning astrology students often conflate signs and houses. I often hear a question such as, "How can you have an Aries South Node in the seventh house? That is completely contradictory!" I explain that there are issues around autonomy (Aries) in how this person relates (seventh house), perhaps a challenge in representing their own empowerment *within the context* of connection.

The tricky part is that the signs and houses are archetypally related. Aries goes with the first, Taurus with the second and so forth, but the difference between sign (how) and house (where) must be addressed. Let's look at the difference between having a ninth-house South Node in Taurus compared to a second-house South Node in Sagittarius.

A Taurus South Node in the ninth house could point to the value of stability and constancy within the context of one's life path. Those with this placement have likely been very reliable in acting in accordance with certain doctrines, and now they are questioning everything (Scorpio North Node in the third). On the other hand, Sagittarius South Node in the second house suggests a pattern of living life completely on self-directed terms. There is a marked need to be the chief decision maker, and that person is learning to let in the thoughts (Gemini North Node) of others (eighth house) to help make necessary course corrections. These situations are quite different, even opposite, in nature. As signs and houses are thematically related, we do see the overlap in the issue of how the life is directed (ninth house, Sagittarius) and the values (second house, Taurus) involved. However, the subtlety of bringing the sign's characteristics to the house's context illuminates the true meaning of the South Node. We cannot say the two placements just discussed point to the same thing.

Let's briefly look at the nodal axis in the houses.

With the nodes in the 1–7 axis, areas of self-orientation vs. interdependence require greater balance. With the South Node in the first house, historical patterns have been more self-directed, so the work is learning to move into others' space and be connected. The South Node in the seventh house suggests familiarity in areas of pair-bonding, deferring to others or identifying as a part of a relationship. These natives are taking control of the reins, learning to move through life more independently and acting decisively on behalf of their desires.

The 2–8 axis involves personal resources vs. merging with others. A second-house South Node may have behavior patterns that are averse to risk, a guarded approach to life. There could be a preoccupation with personal security or earning money, or there could be issues dealing with the person's physicality. North Node in the eighth house is an intention to enter realms of bonding and intimacy and develop greater skills in terms of merging. A South Node in the eighth may have become embroiled in the turbulent waters of psychological crisis and may have dependency patterns or unconscious issues with sexuality and bonding. The second-house North Node is meant to strengthen an anchor in the self and cultivate greater inner peace. These natives are learning body awareness, self-sufficiency and a commitment to following what emerges naturally from inside.

The 3–9 axis suggests unfinished work in the areas of the mind and navigating life. A soul with a third-house South Node has familiarity, and likely some set of issues, with learning arenas. These souls may be quite bolstered here or may wish to be. The work now is to bring knowledge out into the world (ninth house) in the form of publishing, travel or any type of expansive endeavor. The ninth-house South Node suggests a history of participation within religion, higher education or other areas where the "truth" is understood. However, it wasn't fully informed yet, so third-house open-ended study and inquiry rounds out the spiritual education and can be reapplied to the ninth in a balanced way.

The 4–10 axis concerns family vs. vocation. Simply stated, the soul is familiar with operating in one of these realms, and now the other brings greater wholeness. The fourth-house South Node involves private matters, familial expectations and legacies, possibly being hidden or sheltered from the world. Going out in the world (tenth), achieving and being a provider can be helpful for spiritual growth. The tenth-house South Node likely has issues with the type of vocational path. Many times there is discordance with career because of conditioning from external forces. The present life is to find the true calling within (fourth) and reengage with career from a more centered place. This may be supported by the creation of family, but the core issue is the movement into self.

A fifth-house South Node is familiar with, and working on, areas of self-expression and creative pursuits, as well as having experience with children (or displaying innocent or childlike behavior). Those with this placement are learning to mature these tendencies to have a broader reach into the world (eleventh) and to connect with progressive issues, social networks and more worldly concerns. An eleventh-house South Node has experiences identifying with group consciousness and often conforms to such ideation. These natives can be soldiers for a system, a cause or particular sub-culture, adhering to its norms. The intention now is to discover one's own unique personal expression through various creative outlets, to be refreshed by fiery and jubilant experiences. Then those with this placement can participate in the world in a more individuated manner and connect with global issues with renewed joy and self-awareness.

The 6–12 axis involves attention to tasks of daily living (sixth) vs. the release into a more expansive consciousness (twelfth). A sixth-house South Node strives to make matters run smoothly. There are patterns of helpfulness and service, and those with this placement often fill less desirable roles that are lower in the pecking order. These natives are learning of the spiritual vision of the twelfth house to bring greater nourishment, insight and imagination into their projects and work space. A twelfth-house South Node has likely moved through lives in unassuming ways. There are patterns of surrender, which may have been due to some type of removal, retreat, impotence or preference for invisibility. Many times, there is some degree of contemplative ability, which is now being further bolstered. In the present lifetime, these natives must show up in work areas and apply themselves. Ideally, they develop into mentors, tutors, clinicians or facilitators of some variety, actively assisting others in their spiritual growth.

Chapter 5
Planets and the Nodes

In this chapter we will look at planets in connection with the nodal axis—both dispositors and planets in aspect with the nodes. We will also explore the relationship between the Moon and its nodes. Beginning with this chapter, example charts (both of famous and anonymous people) will be used to illustrate the ideas.

Dispositors

Planets dispositing the nodes play major roles in the *Awakening* approach. The nodes themselves are located in signs that convey *general* evolutionary curriculums. Planets further *specify* the spiritual work in a myriad of ways. One out of every twelve people has a Gemini South Node, but each person with this signature has something unique going on with Mercury.

Without looking at the dispositor, the information is incomplete and may actually lead to inaccuracies. For example, Gemini South Node in the sixth house may point to student or apprenticeship karma that is being worked on, a follower. However, Mercury may be in Capricorn in the first house, suggesting that the chart owner actually has been more of a leader. This lifetime may be about further developing the message and teachings, not about resolving patterns of underachievement.

If a person has a Libra South Node in the first house, a standard interpretation might be someone with a pattern of behaving in pleasing and accommodating ways. Though this has some accuracy, there could be more to the story. Let's say the dispositor, Venus, is in Aries in the seventh house—connecting with others (seventh) has much to do with benefitting (Venus) personally (Aries) from them. It's not as selfless as it first appears!

The key is to relate the dispositor back to the South Node. The dispositor provides further information about the karmic situation in an *energetic* way—how the general pattern plays out. Planets convey action, actual forces that we notice in the world. The dispositor of the South Node is not an end in itself. We must look at its entire profile, how it connects with the chart. The dispositor is in a sign and house and in aspect with other planets.

The Leo South Node involves a factor that other placements do not. In this situation, the Sun actually plays two roles. First, it's the dispositor of the South Node and therefore relates directly to how prior lives were actually energetically embodied. It's a window into who we were. However, we are all in a process of becoming more conscious, so we must look at this Sun as less than enlightened (which is universal). It was mismanaged to some degree at the egoic level, which relates it back to the Leo South Node. Next, we also look at the Sun as the agent of awakening into the soul self (which is discussed in the next chapter). There's an entirely separate scope to its development.

The North Node's dispositor gives more specific information to assist the reconciliation of the karmic patterns. I have termed it the "planet of gold" because it points to a bounty of spiritual riches available to mine through concerted effort. This planet is always in the perfect place to address the challenges of the karmic pattern. The key is to do the planet *consciously*. If we are not awakening, then the dispositor of the North Node can actually contribute to regression—as can everything in the chart if we are in a slumber.

The dispositor of the North Node should be distinguished from the Sun, which also appears in the perfect place for our growth. The difference is that the dispositor of the North Node relates specifically with karmic resolution (gardening), while the Sun is the flower that is able to grow in the present. When we manage the dispositor of the North Node well, we accelerate the flowering process of the Sun. All of the factors that have to do with the Nodes involve our karma. The Sun can be a part of this analysis (as seen with the Leo South Node), but it also plays a role as the life force in the present, which potentially brings us to spiritual realization.

Without further ado, let's look at some charts!

The first example is Robin Williams. He had a Virgo South Node in the tenth house—unfinished karma concerning a craft or skill (Virgo) to offer to the world (tenth). Mercury in Leo serves as the dispositor, right on the Midheaven. Verbal (Mercury) entertainment (Leo) is the specific nature of this craft—comedy! Pluto conjoined Mercury suggests that this entertainment-oriented craft likely had shadowy ninth house directives. A possibility is the instruction from authorities not to speak so freely, to keep the voice (Mercury) under wraps (Pluto). In the early part of his career, Williams felt an urgency (Pluto) to speak (Mercury) expressively (Leo), and his style was pressured, some would say manic.

The North Node is in Pisces in the fourth house conjunct his Pisces Moon. Further development entails internal focus and introspection, to solidify his own foundation of love instead of the external focus (tenth) of serving (Virgo) and entertaining (Mercury in Leo). Great upset (Pisces Moon) is being avoided, so the work is to simply be with it.

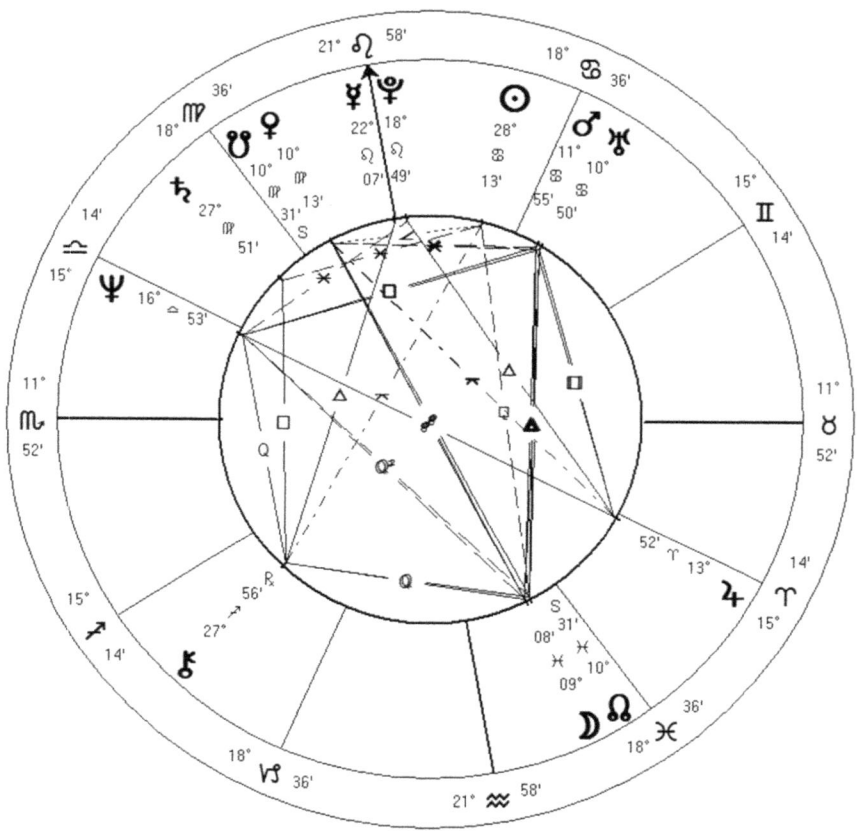

The next point illustrates the importance of the use of modern dispositors, which is discussed at length in *Volume 1*. In this example, Neptune in Libra in the twelfth house plays the important role of dispositor of the North Node. Resolution of the karma taken on in this lifetime involves the completion (twelfth) of this emotional work to arrive at a state of spiritual grace (Neptune in Libra). Neptune (modern) suggests that the way to resolve the karma is through healing, contemplation, and finding deeper spiritual harmony with existence. The ancient dispositor would be Jupiter in Aries in the fifth, a fire planet in a fire sign in a fire house, which sounds incredibly busy and active. It is questionable whether this would be the way to resolve his very tender (Pisces) emotions. In fact, Neptune opposes the Jupiter, conveying the message to calm that fire down in order to truly deepen. Much of Williams' frenetic energy (fire) in his early days could be stemming from the *avoidance* of the deeper emotional work. (From this astrologer's perspective, modern dispositors are clearly more accurate, and this has been verified by countless examples in the counseling room as well as through research. I encourage the reader to conduct similar study.)

The example also illustrates the necessity to do the South Node more consciously. Williams was here to *build* on the foundation of his craft (Virgo) as an entertainer (Leo Midheaven). The more he integrated with his emotions (North Node/Moon in Pisces), the greater depth he embodied as an actor. He wasn't here to "move away" from entertainment, but to do it from greater spiritual wholeness and emotional depth.

Next is the chart for Albert Einstein, another excellent example of doing the South Node more consciously. His chart also shows the value of the spiritual gold available in the dispositor of the North Node. His Leo South Node in the second house is disposited by his Pisces Sun in the tenth house. This profile suggests some initial lack of concern (Pisces) about his public appearance (tenth), not really owning (second-house South Node) his personal light (Leo). We notice this in his often disheveled appearance and downplaying of his celebrity. He grew to embody (second) his fame more confidently (Leo) and used his influence for progressive and humanitarian means (Aquarius North Node).

The Aquarius North Node in his eighth house indicates he was a paradigm-shifter who had a major impact on others. Uranus in Virgo in the third is the dispositor, where the gold is found. He was a revolutionary (Uranus) thinker (third house) on how things work (Virgo). He was blessed with an incredible intellectual gift to cultivate—the planet of innovation and metaphysics (Uranus) placed in the house of the mind (third) in pragmatic earthy Virgo. The "gold" then assists the issues with the South Node. The more he claimed his genius, the more he could mature his willingness to engage his fame (Leo) to make a solid (second house) impact as a public visionary (Pisces Sun in the tenth).

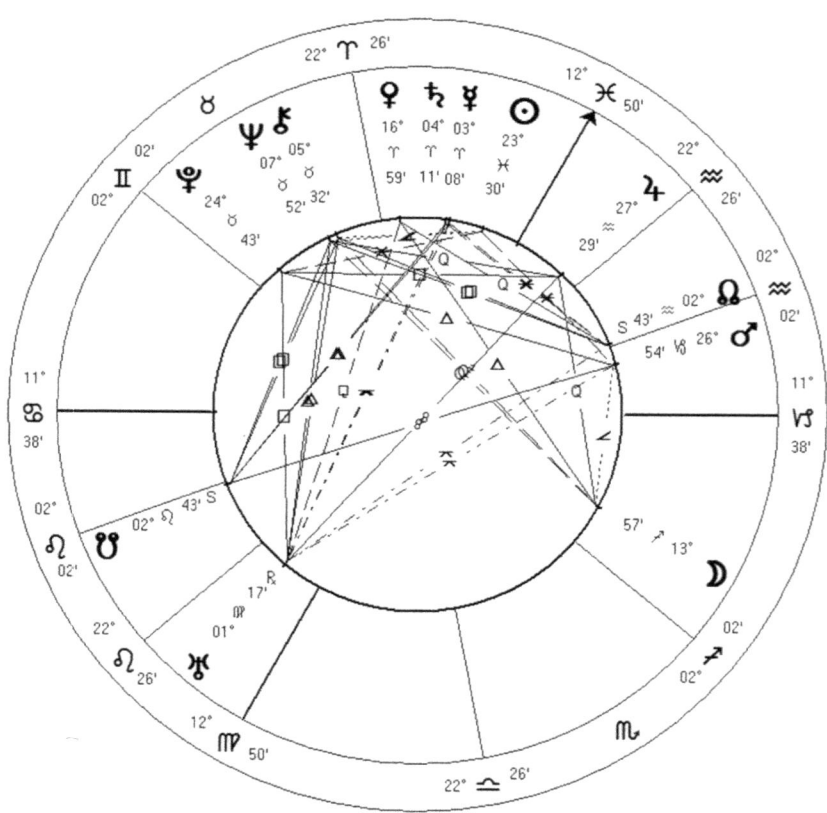

Another significant point to reinforce is the examination of the overall *profile* of the dispositor (sign, house, aspects). Below is the chart for Maya Angelou. She has a Gemini North Node in the tenth, an intention to become a writer. Mercury in Pisces in the seventh serves as the dispositor; it is conjunct Venus, square Saturn in Sagittarius in the fourth, and trine Pluto in Cancer in the eleventh.

The sign placement specifies which type of writing. Angelou was a creative, inspired, intuitive writer, a poet (Pisces) whose work involved transcendent themes. The seventh-house placement shows the intention to share this with others in spiritually intimate ways, which is echoed by Mercury's conjunction with Venus. The square with Saturn illustrates that it is part of the unresolved karma of her Saturn, which is finding greater spiritual meaning (Sagittarius) with vocation (Saturn). The trine to Pluto in the eleventh house in Cancer concerns broader collective issues. There is wounding (Pluto) around tribal/clan membership (Cancer) on the broader world stage (eleventh). This Pluto correlates strongly with themes of oppression involving Angelou's people, and her advocacy of empowerment is a strong theme of her writing.

All of the factors involving her Mercury are helpful for seeing its scope, how it can be the "planet of gold" for her karmic resolution. I also chose this example to illustrate that the system of essential dignities is *not* a part of this approach. As discussed at length in *Volume 1*, essential dignities correlate strongly with the Patriarchal Value System (PVS) that has been in place for eons within the Saturnian world. Using a transpersonal approach, we move beyond such designations, which concern potential benefit in the manifest world.

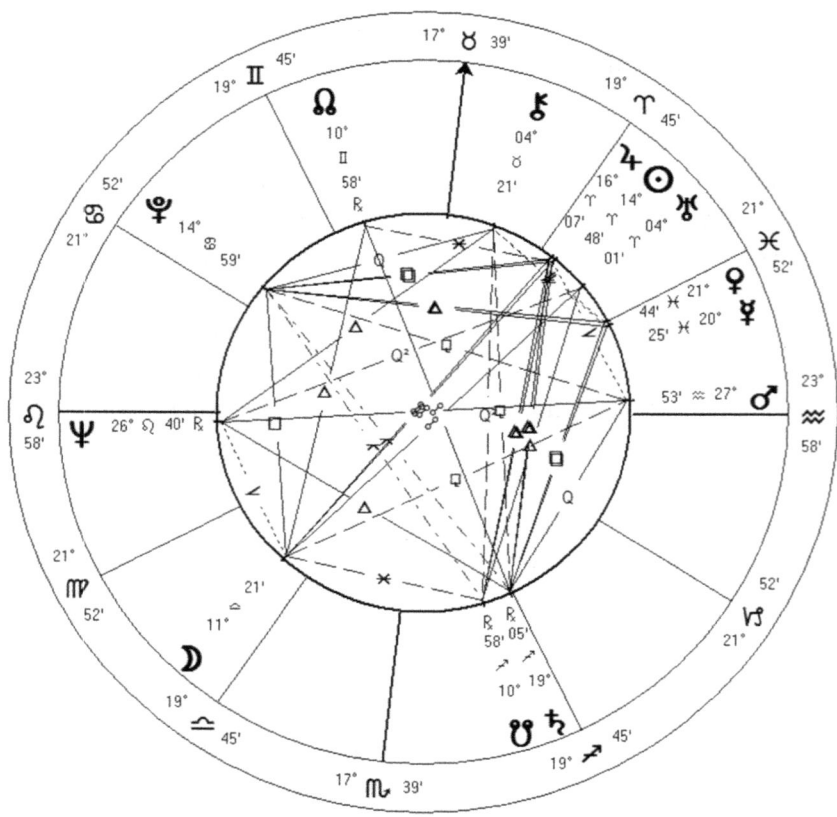

Angelou's Mercury in Pisces is the *perfect* placement and energy for her spiritual growth. There is a brilliant conscious side to it, and she was able to claim that and, subsequently, helped change the world. More conventional astrologers might actually steer her away from Mercury pursuits because they believe this is a "bad" Mercury, or somehow "weak" in its "fall." In this approach, it's her planet of gold, and we would champion its cultivation and the gifts that it brings.

Here are some key points about the dispositors of the Nodes:

*The dispositor of the South Node gives further detail about the nature of the karma. As a planetary energy, it conveys the specific action and dynamics of the more general South Node. It points to roles, conditions and situations from the past.

*The dispositor of the North Node plays a key role in the resolution of the karmic pattern. Whereas the spirit of the North Node balances the disposition established at the South, the dispositor actively engages in the dispersal of energy into new skill sets. It has the potential sculpt a gift to the world.

*It is essential to review the entire profile of the dispositors (sign, house, aspects to other planets).

*Modern dispositors are used, and the system of essential dignities (with its good/bad judgments) is ignored.

Planets in Aspect to the Nodes

These planets further illustrate the energetic forces and dynamics that are part of the karmic pattern being addressed. In the *Awakening* approach, we understand that we are interacting with the self *through* the world. Similar to a dream, everything we encounter and experience is us. Therefore, we realize that the personality may experience people and events as external and seemingly disconnected; these are projected parts of the psyche with which we interact.

The chart owner is not to "blame" for any painful karmic dynamics. Rather, we all initially dream unconsciously, which manifests in a myriad of forms. Anything painful that we dream up potentially teaches and strengthens us, so it is not to be seen as "negative" from the transpersonal level. This approach is non-judgmental and compassionate, and the perspective is empowering rather than blaming. Nevertheless, many of the planets in aspect with the nodes are often experienced as forces that do things to the person; a feeling of fate often accompanies them. In actuality, they are parts of the self returning for integration.

As the nodes represent an axis, planets in aspect to one of the nodes are usually in aspect to both. Planets that are conjunct one node are in opposition to the other. A planet could be square to the axis and, thus, both nodes. A planet trine one of the nodes is sextile the other. It gets a bit trickier when we bring in some of the other aspects. A planet quincunx one node is semi-sextile the other, a minor aspect — one that is relevant (everything is) but not as noteworthy as some other chart indicators. A planet forming a quintile (or biquintile) to one of the nodes is not making an aspect to the other. There are many minor aspects that do reveal important information, and I encourage the reader to apply the points made in this section to independent study. We are going to simplify the discussion and look at the aspects mentioned in Chapter 2.

Planets Conjunct the South Node

Any planets conjunct the South Node add information and reinforce the pattern. The sign is an evolutionary process, while the planets are the energy. So these planets portray the forces at play in the creation of the karmic pattern. Let's review how the major planets might animate the South Node and look at some examples. Of course, sign placement (and planets in aspect) will be modifying variables.

Sun: The person actually embodied the South Node in past lives as the life force. The Dalai Lama is an excellent example: Sun conjunct the South Node in Cancer in the first house. He has been an emotional (Cancer) leader (first house) of his tribe and is resuming his familiar role for another incarnation. Furthermore, he has the Sun conjunct Pluto. Managed on the brighter side, it suggests roles of great power with substantial emotional impact.

Moon: With the Moon conjunct the South Node, there can be karma related to family, roots and heritage, or issues of ancestral or tribal expectations. However, these stem from deeper issues (self-love and nurturing patterns) projected into such areas. Princess Diana was known for battling an eating disorder and struggled with issues of self-worth (Aquarius Moon conjunct South Node in the second house). As she matured, she became an emotional humanitarian as well as a global symbol of love that was revered by her people (Aquarius), although not necessarily by the powers that be.

Mercury: The voice, mind or message is unfinished, so the program involves further development as a writer, or singer, or attaining more accomplishment in education. Aretha Franklin (Mercury conjunct South Node in Pisces in the fourth) holds the intention to bring an unrealized vision (Pisces) around communication (Mercury) forward. With the Virgo North Node in the tenth house, her Mercury connects to a professional display of her craft, a songwriter. Furthermore, she has Mars in Gemini in the seventh house square the nodes, adding a lot of "oomph," especially towards others. She is literally singing to get respect...from herself.

Venus: Possibilities include issues with body and sensuality, relationship patterns, money, resources and worth. Bettie Page had Venus in Pisces in the first house (conjunct the South Node), and she personally embodied (first house) the alluring (Pisces) feminine (Venus at the egoic level). She grew to find greater worth (Venus) in herself (first house) and discontinued giving herself away (Pisces).

133

Mars: There is familiarity with conflict, risky behaviors, or being a warrior of some type—or the native is simply a very independent spirit. These people are learning to be more conscious leaders, more judicious with their decisions. Having the courage to connect the Mars to the North Node will certainly expand its scope. Wildlife expert Steve Irwin, the "Crocodile Hunter," had Mars in Aquarius conjunct the South Node and experienced sudden (Aquarius) violence (Mars) from his riskiness, which led to his death.

Jupiter: There is unfinished work in political, philosophical or cultural realms—making an impact in the world in a meaningful way. The darker Jupiter may have been rigid or narrow and could indicate issues around abundance or the mismanagement of it. The work is to direct Jupiter consciously in ways that encourage growth. Adolf Hitler had Jupiter in Capricorn conjunct his South Node, and he replayed a controlling philosophy that lacked heart (Cancer North Node). He did become a political figure (Jupiter) of substantial authority (Capricorn) but was unable to awaken into the higher promise.

Saturn: Suggests patterns of aligning with authority and institutional protocol. There is likely a soul history of being part of systems and honoring their traditions. These natives are learning to become their own authorities (strengthen the South Node) and stretch beyond the familiar patterns to infuse them with new skills (integrate the North). Lee Harvey Oswald had the South Node in Aries conjunct Saturn on the eleventh house cusp. He was an assassin (Aries), likely selected from a group (eleventh house) that is being influenced and controlled (Saturn) for warfare or other military aims.

Chiron: With this signature, there are often struggles with health and issues of wellbeing, or familiarity with the role of healer. Many times, these individuals are learning to bring more innovative techniques or practices to the health field (defined broadly, anything at all that assists personal development). Richard Simmons has the South Node conjunct Chiron in Scorpio in the second house. He initially struggled with his body (second house), but he transformed himself (Scorpio) from an overweight person to a leading figure in the health and fitness world.

Uranus: The mark of the unfinished revolutionary or innovator. Some of these people have operated outside of the mainstream (Uranus), while others have patterns that have been erratic or turbulent; all of them are smoothing out their routines to make the world more progressive. Simone de Beauvoir had Uranus conjunct the South Node in Capricorn in the second house (conjunct Mercury and the Sun). She developed greater potency (Capricorn) as a revolutionary (Uranus) writer (Mercury) and became one of the leading feminists of the 20th Century.

Neptune: Giving power away (relative to the South Node profile) is likely. Many of these people have been selfless, and they are now realizing a broader vision. Some have been swept away in collective currents; others have been martyrs for causes. Some degree of impotence is noted. The work now is to bring inspiration into reality. Musician Jeff Buckley had the South Node in Scorpio conjunct Neptune (along with the Sun, Mercury and Venus). He was critically acclaimed as an inspired and intuitive singer/songwriter from his debut album *Grace* (Neptune), which included a cover of *Hallelujah*. Sadly, he drowned (Neptune in Scorpio) at an early age and didn't fully realize his talent.

Pluto: Issues of power loom in the soul history. It has likely been mismanaged, which has caused painful drama. With greater authentic empowerment, the soul work is furthered, and those with this placement potentially make a collective impact. Lady Gaga has the South Node in Scorpio conjunct Pluto (and the Moon) in the fifth house. She has developed into one of the world's most successful entertainers (fifth house) and is known for being extremely provocative, raising awareness of sexuality issues and empowerment activism for women and those who have been bullied.

Vincent Van Gogh

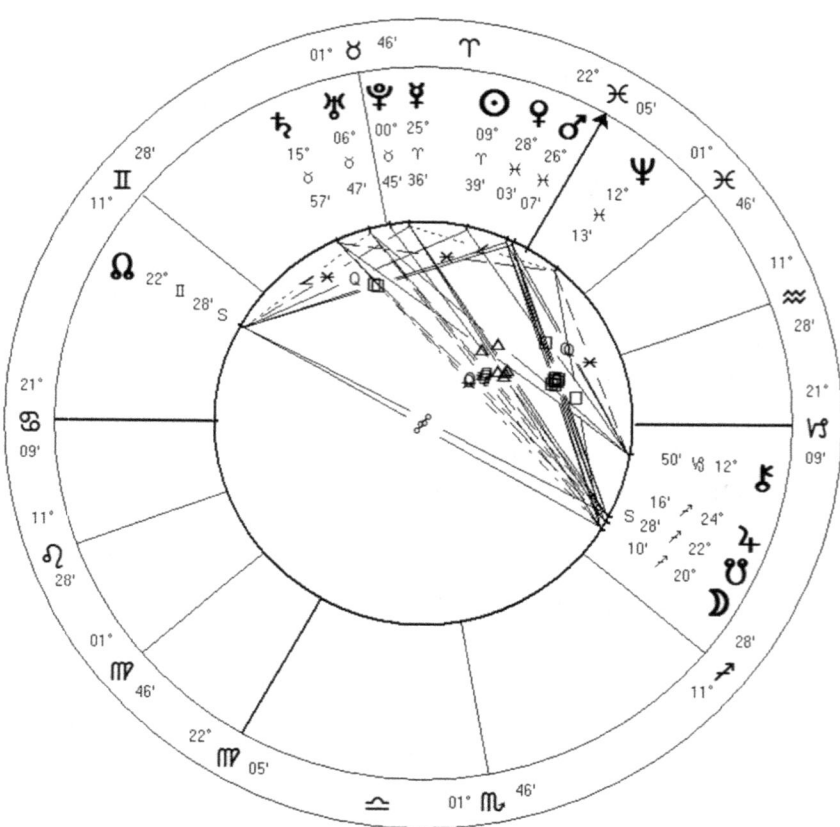

Van Gogh's chart is an excellent one to examine for a few reasons. It features both the Moon and Jupiter in Sagittarius conjunct his South Node in the sixth house, an unfinished need (Moon) to craft (sixth) his purpose (Jupiter, Sagittarius). Again, we see that he is not moving away from areas of productivity and craftsmanship (sixth)—in fact, he made a huge (Jupiter) body of work (sixth) in his short life.

It's important to modify our understanding of the planet conjunct the South Node (in this case, Jupiter) to the context of the house. If this signature were in the tenth, then we would see karma around success or stature, perhaps someone who attained the pinnacle (tenth) and is now building on that with greater spiritual purpose. The sixth house is an area of the underdog, slave, apprentice or worker—the scrapper who is trying to "get by." Indeed, Van Gogh was not successful during his lifetime and was challenged to make ends meet. Instead of ascribing great benefic accolades, it is more appropriate to see his situation as *issues* with success, a theme of the sixth house. Also, religious themes (Sagittarius) are noted in his early family (Moon) life.

In the following section we will address planets square the nodes, and this example serves as a bridge. Van Gogh had Venus in Pisces in the tenth in such a configuration. Money, popularity and acclaim (Venus in the tenth) are at the crossroads of his spiritual work. In prior life contexts, success was likely unattained, and now the intention is to accomplish and realize his vision. Jupiter in major aspect with Venus (square) can correlate with large-scale money and success, and this is exactly what ultimately happened, albeit after his death. His paintings sell for some of the largest sums of any artist in world history, and his art is beloved around the world. We see how astrology conveys an energetic pattern that will live on after the chart owner.

Planets Square the Nodes

All planets in a fourth harmonic (conjunction, square, opposition) aspect to the nodal axis play the most significant and urgent roles in the karmic history. These are the more frictional and challenging types of scenarios and dynamics. Recall that karma derives from navigating from some degree of unconsciousness, and the darker version of these aspects are the most formidable challenges to address.

Planets square the nodes were somehow mismanaged, likely with stressful consequences. These energies represent forces that inhibited or challenged, or were just poorly handled, creating major issues. As for orb of influence, the tighter, the more relevant and central. I have found that a 10-degree orb for a square to the nodes is still quite noticeable in the biography, and whole sign logic, as discussed before, can be applied here as well.

The first piece is to understand how the mismanagement of the planet that is square the nodes relates to the South Node. How would the unconscious version of it contribute to the South Node issues? How can we imagine it as a problematic force in the world? Again, it is important to see the spiritual perspective that the person is not a victim. In his or her own psyche, these planets are not fully integrated yet. They take form in the ego dream externally so the person can learn to work with them. At the soul level, it is helpful to work through these crises and trying situations, as that is the curriculum. At the personality level, we can empathize with the chart owner and affirm just how perplexing they are.

As the planet brightens, it begins to play a role in the resolution of the karma. (If it doesn't, it can actually deepen the pattern.) The planet's more conscious side becomes a very strong force in the biography, one that is unmistakable. It supports the development of the North Node, a major step on that path. It also supports the development of the South Node, as that is in need of more conscious management. So the planet becomes a key to balance the entire axis. Let's look at an example.

David Koresh

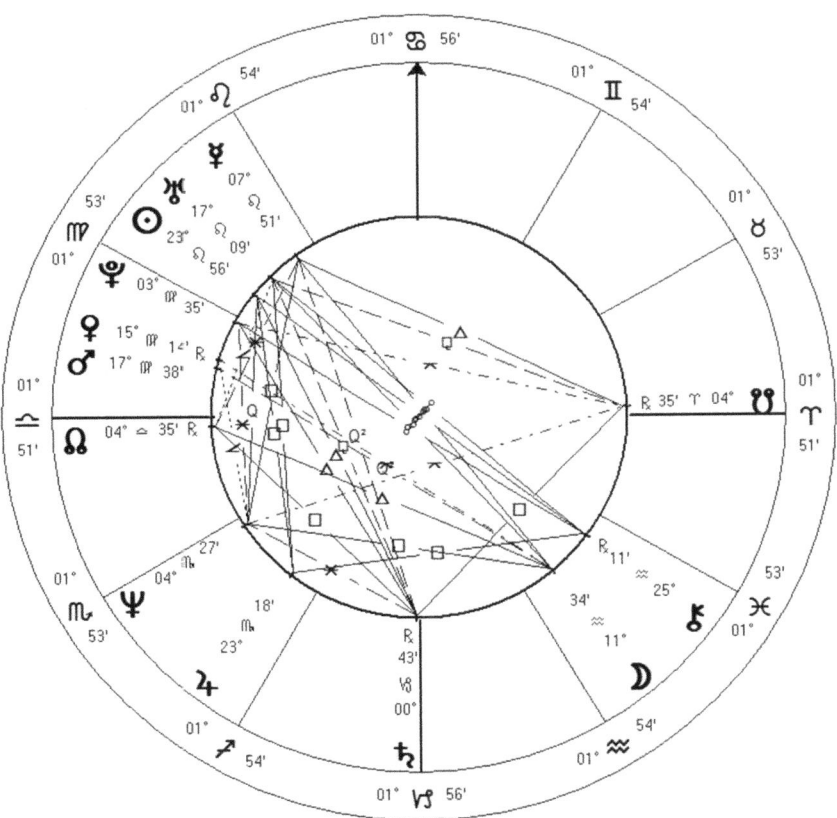

Koresh is the cult leader infamous for the 1993 Waco standoff with the government that led to his, and his followers', deaths. We see the South Node in Aries in the seventh house, which speaks of conflict and opposition with others. Saturn in Capricorn on the fourth house cusp (within only a few minutes) is at the square position (with the Libra North Node on the Ascendant). The conflict suggestive of the South Node is in a major relationship with authority (Saturn in Capricorn) in the area of home. The issue played out with the U.S. government on his ranch, a perfect reflection of the symbolism. As noted above, it is his battle with his own maturation (Saturn) that is being worked through. The soul intention was to deepen (fourth) into himself and find greater inner strength (Saturn) to hammer into a solid contribution (Capricorn). The North Node is suggestive of developing a far more pleasing (Libra) persona and approach to life (Ascendant) that is considerate of others. This would help him be able to share whatever mature work he would develop.

Paul Joseph Goebbels

Goebbels was the Reich Minister of Propaganda in Hitler's Nazi party. He earned a Ph.D. in literature and went on to be an orator and writer of propaganda. He ordered the burning of "decadent" books at one point and is known as a master at psychological manipulation. Goebbels had Mercury in Scorpio exactly square his nodal axis.

Mercury themes were dominant in his biography, marked by great intensity (Scorpio). His Mercury is connected to karma around social inclusion (square Leo South Node), and his writing brought him acclaim within the Nazi regime. The twelfth house placement of the South Node suggests that he is comfortable operating behind the scenes, while Mercury's placement is in the fourth house, the area of the homeland. The North Node intention was to be an advocate of liberation (Aquarius) by developing the ability to work with others (sixth) in progressive ways. To do this, he would need a death and rebirth (Scorpio) of his Mercury and would have to use his psychological savvy in completely new and conscious ways.

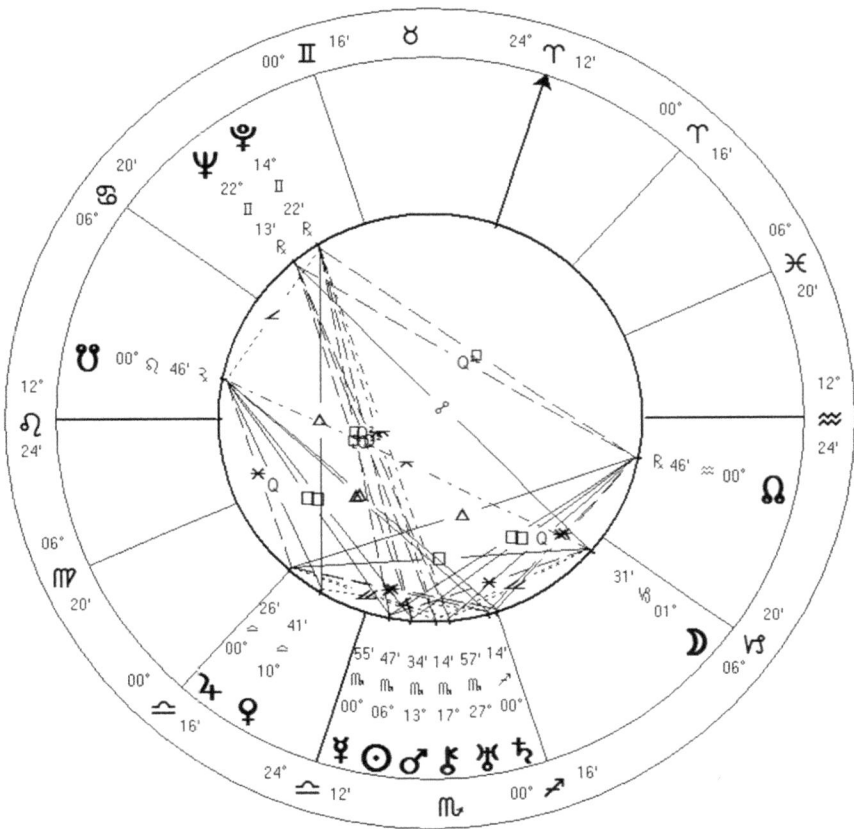

Planets Conjunct the North Node

These planets play two very different roles. First, they are in opposition to the South Node; next, they are conjunct the North Node.

Initially, these planets are forces that oppose the South Node pattern. Natives do not identify with these energies, so they become projected out in separation consciousness onto external situations and people. As the life plays out, strategies to address these forces become necessary, which enables the chart owner to claim their promise. Another possibility is that the chart owner unconsciously mismanages these planets in ways that have been counter to the owner's own spiritual aims and development.

Next, in conjunction with the North Node, the planets are a major part of the spiritual curriculum. In a sense, the chart owner is learning to become a more conscious version of the very thing that has been oppositional or estranged. Integration involves the retracting of projections, seeing through the illusion of separation consciousness and humbly accepting the sacred reflections as the self. It can be very difficult, especially when the karma is painful or catastrophic, for a person to accept that this stems from the self. Ways to address this in the counseling arena are found in Part 2 of this book.

Planets conjunct the North Node give it an energetic boost. Similar to the dispositor, they drive it forward. When the planet is done consciously, the North Node intention is strongly carried forth—the reward for having to struggle with this planet for so many lives! However, all of the planets in aspect to the North Node will support it. The difference is that adept management of the planet conjunct the North Node will automatically further the intention without as many variables to negotiate. For instance, in a prior example, Koresh needed to mature his Saturn and connect it with a more pleasing disposition. If he had Venus in Libra on his North Node, then the situation is more directly related.

Madonna

Madonna has a Jupiter/Neptune conjunction on her North Node in the second house. Initially, this cluster is at odds with the South Node pattern, which has to do with working through conflict (Aries) with others (eighth house). As the second house pertains to self-worth, the karma suggests materialism (Jupiter in Libra) and sexual mystery (Neptune in Scorpio) were assets (second house) that contributed to the pattern. Having an appetite for possessions and being valued for sexual allure can hook into the demands of others (eighth house) in conflictual (Aries) ways. Here, we see a situation in which the native's own mismanagement of the energies led to the relationship pattern (the sexy Material Girl desired by others). The conscious side to Jupiter and Neptune were lacking.

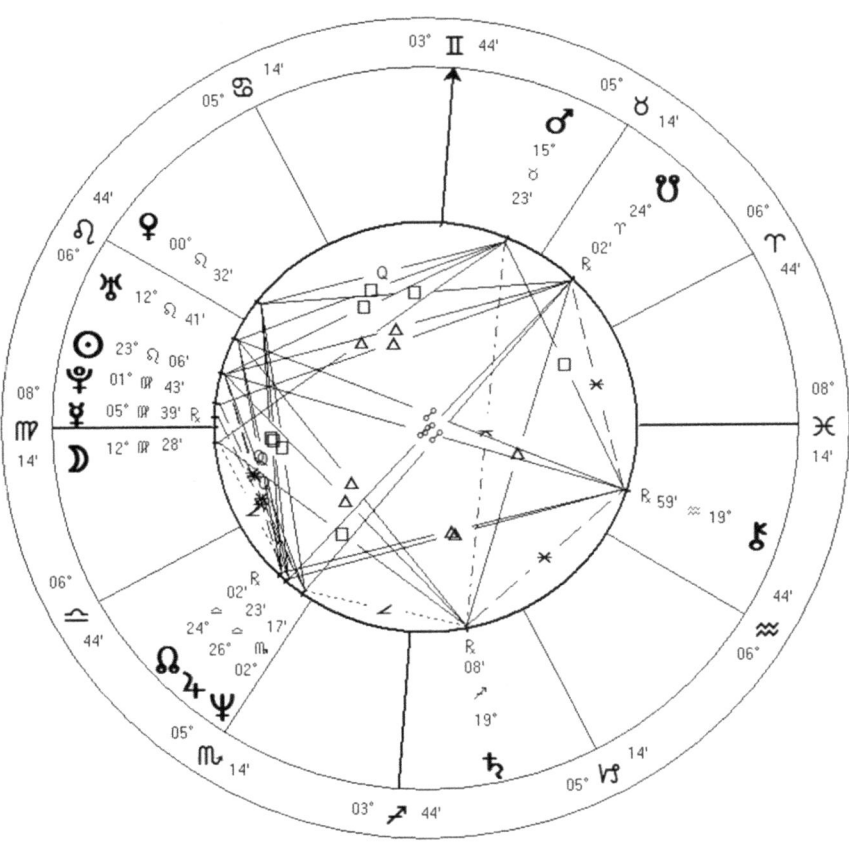

In a more awake fashion, these planets are key for the karmic resolution. When she learns to value a transcendent (Neptune) philosophy (Jupiter), she finds a connection with her own power (second house) and achieves more autonomy. Madonna went from being the Material Girl to studying mysticism and Kabbalah and brought those themes into her music (Libra North Node). She has a message of non-attachment, and her spiritual focus is not a fad — it's the point of her chart.

Planets Sextile/Trine the Nodal Axis

Planets trine and sextile the nodal axis also play significant roles in the spiritual work, but they do not have the same degree of crisis and challenge as the square or opposition. Rather, they point to forces that have been developing, and the work is to take them further. The harmony of the sextile and trine can be tricky. Everything can be done in a more enlightened way, so these planets do indicate some degree of unconsciousness that can be addressed. They have not been problematic like other situations. However, in many cases, there is egoic pride, attachment or comfort with how they have historically operated.

Here are a few possible scenarios to illustrate. Consider the situation in which someone becomes prominent but is unable to integrate deeper meaning into his or her work. That person might have a planet in the tenth house trine/sextile the axis. Another might have no resistance to, or issue with, being on the sidelines of life as an observer, cultivating inwardness and wisdom. That person could be picking up on this pattern and doing more with it, perhaps sharing what has been discovered. Someone else might have a brilliant mind as an asset and is building on it in new, more holistic or intuitive ways. Below is an example.

Jimmy Page

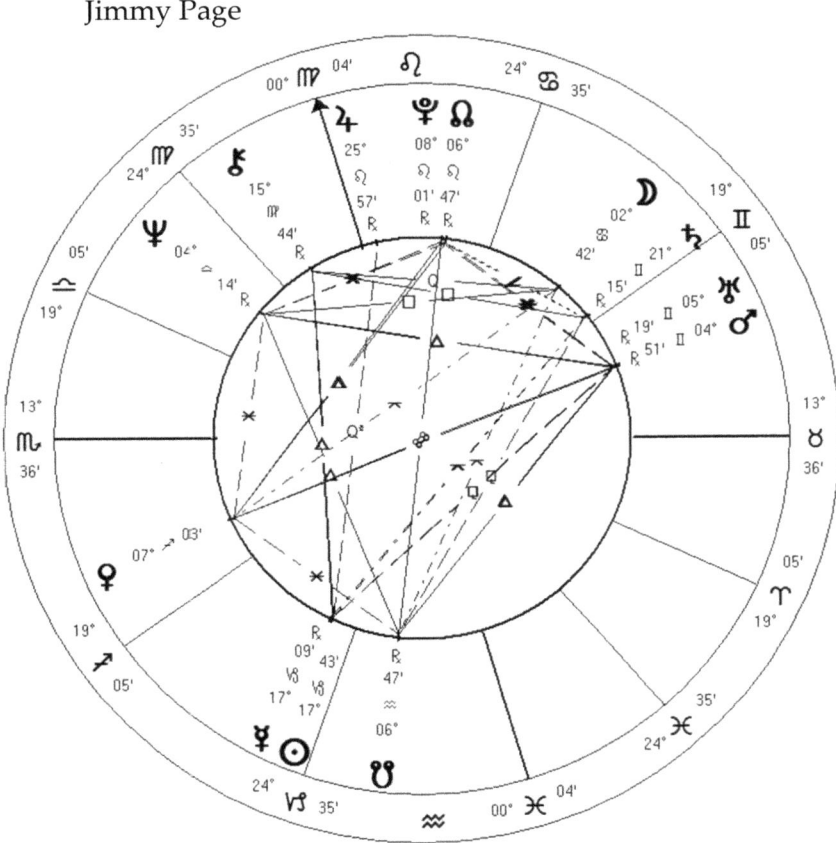

The Led Zeppelin guitarist has Venus in Sagittarius sextile his Aquarius South Node, as well as a trine from Uranus/Mars in Gemini. Aquarius has to do with innovation, and the third house represents sound and communication. There has been interest in artistic (Venus) discovery (Sagittarius), further emphasized by Uranus in Gemini (also the dispositor of the South Node), which is also interested in sound and communications. Mars (initially projected out in the seventh house) suggests some challenges regarding initiative. When he does the planet more consciously,

145

he becomes a leader. The Leo North Node (conjunct powerful Pluto) invites greater visibility and charisma.

Page also has Neptune in Libra trine the South Node from the eleventh house portraying a yearning (Neptune) to share his art (Libra) with the world (eleventh). In this example, note that the planets making the trines and sextile to the South Node are not problematic; rather, they are unfinished in their development. They are assets that can be connected to the North Node to complete what Page has been working on.

Other Situations

As mentioned in Chapter 2, all aspects are relevant and can be explored. The reason for focusing on the major aspects is because they tend to be more central or significant, but minor aspects play very important supporting roles. I encourage the reader to conduct research on every way that planets can connect with the nodal axis. In this final section, we will look at two other situations (quincunx, quintile), as they warrant greater attention. (Recall that they are included as major aspects in the *Awakening* approach.)

Martina Navratilova

An example with the quincunx is found with tennis legend Martina Navratilova. She has Sun/Neptune in Libra in the seventh house quincunx a Taurus South Node in the second. Her South Node pattern tends to be independent, perhaps grappling with issues of self-worth, money or the body. Saturn in Sagittarius in the eighth opposes the South Node, suggesting stern directives, and restrictions, about how to live her life. Venus (dispositor of the South Node) is conjunct Jupiter in Virgo (sixth), portraying obedience to these suggestions.

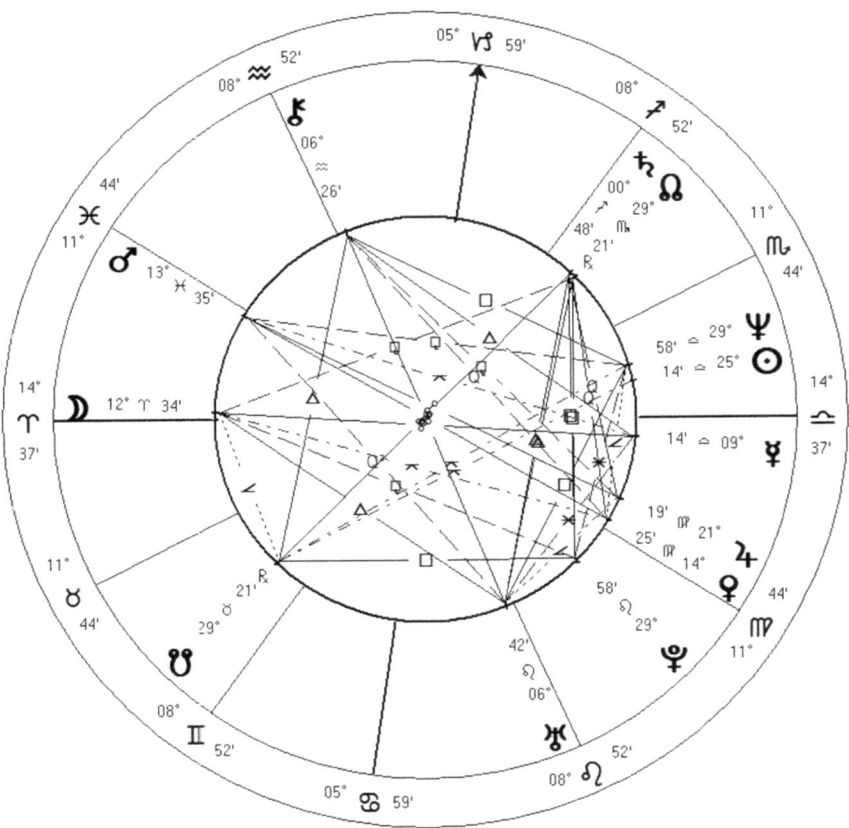

The Sun is the life force. Its position conjunct Neptune and quincunx the South Node suggests that in her karmic history, Navratilova has been unable to be herself, surrendering (Neptune) her true relational identity (Libra, seventh), with resulting sadness or yearning. The quincunx can be frustrating or perplexing, leaving the native feeling stretched in impossible ways. Navratilova's way through is to further develop the South Node (increased confidence, self-alignment) and venture boldly into the intimate North Node (Scorpio, eighth house). Then the awakening of the Sun/Neptune conjunction in Libra is on more

147

solid ground. She did develop the courage to come out as a lesbian (well before broader public acceptance) and became an inspiration to many.

Emily Dickinson

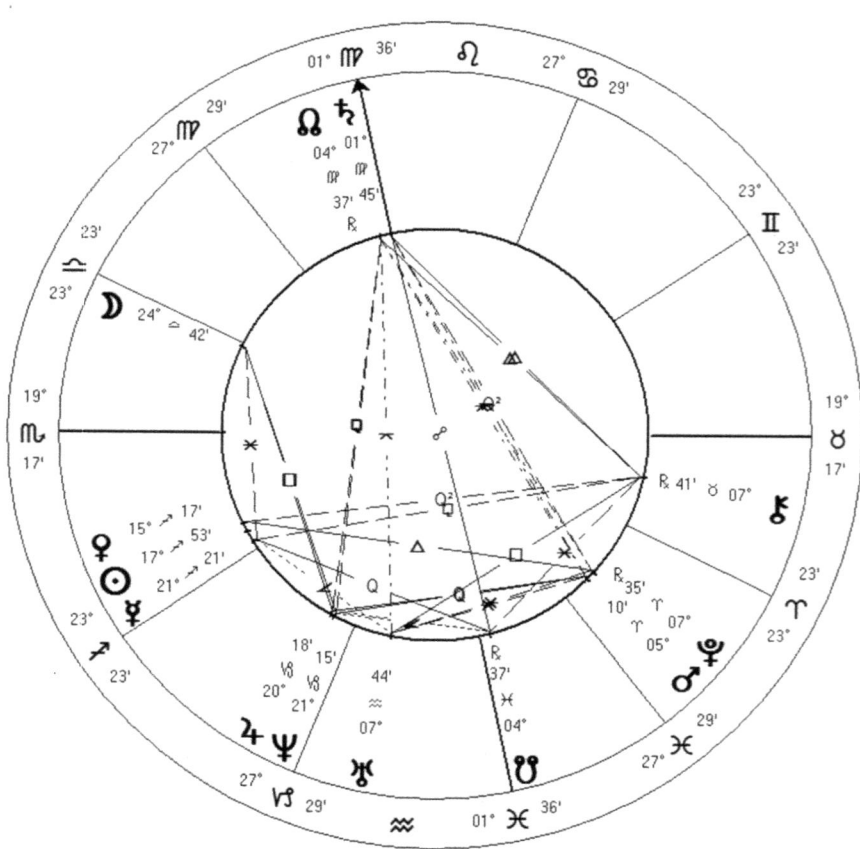

The poet had Mercury in Sagittarius quintile the (visionary, yet likely unaccomplished) Pisces South Node, providing an excellent example of how the aspect operates. Dickinson wrote hundreds of poems, yet only a few were read while she was alive. She had a poetic genius that operated in its own way. In fact, the poems that were published had to be altered to fit more conventional standards. She used unconventional capitalizations, punctuation and rhymes, and some poems lacked titles. They were completely unique, which is the defining characteristic of the quintile. Interestingly, after her death, her body of work was discovered and published (North Node in Virgo in the tenth). Her Mercury was the dispositor of her North Node (and MC), so the intention for greater visibility to her poetic brilliance was eventually realized.

Relating the Moon to the Nodes

In the landmark *Astrology, Karma & Transformation*, Stephen Arroyo mentions different types of karma as understood from the Buddhist tradition. He writes, *"Pralabd karma* is considered the fate, or destiny, karma which must be met in the present lifetime."* In this approach, the karmic patterns and habits selected to be worked on in the present incarnation are found through the lunar nodes. As mentioned previously, the nodes are the points of intersection where the Moon (past) crosses the ecliptic, the Earth's revolutionary path around the Sun (present). We bring specific material from the basin of collected experience (Moon) into energetic activation (Sun).

The Moon is the dreamer, gradually awakening from unconsciousness into greater awareness and presence, like an infant growing into a child and then an adult. As we go through life, our unconsciousness plays out in habits and patterns that become our karma to resolve. As we look at the Moon in a chart, we can feel deep empathy for the spiritual child who is trying to cope, survive and grow. The South Node (and attendant factors) is seen from this foundation. We can see the unfolding of the drama going on, how *the dynamics and circumstances of the South*

Node are rooted in the inner emotional landscape. When we further awaken into soul realization, not only do we have the awareness to heal the prior patterns, we lessen (if not remove) our karmic footprint, as the great Indian sage Sri Ramana Maharshi informs us. It would make sense that we cease to create personal karma when we act as a conduit for the divine.

The Moon is often not seen in relation to the Lunar Nodes. In fact, I have rarely seen astrology-related presentations, literature or discussions make this connection. Most astrologers tend to view the Moon and Sun from the conventional perspective, i.e., in terms of personality and gender. The nodes are generally explored as the karmic significators. The *Awakening* approach attempts to bring the Moon (seed) directly to the nodes (gardening), which in turn assists the Sun in blossoming.

The Moon opens a window into the most vulnerable, regressive and less mature facets of our past. If a soul grows and resolves the egoic coping strategies and stories, the material ceases to be part of the Moon. It would be processed through and given back to Spirit, no longer concretized within. As we are all in (what tends to be) a long journey of spiritual evolution, it is universal to carry remnants of the past.

To summarize, the Moon (and attendant factors) is who we are inside, while the South Node (and attendant factors) is *what we did*. There are a variety of pathways we might take when we are fumbling around in the dark. We do the best we can, but we also have to "clean up" after ourselves. The best way to illustrate this connection is through chart examples, and the ones which follow are from my counseling practice.

Client Example #1

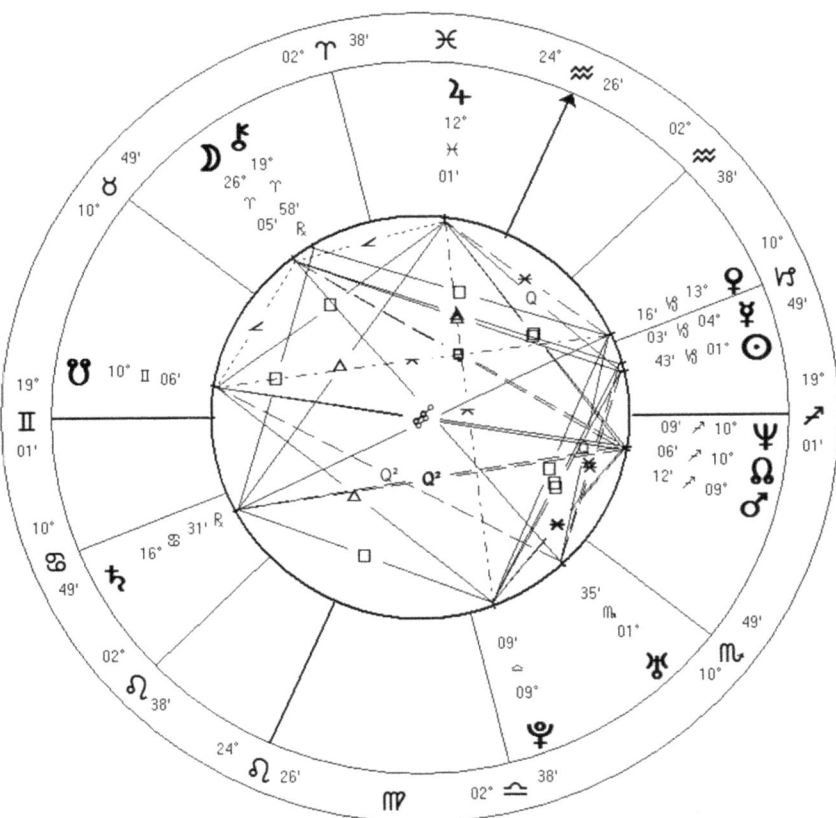

The first example features an Aries Moon conjunct Chiron in the eleventh house. There is an unresolved need for public leadership, perhaps some unprocessed frustration about meeting that aim. Moon/Chiron is not yet a confident warrior (Aries), and the square from Saturn in Cancer in the second house further suggests emotional challenges around self-worth and confidence. Eleventh-house conditioning has sculpted this Moon to follow the cultural norms, to quell individual expression and defer to the community. The frustration around this is further emphasized with the opposition from the Moon to Uranus in Scorpio in the fifth, which wants to upset the apple cart (Uranus) to claim empowered (Scorpio) individual expression (fifth).

The Gemini South Node in the twelfth house shows the pattern of surrendering (twelfth) the voice (Gemini), and giving one's power away (twelfth) to what is being taught (Gemini). As the dispositor, Mercury in Capricorn in the seventh suggests that others have been in positions of authority, and the expectation is that the native will listen to them. Mars in Sagittarius opposes the South Node, illustrating an initial distancing from leadership. Neptune's presence further accentuates the theme of surrendering to a belief system (Sagittarius), to be humble and sacrificial. Jupiter in Pisces square the Nodes is another statement about deferring or surrendering to the guiding philosophy, while Pluto in Libra in the fourth trine the South Node suggests that this is reinforced in the family system. The North Node situation involves claiming his spiritual (Neptune) leadership (Mars) and working similarly with others (sixth) around empowerment and development.

In states of less development, the lunar coping mechanism was to seek security in numbers (eleventh). Having like-minded allies does make us feel supported. The cost was the submergence of autonomy (Aries), the inability to develop leadership, and hence the unfinished Aries need. We can see a clear link between the emotional vulnerability of the Moon and the behavior preference (twelfth house South Node) not to make any waves.

The Sun is the perfect energy in the present to rectify the situation. Growth involves learning to hold authority (Capricorn) in connection with others (seventh), while integrating with the previously estranged need for individuation (Sun sextile Uranus in Scorpio in the fifth) and claiming greater power (Sun square Pluto). Furthermore, Sun quintile Jupiter in the tenth provides the opportunity to professionally expand and have outreach for his

152

leadership. In fact, there are novel abilities available to claim (quintile) that would make it all the more exciting.

Client Example #2

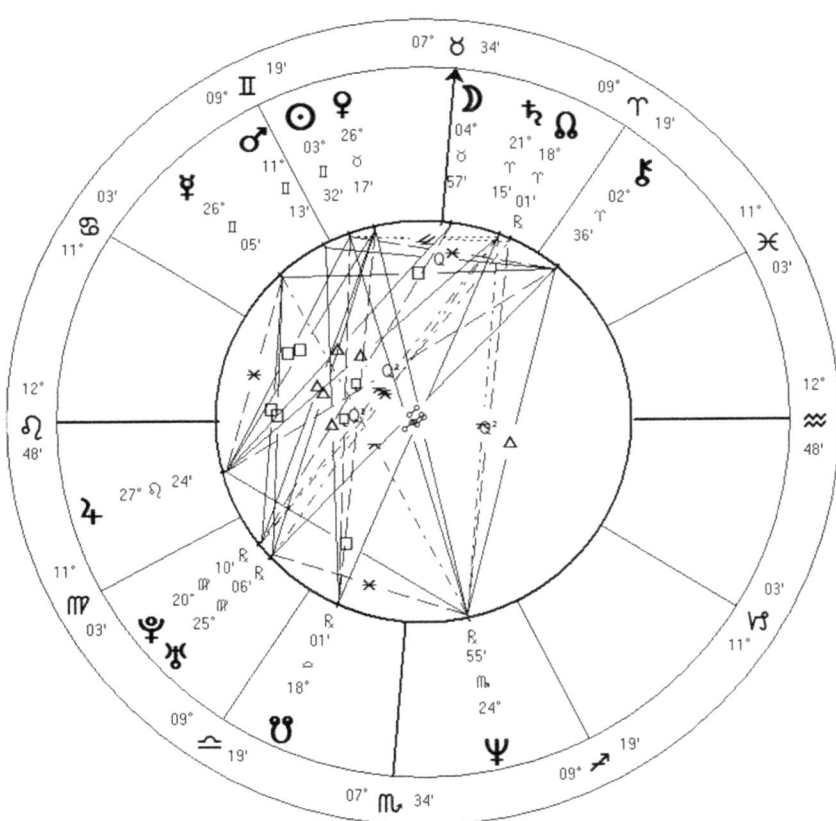

The next example has a Taurus Moon in the ninth house, a need to find emotional security in a guiding life philosophy. There is an adherence (Taurus) to a particular way of operating (ninth house), a conditioned need to not vary from what has been instructed. The Moon is trine Jupiter in Leo in the first house, suggesting that pleasing behavior patterns (first) have been

153

sculpted to be in accordance with this doctrine (Jupiter). (This person is one of the nicest you will ever meet!)

Indeed, the South Node is in Libra in the third house, indicating a pattern of being polite and responsive to the needs of others. The instruction received by the Taurus Moon has been integrated into the mind (third), a pattern of *not* questioning and of compliance. As the dispositor, Venus in Taurus in the tenth house indicates public roles in support of the influences she has received. She appears stable and strong and has taken jobs that are mainstream and "acceptable."

Saturn in Aries in the ninth house opposes the South Node. The lunar need to adhere to doctrine opens the door for stern authorities (Saturn in the ninth) wielding power (Aries), thereby restricting the chart owner's. The spiritual work is to become her own authority and courageously live life as she sees fit. Mars, the dispositor of the North Node, is in Gemini in the eleventh. To reconcile the karmic pattern, she is boldly bringing new ideas forward, becoming willing to face the world (eleventh) in more self-aligned ways. The Sun illustrates that this woman is awakening into the Gemini program of diversity and questioning, in conjunction with Martial empowerment. In turn, the Sun brings more awareness to the tenth-house Venus, new information (Gemini) to the older pattern. We can also note Uranus/Pluto in the second house square Mercury in Gemini in the eleventh, another statement about bringing forth progressive (Uranus) and challenging (Pluto) ideas.

As the attachment to stability and comfort is released, she becomes freer to communicate her brilliance — which is certain to disrupt the previous pattern of pleasantness and accommodation of the South Node. We can see the direct link between the Moon's need for security and rule-following and the South Node's tendencies for intellectual compliance. The present lifetime involves the uprooting of this pattern, allowing the client to take back her mind.

Client Example #3

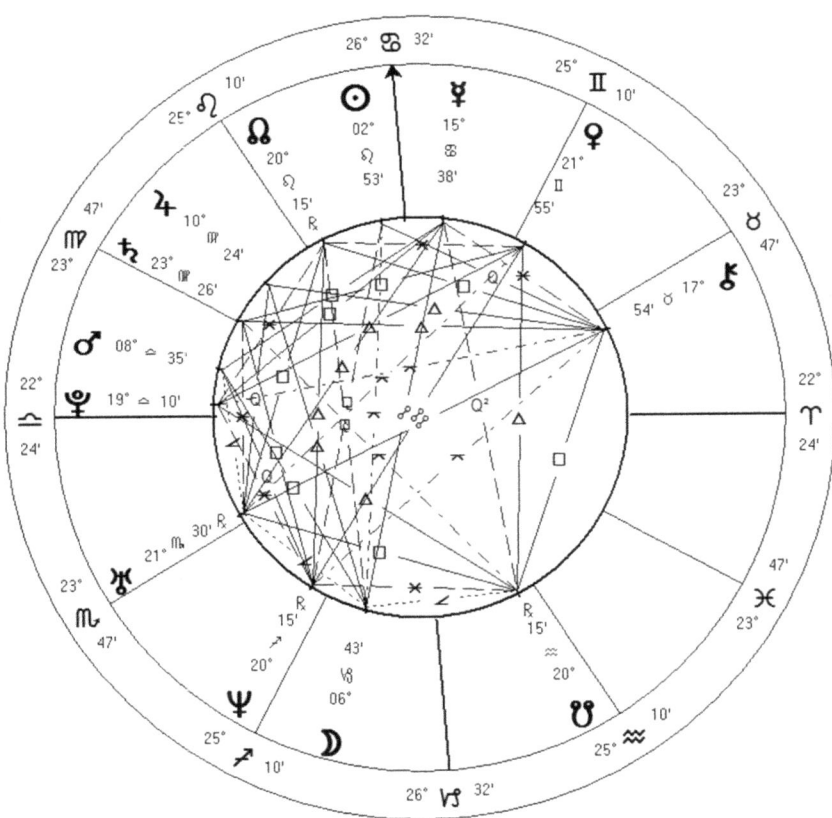

Here is a Capricorn Moon in the third house trine Jupiter in Virgo in the eleventh, indicating an allegiance with pragmatic and conventional influences shaped by a communally organized belief system of humility, deference and service. The expectation is to work hard, play by the rules and respect tradition. Underneath, there is an unresolved need to think for himself

155

(third house) and realize his own power (Capricorn). The Moon opposes Mercury in Cancer in the ninth, further illustrating an initial distance from intellectual autonomy as well as tension with the teachings. The Moon is also square Mars in Libra in the twelfth, suggesting frustrated leadership and the tendency to keep his power off to the side (twelfth). The client's Martial rawness has been conditioned to be socially acceptable (Libra) and thereby weakened.

The South Node is in Aquarius in the fourth house, showing a pattern of estrangement (Aquarius) from the inner self (fourth house). This is very likely to play out within family contexts (fourth) with alienation or abandonment themes—all a reflection of self. Uranus in the first house in Scorpio (which disposits and squares the South Node) portrays deep psychological challenges around acting in alignment with his authenticity and power, which is exactly the work he is addressing. The North Node in Leo in the tenth indicates that the client is learning to reveal his true colors visibly, joyfully, as part of a career. As he develops, the frustrated Capricorn Moon ideally becomes received by the world. The Leo Sun is quincunx the Capricorn Moon, assisting it in lightening up and also helping to claim greater visibility (tenth house).

Also of note is the Grand Trine: Venus in Gemini, Pluto in Libra and the South Node in Aquarius. Spiritual work includes having more relational possibilities and openness. Ideally, he is able to come out of the proverbial closet (Pluto in the twelfth) and connect with his relational curiosity (Venus in Gemini), allowing him to heal the prior disconnect (Aquarius South Node). The North Node in Leo invites warmth, participation and visibility to the bonding needs that were previously more conceptual (air) than manifest.

The conditioning of the Moon convinced the client not to be his true self but to be "appropriate." In particular, there is an

156

estrangement from the desire function (Mars). Prior emotional frustration was difficult to process, so it was banished away (twelfth). The resulting karma stems directly from this dynamic—the Aquarian South Node disconnection. He is learning to manage the South Node more consciously—to sink deeply into himself (fourth house) and connect with his truth (Aquarius), then to go out in the world (tenth-house North Node) and to be himself, connected with the possibilities of the present moment (Leo).

Chapter 6
The Sun

The Sun is the star of the show...literally. Though often termed a "planet," the Sun is actually a star, which brings it to a whole other league. Stars connect us to the broader universe; our souls are like solitary candles lit from the eternal flame of Spirit. In the *Awakening* approach, the Sun relates to soul realization. It is the life energy itself, shining out and connecting with all of life.

Many think of the Solar System as static, a group of planets revolving around the Sun. (This is an upgrade from astrology's early years, when we thought the Earth was at the center.) Actually, we know that the Sun is moving through space at the rate of 828,000 kilometers per hour. All the planets are being pulled through space, continually spiraling. The Sun travels around the Milky Way galaxy in 230 million years, an incredible orbital reach. Compare that to the motion of the Moon around the Earth, which takes about a month and stays very close. If we contrast a 230-million-year cycle versus a month, we recognize that the Sun and Moon have a completely different scope. Holding on to the idea that they are equal shows the incredible difficulty the ego has in accepting its diminished status (while being trapped in the illusion of this one relative vantage point).

On the Nature of Soul

What is our inherent energetic composure: Spirit or ego? Who are we *really*? Volume 1 of the *Awakening* series addresses the *egoic takeover*—how an individual tends to claim ownership of life energy and mistakenly believes there is complete autonomy and jurisdiction of that energy. The view here is that we are energetically connected to all of life, which turns out to be us! Instead of soul realization, the conventional view of the Sun equates with personality (Sun sign astrology). The culture around becoming a "star" in any given field is an example of how the promotion of ego is celebrated and rewarded. All the while, there is little or no awareness that we are *borrowing* our life energy from the universe and that the curriculum is to partner with it consciously.

The conventional view of Sun as ego is a reflection and perpetuation of the fundamental spiritual crisis on this planet. As we learn to collectively identify as part of unity rather than just separation, our views of life will shift, and astrology will reflect this advancement. In equating Sun with soul, we should clarify how we understand the idea of "soul." Some believe it has to do with woundedness and darkness—the soul needs to be healed. Perhaps it is the ego which needs to be healed in the soul journey. Spiritual teachers overwhelmingly discuss the soul in terms of brightness, awakening and becoming, and here are a few examples.

Gary Zukav: "The soul is the highest, most noble part of yourself you can reach for."

Iyanla Vanzant: "The soul is filled with the divinity of all that is."

Deepak Chopra: "The soul does not exist in space-time."

DeVon Franklin: "The connecting line to God."

Eckhart Tolle: "The essence of who you are beyond form."

Wayne Dyer: "The soul is infinite, there is no place where it is not."

Marriane Williamson: "The light—the soul."

Jean Huston: "The soul is how we wake up, it's the lure of our becoming."

Swami Rama: "The Soul does not need to be cured or healed; it seeks only to be experienced and known."

Andrew Cohen: "All the world's great wisdom traditions have insisted that higher human development is dependent upon the cultivation of the soul."

Even the dictionary (Webster's) defines soul as "the spiritual or immaterial part of the human being or animal, regarded as immortal." There are many gradations of "wattage" to the Sun, depending on how connected we are and how we relate to the universe. As Alan Watts (quoted earlier) described, we are apertures of light. We bring this creative and radiant Source energy into whatever projects and abilities the natal Sun depicts.

Conventional astrology tends to see the Sun in terms of particular chart factors. Someone might have the Sun in Gemini in the second house square Neptune, and that is who that person is. Period. The variable of consciousness is excluded—the Sun is not seen in a developmental way. Certain descriptions are thought to capture its scope. In the *Awakening* approach, we see an incredible spectrum of possibilities with the Sun, contingent on how we are developing. As mentioned earlier, the Moon is the "seed," while the Sun is the "flower." Meister Eckhart writes, "The seed of God is within us. Given an intelligent and hard-working farmer, it will thrive and grow up to God, whose seed it is; and accordingly its fruits will be God nature."

The focus of the *Awakening* approach is developing spiritual realization. There is an emphasis on the Sun's higher potentials, as that is the central intention of our flowering. We are enrolled in the liberating channel described in Chapter 1. The geocentric chart depicts our curriculum for awakening. In a future volume of this series, we will explore heliocentric astrology. The emphasis becomes reversed, focusing on how Spirit becomes manifest in separation. For now, we are looking at evolving egos becoming more enlightened.

The Sun in the Chart

In the *Awakening* approach, the Sun relates to:

1) A developmental process of increasing awareness: As noted in the human chronology, we start out as infants with no awareness of self and do not retain any memory of what is occurring. This depicts the initial amnesia of enrolling in separation consciousness. We develop an autonomous self (ego), which enables us to see to our survival and happiness. As we grow, we expand our awareness of both self and the universe. Ultimately, we realize that they are one and the same.

2) Mindfulness and presence: The main qualities of the Sun are its light and heat. Light is paired with awareness, while heat is equated with presence. Simply stated, we show up to life (heat) and learn to be mindful to what is actually happening (light). We can learn to just *be* with what life is offering without any resistance or need to change it whatsoever. The ego potentially learns to take a backseat to what the soul is orchestrating. We become mindful of the incredible intelligence that potentially informs our lives.

3) The energy body: Sometimes called an aura, each person's energy radiates into the world. Whereas the Moon pertains to the physical body, the Sun is the energy body—the soul connection with life. The soul is like a mediator between the unity of Spirit and the location of the separate self in the relative world. The soul has access to endless wisdom, the matrix of interconnection that envelops us. We sense our soul operating intuitively, a knowing that can be experienced in a variety of ways or channels when we develop greater clarity: clairaudience (clear hearing), clairsentience (clear feeling), clairvoyance (clear seeing), or claircognizance (clear thinking). Through the energy body, we send out intentions into the world to shape our realities. The Sun energizes the dreaming process, consciously or not, depending on the person.

4) The highest expression of self: If we were to encounter an apple seed for the first time, we would have no concept of the fruit that will dangle off a tree someday. The seed goes through a lengthy growth process. Likewise, each of us matures the seed (Moon) to branch out into progressively tastier, sun-ripened gifts. Every Sun profile portrays a unique kind of "tree," and what a joy for us to grow into it and maximize the harvest! The Sun portrays what we may develop into if we fully engage our curriculum. We need to "feed" our Sun, to engage in activities and experiences that promote our becoming.

5) The ideal life energy to address our karma: Each of us is given the gift of being perfectly enrolled in the solar curriculum that maximally assists spiritual development. The catch is, we have to release the familiar egoic attachments, identifications and pulls to the past. As examples provided later in this chapter illustrate, the Sun always shows up in ways that connect the chart owner to who he or she can be in the present. It's as if the native is already in the awakened state. Our task is to more fully embody the promise.

163

6) A profound gift to shine into the world: Every "fruit" that ripens in the evolutionary process is completely unique. Not only does each fruit fulfill the individual curriculum, it extends to broader collective themes of evolution. Each of us has the potential to dynamically change the world in some way. A fully realized Sun leaves an indelible and unmistakable mark on the planet, which is not necessarily about fame or recognition. In fact, the awakened person is non-attached and is operating from "divine GPS." It is actually Spirit operating through the person, and it may not be noticed any more than a beautiful coral reef at the bottom of the ocean. Developing the Sun makes the planet a glorious reflection of Spirit—we bring heaven down to earth in infinite ways.

As we get into chart factors, it's worth discussing the central challenge of the Sun. Simply stated, none of us starts out very awake, and therefore the Sun gets distorted. The instinctual Moon, preoccupied with itself, radiates its agenda through the Sun's energy. Therefore, the person initially tends to play out the darker (or more unconscious) facets of the Sun, blended with lunar material. For instance, someone with a Cancer Moon and a Sagittarius Sun may be dependent (Cancer) in youth and gravitate to religion or belief systems (Sagittarius) for security. As that person matures and awakens, living a path of heart (Cancer) increasingly develops through more conscious Sagittarian decision making on how to proceed.

Claiming the Sun's potentials can be a lengthy and challenging process. So often I hear clients claim that they don't quite identify with their Sun signs. I explain that it's a process of *development*—who we are inside (and have been) is the Moon, while the South Node portrays familiar ways of behaving. These signatures are immediately recognizable, while the Sun becomes progressively realized.

In this chapter, we'll look at the Sun in the astrology chart. It would be redundant to discuss the Sun in the various signs, as the spiritual purposes of the twelve signs are provided in Chapter 2. The intention is always to develop their most conscious expression, while our spiritual education includes learning the less conscious sides. Below are remarks on the Sun in the twelve houses, followed by the planetary dialogues the Sun makes through aspect.

The Sun in the Houses

The Sun's house position is an area of great discovery and development. The nature of the sign will create the house's décor, and the chart owner will be spending a good deal of time getting more familiar with the lessons of the sign/house blend. A conscious response to the Sun would increasingly illuminate the gifts that reside in that house. Unlike signs, which are fixed evolutionary programs, houses are fluid. If someone has the Sun in the fourth house, that person is not limited to a life indoors, and people with the Sun in the tenth generally do have homes! The house placement is where the life energy finds connection with soul, and the person feels drawn to this area to do the spiritual curriculum. The aspects to other planets (and dispositor schemes) show how the Sun connects to other areas—the life energy is not bound to one place.

A Sun in the first house is learning to embody solar characteristics as part of the persona and approach to life. The lesson is to be the captain of one's ship, completely in control of behavior decisions. These people can be quite magnetic and attractive as they develop. The more they claim their "big" selves, the more impact they can direct.

With the Sun in the second house, the chart owner is learning greater self-sufficiency and confidence. There is a focus on the body, self-alignment with one's inner strength. The native is bolstering personal security and sturdiness, and making money can be a part of this. The person is realizing that the self is the greatest source of wealth.

In the third house, the Sun develops communicative power and greater reasoning skills. The chart owner is learning about the world, strengthening cognitive abilities, and getting involved in a variety of active pursuits. The program is to trust one's own perception and thinking, and operate strategically to deliver a newfound message.

A Sun in the fourth house is illuminating areas of the heart, family and connection with location. These natives are learning to be more rooted in themselves, experiencing deeper love and attachments. When they discover that sustenance comes from within, they have solid internal foundations to approach the world.

A fifth-house Sun is developing spontaneous expression and participation with life. The chart owner is becoming reacquainted with the sheer joy and abundance of living. Developing some form of talent or creative outlet helps the soul shine. A fifth-house Sun may be drawn to children, which is a reflection of one's innocence.

The sixth house is an area of training and skill development, finding greater mastery of a craft. The Sun here is rolling up the sleeves to become more professionally specialized and adept in order to help others, and potentially the world itself, grow. This is a hands-on intention to assist evolutionary momentum, which is a reflection of the personal awakening process.

In the seventh house, a Sun becomes more vibrant through interpersonal exchanges, joining together in partnerships of many forms. Whether through romance, business associations, or friendship, these natives are becoming more visible and engaged.

They are learning how to share their light with others and see the sacred reflection.

The eighth house involves the interpenetration of souls, making profound contact at any and all levels. With the Sun here, the learning involves overcoming fears or inhibitions to meet that promise. With a revealing, present and soulful disposition, sacred union and intimacy are continually developed.

A ninth-house Sun finds its vitality through following its own spiritual path. Aligning with purpose and taking steps to realize a soul mission is indicated. There could be the intention to become more adventurous, to enter cross-cultural experiences, or investigate areas of higher learning—a lifetime of expanding horizons in fiery ways.

The tenth house is the pinnacle of the chart, indicating an intention to earnestly contribute to society. Those with this placement are developing excellence and commitment to important ambitions that stem from their more awakened selves. The world desperately needs more enlightened executives, bosses or visible people in the news, and perhaps these natives will occupy those roles.

The eleventh house is like the "world stage" as it involves networks, communal efforts and the broader public milieu. The Sun placed here is learning to assist the world in becoming more conscious by joining in humanitarian and collective causes. The more these natives engage the awakening process, the more their light shines brightly as a beacon of hope and possibility.

In the twelfth house, a soul is learning to increase its luminosity through the direct experience of Spirit. Those with this placement are learning about contemplation, retreat, connecting with nature, and recharging their batteries through conscious resting. They are not necessarily here to stay on the sidelines, but rather to become spiritually energized to engage the rest of life.

Planets in Aspect to the Sun

The Sun is generally in aspect to a few planets. They are the forces that ideally become assimilated into the life energy to carry out its intentions. As we'll see later in the chapter, the Sun profile is always the perfect energetic vehicle to grow into the present, given the issues and challenges of the past. The planets in aspect are instrumental in the evolutionary process, partners on the path of becoming.

Though it's popular to identify as a Sun sign, the planets are the actual energy of the system. We can think of being Martial or Saturnian if the Sun is in aspect to these planets. The Sun sign indicates the evolutionary program that modifies the energy.

An unaspected Sun is very rare. It is appropriate to extend the Sun's orb, even to 15 degrees, making it nearly impossible to have a Sun with no aspects. The Sun is the life energy, and the astronomical Sun is bigger than everything else in the Solar System combined, so this orb is warranted. Yet we can look at minor aspects (with wider-than-usual orbs) if any question remains. There is also, as discussed before, whole sign logic, and the planet that disposits the Sun has a connection as well. I personally have not seen any examples of a Sun that is truly unaspected—most anyone has a soul intention to work with particular planets as part of his or her evolution.

Sun/Mercury

On the geocentric chart, Mercury is always near the Sun, never moving more than 28 degrees away. Therefore, a conjunction is the only aspect the Sun and Mercury can make. Our awareness (Sun) seems to have that little inner voice (Mercury) nearby and most of us initially identify with the mind's activity.

Spiritual awakening involves seeing Mercury as a tool that the soul uses to navigate in the relative world.

Much of the time, the Sun and Mercury are located in the same sign (or house), so they're working with the same developmental program (or area of life). Considering the large orb we allow for the Sun, it is conjunct Mercury quite frequently. When the planets are close together, there can be a strong focus on intellectual matters or verbal skills, a clarity of perception — but also the over-identification with one's thoughts.

The Sun and Mercury in adjacent signs (or many degrees apart) can be different. Such a placement is not more or less favorable; there is just some variation as to how awareness and intellect work together. There can be some distancing from busy cogitation, or a multi-faceted, rather than sharply focused, approach to learning, thinking or perception. The challenge is to get the planets to operate on the same page.

Sun/Venus

Venus is never more than two signs away from the Sun. Just as we have our minds as part of our life energy, so too do we innately orient sensually and relationally. Venus is tactile (earth) and also deals with object relations (air). Venus is frequently in a sign different from the Sun. Since Venus moves swiftly near the Sun and slows for its stations (while furthest away), having the Sun closely conjunct Venus is unusual. Most of us have a Venus profile quite distinct from the Sun, which adds more variety and nuance to character, interests and self-expression.

When the planets are in conjunction, the life energy has greater access to a pleasing and engaging disposition (modified by sign). These natives have access to increased popularity, social participation, developing talents and diplomatic skills. There can be indulgence or slickness if taken too far. When the planets are further apart, there can be less attachment to social needs and often less charm and appeal. Being less Venusian simply means the work is on other matters.

Sun/Mars

This combination is a powerhouse! These fire planets team to learn personal assertion, courageous action, putting the life in drive. Perhaps the most active of all planetary pairings, this aspect indicates a soul intention to carve one's own unique way. In the spiritual history, this boldness was likely absent or mismanaged. The present lifetime aims to correct this by showing up to life in an entirely new, more spirited, way. The challenge is unconscious behavior that is selfish, unnecessarily edgy or brash. Sun/Mars can choose the wrong battles to wage if it's operating from unconsciousness or woundedness.

Sun/Jupiter

It doesn't get bigger than this. Jupiter is larger than all of the other planets combined, while the Sun is larger than everything in the entire Solar System with a lot of room to spare. So the intention is to develop a noticeable presence, acting from spiritual purpose. If otherwise motivated, then this pairing can manifest in grandiose and entitled ways. In prior lives, the chart owner may have been misguided, confused or somehow lacking conscious convictions. Many have been hurt from religion, experienced a limited sense of free will, or were upset by misfortune. The present life path is to enthusiastically get back on the horse that threw him/her. There may be some degree of having the "Midas touch," so those with this pairing need to be careful what they wish for. Awakening into greater presence and having an impact on the world can take a variety of forms. The spiritual lesson is to find clarity on the path.

Sun/Saturn

Saturn involves the development of integrity, endurance and wisdom, occupying the mature self. Sun/Saturn is an intention to deliberately pursue and structure works that bring self-respect and make a solid contribution to society. Lessons involve self-reliance, embracing solitude and getting real about the ways of the world. Often challenging when young, this combination potentially becomes sturdy and effective, able to make an impact. The spiritual history may have themes of giving power away to others, immaturity or complacency—some dynamic around responsibility. If these natives are stuck in the past and refuse to grow, then the biography may have themes of limitation, blockage and sometimes depression. Sun/Saturn is learning to claim more influence in the world.

Sun/Chiron

This combination appears frequently with healers and practitioners of self-development. A theme with Chiron is reconnection, so performing the necessary tasks and processes to achieve such self-alignment is the native's divine gift. However, we teach what we are learning. Sun/Chiron people are healing their own splintering or wounding. If they don't take measures to address this, then it's likely to radiate out to create an ego dream that reinforces their personal challenges. Upon integration, they become sensitive to themes of disconnection and act as bridges from the personal to the transpersonal in their private lives and, potentially, in their professional lives.

Sun/Uranus

A lifetime of experimentation and reinvention is indicated. The life force is learning to consciously embody the unconditioned authentic self. On the way, sweeping changes and redirections are likely. There may be career choices, lifestyles or interests that vary from traditional standards. The intention is to be true to the self, even if a resulting action is unpopular. Those with this pairing are learning about freedom and non-attachment. These lessons can inform contributions for our collective evolution. The challenge is in making erratic and unwise decisions that are "out there" to the point of being simply misguided. These detours are a part of the education. Often in the spiritual history, there are themes of conforming, playing it safe, or lacking metaphysical understanding. Now these natives are jazzed to bring the future into the present. The better they understand (and embody) the transpersonal, the broader the scope of their impact.

Sun/Neptune

The intention is to be "in the world but not of it." These people exist in the hallway between this world and another. As the veil is thin, they have the ability to bring in great inspiration, unconditional love, and grace. The program is to infuse the life force with mystical wonder, to operate in connection with the transpersonal. The challenge is learning how to do this lofty program! Learning to navigate the dream world and raise one's consciousness is a tall order. On the way, there may be times of feeling lost, not really knowing who the self is and feeling disillusioned about the world. In the soul history, there may be a pattern of strong attachments to outcomes, mundane pleasures, or the whims of the personality that are now being let go. It is crucial to arrive at a clear vision with Neptune; then the life energy can truly shine.

Sun/Pluto

The Sun and Pluto relate to power, albeit in very different ways. The Sun is overt radiant energetic power, while Pluto is of the deep, subtle and emotional variety. The promise is to develop into a force that catalyzes shifts and dredges up necessary issues to work through. The more someone with this pairing is wise about the shadow and in touch with his or her own, the more that person can steer through the unconsciousness of the world and be a light through it. The challenge involves the personal stumbling through such territory—there can be crisis or extremity that marks the biography. Plutonian material may have been avoided or problematic in past incarnations, so now the native has a psychologically charged lifetime to season and mature—and potentially help the world do that, too.

Working with the Past

As the Sun is the energy of presence, we will look more closely at its role in arriving in the moment. Most of us are unconsciously playing out what is unresolved, and we don't realize it. We meet this material in the world and often see it as an annoyance. The astrological Sun portrays a pathway to cut through all of this if we can learn to see the external world as the self. The Sun's unique condition provides a prescription for how to approach the projections of our unconsciousness.

When we pay close attention to the nuances of what is actually occurring, we can see how our consciousness is creating our experience. Then we can be in charge of it rather than having *it* be in charge of *us*. We are continually integrating Sun (awareness, presence) into the Moon (well of the unconsciousness), a process that enables the seed to blossom into a flower. I have termed this "spiritual photosynthesis." The process can proceed rather quickly or may take many lifetimes, depending on how deeply the emotions are buried and what defense mechanisms are in place. Ultimately, the Moon learns to open from its prior contraction, and we awake to life.

Anything we encounter can stimulate awakening should we pay attention to what our souls are bringing to our awareness. The Moon is a rock, analogous to how our unconscious emotions can harden and remain stagnant. Energy (Sun) stimulates motion, and emotions are the result. We can either get our resistance out of the way to allow the process to unfold, or we can renew defensive measures. Abraham Maslow says, "In any given moment we have two options: to step forward into growth or step back into safety." Partnering Sun with Moon allows the present to heal the past.

The emotional stimulation that initially troubled or harmed us becomes the buried treasure that may enhance us. On the spectrum of consciousness from dark to bright, every facet of astrology is like a double agent—one side can cause problems, while the other promotes well-being. The Sun seeks to awaken the brighter possibility. The following table lists the twelve major themes, how the emotional issues transmute into empowered gifts when the past is processed.

Sign (related planet)	Emotional issue	Empowered gift
Aries (Mars)	anger, frustration	direction, assertion
Taurus (Venus)	stagnation, indulgence	peace, comfort, security
Gemini (Mercury)	disorganization	knowledge, curiosity
Cancer (Moon)	upset, hurt feelings	heartfelt receptiveness
Leo (Sun)	egocentricity, insecurity	warmth, likability
Virgo (Mercury)	shame, guilt	competence, diligence
Libra (Venus)	co-dependence	interdependence
Scorpio (Pluto)	intense wounding	power, impact
Sagittarius (Jupiter)	dogmatism, grandiosity	spiritual direction
Capricorn (Saturn)	coldness, fear	mastery, wisdom
Aquarius (Uranus)	detachment	perspective
Pisces (Neptune)	sadness, grief	compassionate love

Carl Jung says, "Emotion is the chief source of all becoming conscious. There can be no transforming of darkness into light and of apathy into movement without emotion." The more we empty the proverbial cup, the better we feel because we are cleared out. We have greater access to the spiritual grace and beauty continuously available when our energy isn't contracted. This is the paradox: most don't want to feel what is buried because they want to feel okay, but releasing it is the methodology to actually feeling better. We already met it once, at the time of impact, and we survived. So why not dive into it to process it and be free?

In contrast, keeping unconscious defensive measures in place saps our energy. We continuously strategize to have only "good" experiences, which prolongs the defensive pattern. We stay on a merry-go-round of avoidance. Some say we should "grow up" and out of our limitations and issues, while the truth may be that we actually mature by growing *into* who we really are. There's a saying, "You may be done with the past, but the past isn't done with you." This brings to mind another quote from William Faulkner: "The past is never dead. It's not even past."

When we do allow buried emotions to be felt, we can take measures to release them. This takes a number of different forms: emotional catharsis and release, methods that stimulate purging, self-expression, dance, conscious temper tantrums, art, physical exertion, venting, toning and other vocalizations, bodily cleanses, getting issues off of our chest or simply breathing them out. As we are *energy-processing systems*, any type of energetic motion outwards can be helpful. Short-term pain leads to long-term gain, and if it is done well, some kind of treasure emerges. Sadness transmutes to compassion, anger to direction. We have the choice to either clear it out or play it out.

Though we "empty the cup" by processing the past, the residue of wisdom remains. Each of us has a memory of the past and access to the emotions involved with such experiences. This allows us to be empathic and loving towards others and to physically (Moon) embody soul (Sun) intentions. Though some have a picture of an enlightened being as above it all, the view in the *Awakening* approach is the integration of awareness (Sun) with the physical system (Moon), to bridge worlds. As long as we have bodies, we are human, oriented to the relative world and subject to all of the feeling states involved with life.

The Past & Present in the Chart

The Sun's position in the chart reveals how the present life builds upon the past, which can be indicated in a few ways. For instance, the Sun can be in direct dialogue with the Moon, by aspect or dispositor. The Sun engages with the unfinished needs and intentions and attempts to see the work through. There is enrollment in a new program (new awareness, roles and attributes) that may bring perspective to what has been left in the unconscious.

When the Sun appears in the same sign as the Moon (either a new Moon or balsamic), then further work with that archetypal program is necessary. Present evolution (Sun) requires sharing the inner contents (Moon) in overt and radiant ways. Only in the rare situation of having an exact new Moon would the luminaries be in the same place. Usually, they occupy different places in the 30-degree range of a sign and therefore have their own distinct profiles in the chart (different aspects and house placement). The present then has some unique suggestions as to how to work with the past.

The Sun can be in relationship with the Moon's nodes, as discussed in the last chapter. In this case, the chart owner is actually embodying who he or she has previously been in terms of *biography* (e.g., the Dalai Lama). The conjunction would portray that most strongly, while other aspects to the nodes suggest that certain facets of who that person was are being renewed in the present to heal something mismanaged. For instance, a Capricorn Sun square an Aries South Node indicates that karma accrued in vocational ways is being addressed. Anyone with a Leo South Node has the Sun as the dispositor and therefore is carrying past themes forward.

With no connection (by aspect or rulership) to the nodes, the Sun is the energy to complement what has come before in novel ways. For whatever reason, it is less necessary to directly "relive" the familiar energy from the past. Whatever the situation is between the Moon and Sun, the Sun can always point to more enlightened usages.

Next we will use examples to explore the Sun's central importance in chart analysis. It is always in the perfect place!

The Sun's Centrality

Each of us shows up in the ideal energy body for continued development in the soul journey. By virtue of being alive, we embody our soul selves, and our task is to remove the blockages to realize that. As so many spiritual teachers say, awakening is a *deconstructive* process. The piercing light and heat of the Sun can blast away the distortions and issues that get in the way of being a vessel of shining awareness.

Not only is the Sun the center of the Solar System, it plays the central role in each person's development. It is the flowering into spiritual potential. Everything that has been worked on in the soul history serves as a foundation. We bring greater consciousness to the past and springboard from it into new avenues. As we'll see in the following examples, the Sun is always in the perfect position to spark the chart owner's spiritual evolution. Not only does it assist the native in growing further, it also helps manage the outstanding lessons. Below are some examples from the counseling room.

Example #1

Our first example has a Gemini Moon in the fifth house, indicating an optimistic youthful disposition and a need for greater learning and expression of knowledge. The trine to Pluto in Libra in the ninth house shows an emotional allegiance with those in positions of power, exactly what is expected of students in the developmental years. However, the Moon's square to Mars in Aquarius in the second house illustrates a frustrated need to break away into more progressive areas. The underlying issue is confidence and self-alignment, which the strengthening of the Moon/Mars square will ultimately provide.

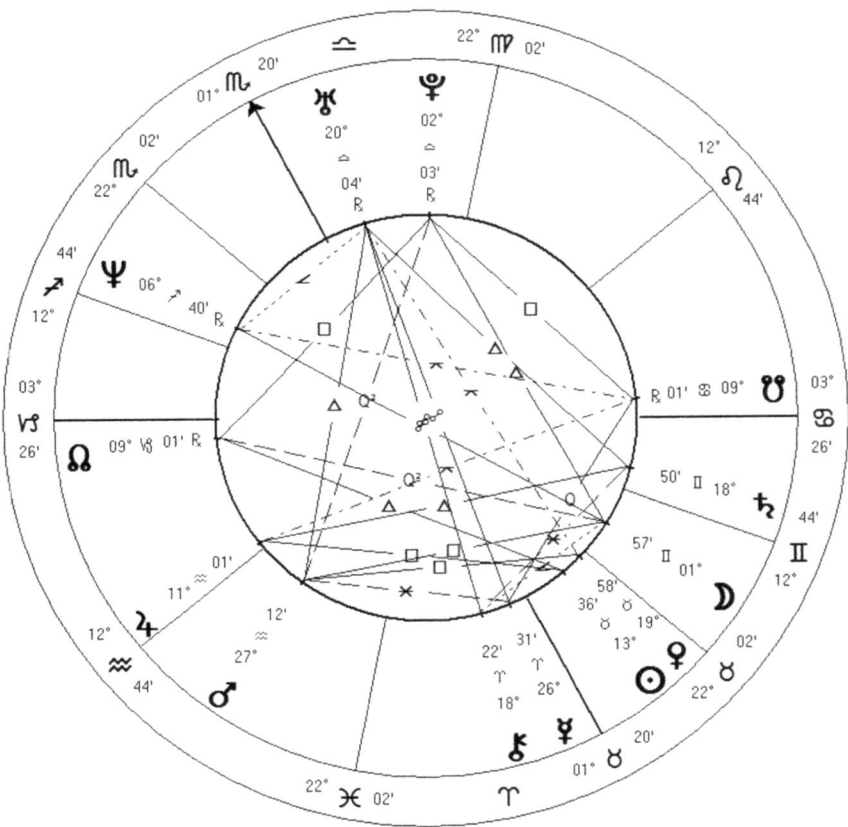

From the youthful disposition of the lunar profile, the karmic pattern (seventh-house Cancer South Node) is to give power away to others, trying very hard to be loving and supportive. The first-house Capricorn North Node intends to develop greater toughness and self-orientation. The dispositor of the North Node (Saturn in Gemini in the sixth) seeks ardently to develop expertise and diligence in intellectual matters, perhaps to become a teacher or author.

Given the information from the past (Moon, South Node) and the intention to reconcile the karma (North Node), the Sun placement is ideal. The Taurus Sun is an intention to develop

179

greater inner strength, while residence in the fourth house suggests deeper rootedness to self. Sun square Jupiter in Aquarius in the second is learning to become more confident and to venture into progressive philosophical territory. The Sun is also trine the Capricorn North Node in the first, bringing energy and focus to the development of greater authority and self-direction. The dispositor (Saturn in Gemini) takes this forward, and the Gemini Moon can ultimately fulfill its outstanding need for greater learning.

Example #2

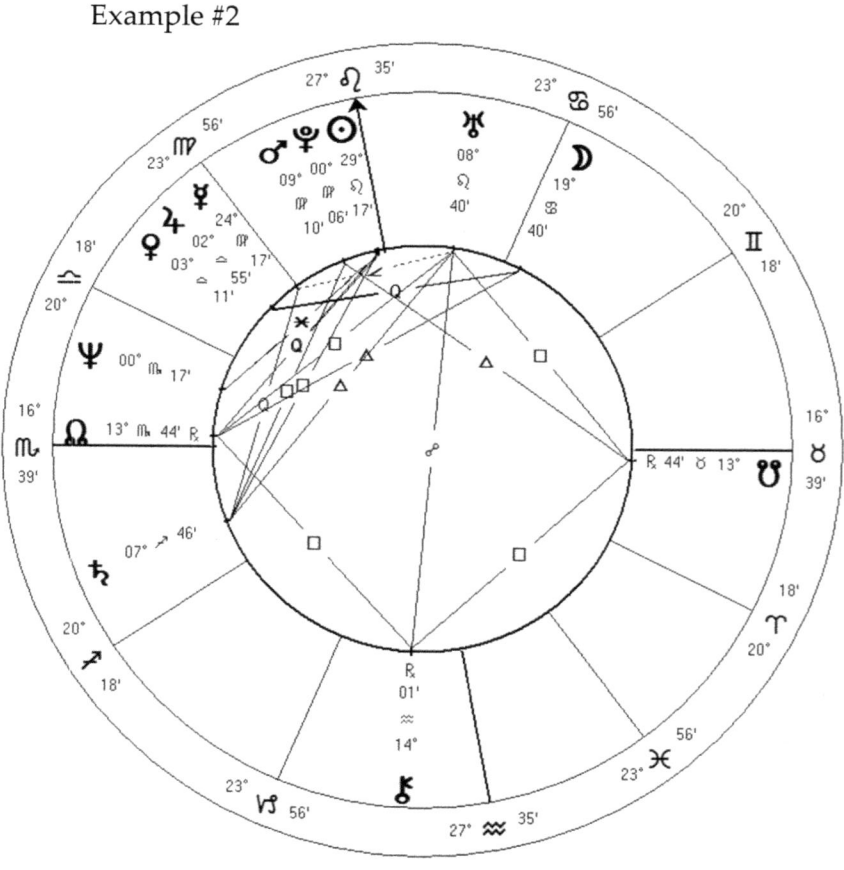

The Moon is in Cancer in the eighth house, indicating a strong need to feel loved by others and a willingness to be dependent on them for that love. The quintile to Jupiter/Venus in Libra in the eleventh portrays emotionally satisfying community experiences that reinforce this need. The ego is quite focused on connection and security (Cancer Moon), which led to the karma in question. Taurus South Node in the sixth is a very hard-working pattern, totally committed to handling responsibility in order to promote stability. There is experience being deferential and serving others (sixth), which stems from the lunar need to be a caretaker. The South Node dispositor is Venus in Libra (mentioned above), an agreeable public persona working within group contexts.

Uranus in Leo in the ninth, and Chiron in Aquarius in the third, are both square the nodal axis. These planets have to do with breaking through prior conditioning to claim more authenticity, fun, progressive ideas, and autonomy about what to think and who to be.

The Sun is in Leo in the tenth house, indicating the intention to become more commanding and empowered and for public life to be joyous. The Sun is next to a Pluto/Mars conjunction in Virgo, a desire to transform vocation into service and skills that dig deep into the human condition. The Sun is also square Saturn in Sagittarius in the first, which matures into greater leadership and more self-directed purpose. Ultimately, the Moon is able to experience the depth and connection it desires, made more available when the native claims greater personal power and autonomy of the solar intention.

Example #3

This chart features a Virgo Moon in the ninth house, a need to follow the rules and do things appropriately and in accordance with the teachings received. Underneath, there's a need for greater autonomy (Moon opposite Mars), and to have more fluid and unrestrained experiences (Mars in Pisces). The Moon is also quincunx Mercury in Aries, illustrating the need to think for oneself.

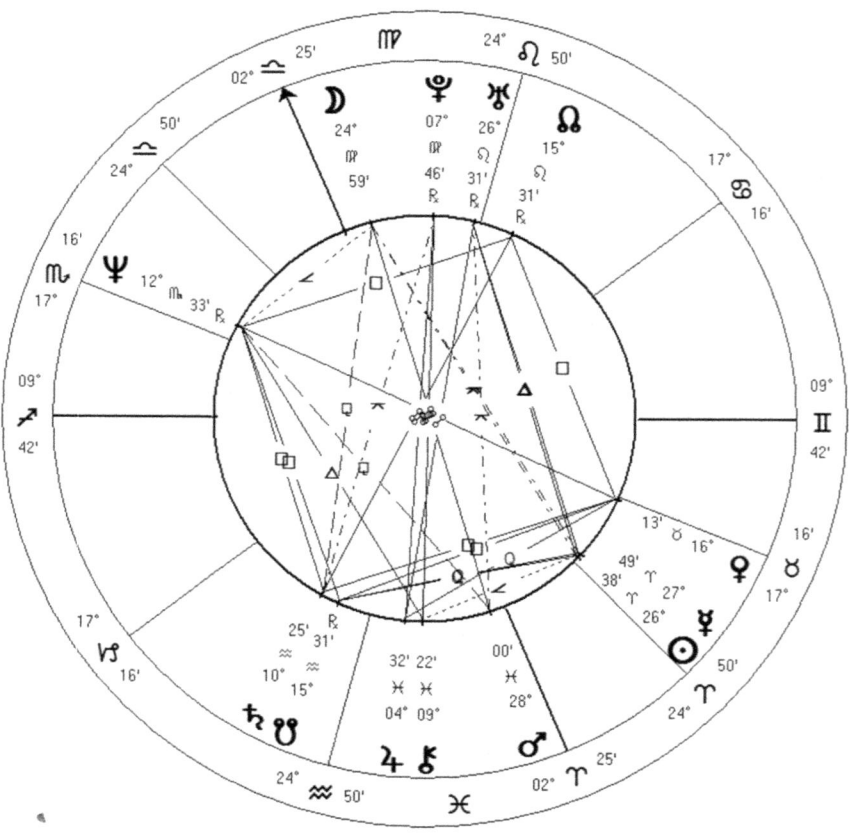

The karmic pattern reflects restricted freedom (South Node conjunct Saturn in Aquarius)—due to a challenge around self-sufficiency (second house) and self-governance (Saturn). The work is to become mature and confident about claiming one's freedom (Aquarius). The Leo North Node in the eighth house invites greater presence and drama in intimate exchanges, being oneself with others and experiencing more depth and connection.

The Sun is in Aries in the fifth house, showing an intention to claim the unresolved independence and to learn greater spontaneity and zest for life. The Sun is conjunct Mercury and trine Uranus in the ninth, highlighting the issue of independent thinking. Through questioning everything (Uranus/Mercury), a new belief system or guiding life philosophy (Uranus in the ninth) is achieved. Then the Virgo Moon can release the attachments to limiting patterns. The conscious Moon grows to become more adept (Virgo) at following a meaningful path (ninth house), which is illuminated by the freshness and vigor of the fifth-house Aries Sun.

Client Example #4

A Capricorn Moon in the eleventh house is strongly influenced by mainstream cultural sensibilities, a need to fit it with the fabric of society and contribute to its preservation. With the Moon trine Saturn in Virgo in the seventh, there is a particular need to be responsible to others and to partner with those who represent and provide the traditional forms of security. Moon square Pluto in Libra in the eighth shows wounding from giving power away, a sense of unfairness and emotional upset around deeper bonding. The Moon's sextile to Uranus/Venus in Scorpio in the eighth desires deeper intimate connecting. This can be disruptive to the Saturn in Virgo pattern, so it's more removed (Uranus), even in the shadow (Scorpio).

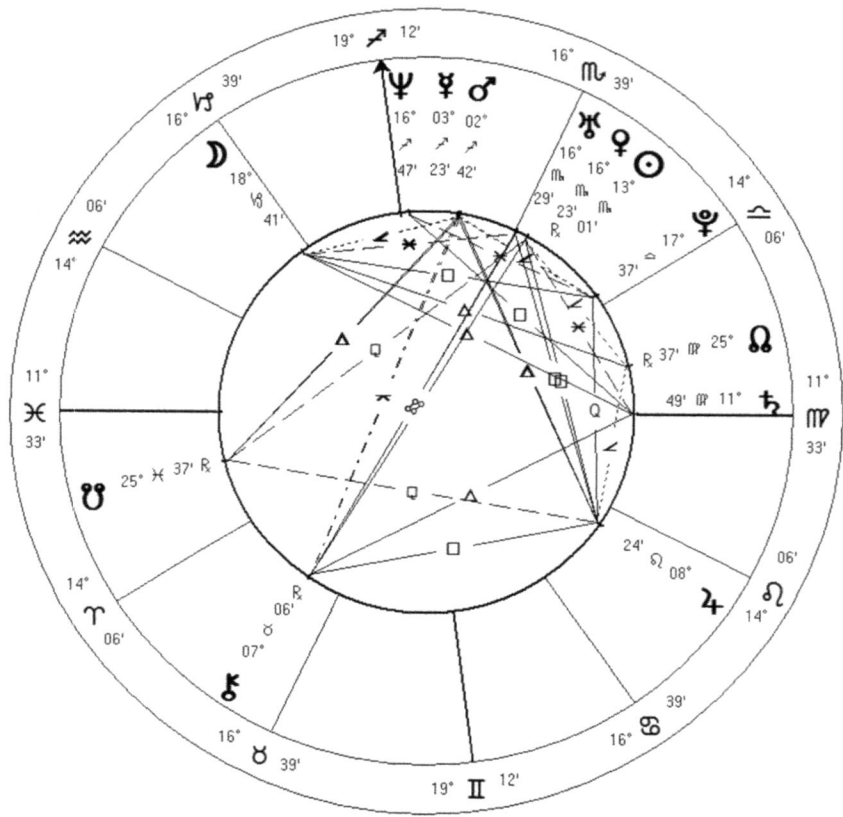

Stemming from the responsible lunar need, we see a karmic pattern of surrender to the conditioning (South Node in Pisces in the first) connected to ideology (Neptune in Sagittarius in the ninth). The North Node reverses the pattern by learning to be more skeptical and discerning (Virgo) and to connect with others while holding greater equality (seventh) by virtue of this questioning demeanor. As the North Node dispositor, Mercury (in conjunction with Mars) is learning to speak up more and share its own views (Sagittarius in the ninth).

The Sun in Scorpio in the eighth picks up on the work in the ideal way. It is conjunct the unresolved Uranus/Venus desire for interpersonal breakthrough, providing energy to that need. Also, Scorpio concerns the development of power, which is important given a historical pattern of giving it away (Pisces South Node). Furthermore, the Sun is sextile Saturn, an intention to integrate greater authority as part of one's own energy instead of projecting it onto others (seventh).

Client Example #5

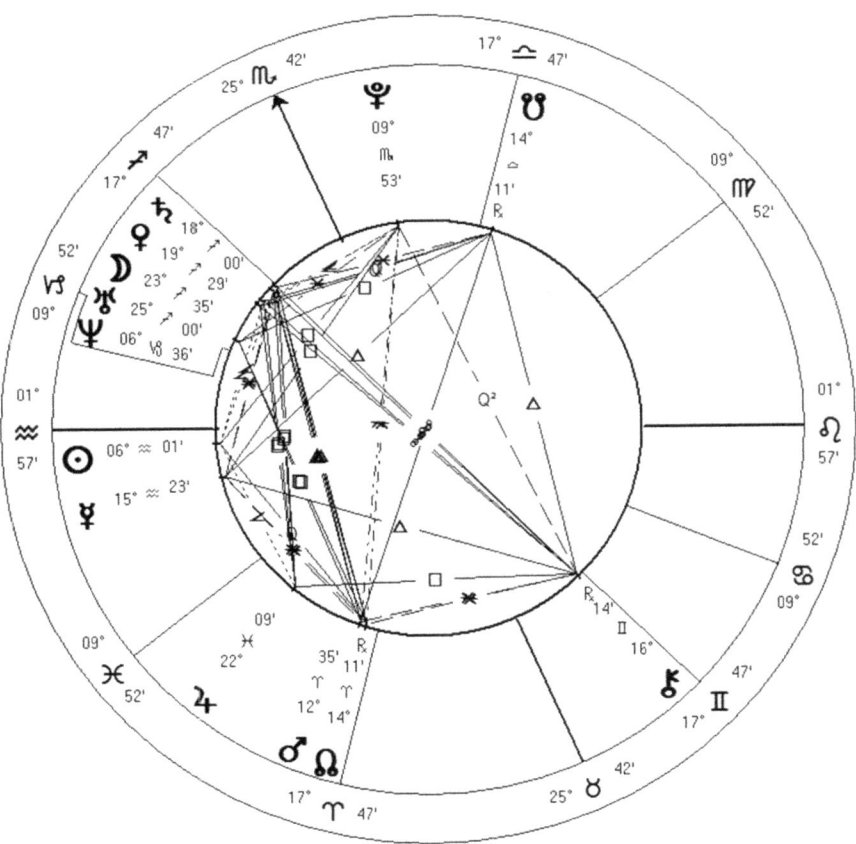

This chart has a Sagittarius Moon in the eleventh house conjunct Venus, Saturn and Uranus, indicating an unfinished need to join with like-minded allies to help change the world. Security is found through affiliation (Venus) and structure (Saturn), participating in social arenas and adhering to their norms. This would play out in educational, political or cultural spheres. The chart owner would have liked for participation to be more progressive (Moon conjunct Uranus), but Uranus is initially beyond the manifestation of Saturn, so the need is unintegrated.

The karma generated by the Moon's strong need for affiliation is found in the Libra South Node in the eighth, a pattern of accommodating (Libra) other peoples' agendas (eighth). Venus serves as the dispositor, suggesting that this is played out within community or group contexts, fitting in (Venus) with group consciousness (eleventh) and direction (Sagittarius). Opposite the South Node is Mars in Aries in the second house, a historical challenge around self-alignment and potency (Mars) in declaring one's independence (Aries). Mars is being strengthened in the present lifetime. What would be most helpful is greater non-attachment and a broader metaphysical perspective, as so much of the pattern is of compliance.

Yet again, the Sun is in the perfect place—in this example, Aquarius in the first house square Pluto in Scorpio in the ninth. Further steps are taken with authentic (Aquarius) independence (first). There is an intention to completely transform the guiding life philosophy (Pluto in the ninth) in order for a transpersonal (Aquarius), non-attached, and more empowered (Sun square Pluto) way to emerge. The Sun is also quintile the North Node in Aries, so innovative leadership abilities are available. With such abilities manifested, the unresolved lunar need to help change the world becomes more possible.

The Lunar Cycle

The rhythm of life is established by the lunar cycle—a waxing and waning, breathing in and out, moving to manifestation and back to renewal, an ongoing cycle of rebirth. The new Moon illustrates the emergence of the separate self (Moon) from Source (Sun). We venture out and accrue experiences before returning. The degree of awakening and development sets the course for another cycle.

The lunar cycle is often neglected in astrology practice. A cyclical and evolutionary perspective is less popular than the predictive and personality emphasis found conventionally. Also, the focus on Sun and Moon gender designations doesn't easily apply to the lunar cycle. With a spiritual view, we see how it illustrates a partnership between the separate self and soul/Spirit.

There are many ways to split up a pie. It's quite common to use eight lunar phases—four in the waxing half (new, crescent, first quarter, gibbous) and four in the waning (full, disseminating, last quarter, balsamic). The four-fold division (new, first quarter, full and last quarter) is popular (weather page in the newspaper, calendars, etc.). Since the zodiac is based on the number twelve, we could also use twelve phases that match the procession of the signs through the zodiac or the movement through the houses.

The Moon's position in the cycle is part of a particular developmental stage. Astrology is based on this rhythm, and the Moon's phasal position is most instructive about the native's general temperament and emotional characteristics. Of course, there are many factors to take into consideration with the Moon (sign, aspects, house), as well as the general tone of the overall chart. Nevertheless, the lunar phase is important.

We will consider two variables: whether the Moon is waxing or waning and whether the Moon is dark or bright. The Moon is waxing when it goes from new to full, and a waning

Moon is advancing from full to new. The Moon is brighter from the first quarter through the full Moon to the last quarter; it is darker from the last quarter through the new Moon to the first quarter. The condition of any Moon can be viewed through these two factors.

Waxing Moon

The waxing hemicycle is noted for its upsurge of energy in pursuit of goals and accomplishment. The motion is towards the climax of the full Moon, with a strong determination to see aims reach fruition. The focus is on development, whether that means personal growth, projects or other intentions. Building something is the spirit, and the natural motion is towards greater realization. There can be a sense of urgency, as if life is continually marching on and there is much to do.

The gift of the waxing Moon is a forward focus, and the challenge is attaining clarity of direction. A waxing Moon can be immature and naïve, like a young upstart full of eagerness and less full of wisdom. Often, there is learning by trial and error, simply going for it.

Waning Moon

The waning hemicycle features the diminishing of light, which symbolizes shedding and distributing. With a broader focus on outreach, waning Moons are more concerned with how personal growth or projects fit into the collective milieu. The flavor can be less assuming and less involved with the personal story. They are keenly aware that the fruits of the tree have ripened and can now be disseminated. A task is to find this outreach and maximize impact.

The gift is a more universal focus, and the challenge has to do with the situation's eventual finality. Light is diminishing, and the end is sure to come, so the lesson is to be wise and judicious as to how matters may come to completion. Whereas the waxing cycle has to do with action, the waning concerns awareness and integration.

Bright Moon

From the first quarter to the last quarter, the Moon is more bright than dark. This hemicycle has to do with illumination of unconsciousness and, ultimately, finding resolution. Bringing issues to light, or projects to manifestation, is the program. The brighter part of the cycle tends to be interpersonal in scope. Others and the world itself are reflections of self. With the increased light, this becomes more obvious—if awareness is lacking, then issues will play out strongly to help catalyze more awareness.

The gift is clarity and illumination; greater fullness brings results. The challenge is whether the cycle has been navigated consciously. If not, then whatever is problematic, incomplete or wounding is in greater exposure.

Dark Moon

From the last quarter to the first quarter, the Moon is more dark than bright. The theme here is of potential, which can be seen in two ways. From the new Moon to the first quarter, intentions are being developed, so the question is one of viability. From the last quarter to the new Moon is the contemplative part of the cycle. We review what has come before and integrate lessons. We get a "progress note" of how we've done and therefore realize what we're made of, what our potential actually is. Whatever the status is becomes renewed for another go-around with the new Moon.

A gift of the dark moon is being covert. During the night we are not seen, so we are able to switch courses and rethink our steps. There is an internal focus on our process, something the more exposed bright Moons no longer have. Dark Moons involve the process of getting started or releasing, and either way, they reside in the internal landscape of potential.

For our purposes in this book, we are going to note the general condition of the lunar phase as a factor to consider in chart analysis (waxing/waning, bright/dark). To this author, it is of major significance and must be included. In fact, lunar phase is so important that I am dedicating the next volume of this series to studying it more fully. *The Astrology of Awakening Volume 3: Seasons of the Moon* will not only detail the lunar cycle, it will specifically focus on this cycle by progression. We will review each phase in detail and understand the overarching storyline of our evolution. In addition, this volume will cover the fascinating and mostly undeveloped terrain of the Moon's declination—the heights and depths of emotionality, which, after all, is what the Moon is about. The volume will also provide additional material on the nodes of the Moon.

Chapter 7
Pluto and the Chart Skeleton

This chapter completes the introduction of the major players in this approach, structuring the material in a coherent way as a strategy to enter charts. The overarching motion of awakening from unconsciousness must address the shadow. Deep beneath the well of the emotional unconscious (Moon) lies the Underworld (Pluto).

Carl Jung remarks, "No tree, it is said, can grow to heaven unless its roots reach down to hell." The lifeblood of growth is water, and astrology portrays three central components of this element. Moon/Cancer is the foundation of the personal self in an emotional body. Pluto/Scorpio details the psychological impact of exchanges with others and the external world itself. Neptune/Pisces is the dream space, the imaginative processes that influence and sculpt the Moon's ego dream, and also where we release prior dream material. The emotional body is inspired by "heaven" (Neptune, loftier states of consciousness) but must deal with the dream material produced by unconsciousness, what many refer to as "hell" (Pluto, deeply buried). As we enter this discussion, it's important to bring a non-judgmental perspective. Plutonian material is not "bad," rather, a natural part of learning. The way to grow is to love it and embrace its wisdom.

Pluto and the Moon

During spiritual childhood, it is natural to have misguided dreams because we just don't know better. If we are not radiating out love, then what is reflected back is not loving. The material that is most painful and "unacceptable" goes underground to the proverbial Underworld. Disconnected from one's identity, it is all too easy to project this material onto others and the world itself. It is each person's task to venture into the darkness, to the depths of the psyche and claim it as his/her own. The proverbial "dark night of the soul" is about this universal process.

In astrological discourse, there are many different understandings and perspectives on Pluto, and often, it has no connection to the Moon. There are two reasons why the Moon/Pluto relation is central in the approach here. The first, mentioned above, is the connection through the water element as seen in the signs of Cancer and Scorpio. We have personal emotional experiences (Cancer, Moon) of how others and the world have affected us (Scorpio, Pluto). We can process (Moon) the impact to become more wise and empowered (Pluto), or we can banish it to the Underworld if we are defensive, protective and assign blame externally. Either way, there is a strong link between emotion (Moon) and psychology (Pluto).

The other reason pertains to the natural interplay of light and dark. The Sun is the source of light, eternal awareness and presence, spiritual realization. As it illuminates everything, it naturally casts a shadow when it strikes anything physical. The Moon is our rootedness in a physical, emotional body, and the shadow (Pluto) is a natural product of simply being alive (Sun). The opportunity of being physical allows us to work with spiritual creativity tangibly; the challenge is to be cut off from soul. Awakening involves bringing awareness to the darkness in order to consciously reconnect with light.

From the position of our physicality (Moon), we might perceive the shadow as separate from us. "There it is, over there. If I can point at it, how can it be me?" We heal this disconnection by looking very closely at the shadow and seeing that it actually does connect with us. In fact, it follows us everywhere! The phenomenon of the shadow is a graphic illustration of projection.

192

Also, it serves as a bridge between self and the world when we recognize its origins in our own psyches.

The *Awakening* approach examines Pluto as the shadow derived from unintegrated awareness (Sun) interacting with our physical and emotional foundations in separation consciousness (Moon). The Moon is the mediator between darkness (Pluto) and light (Sun), and has various degrees of awareness as depicted in its phases. We will be exploring how the chart portrays the relationship between the basin of unconsciousness (Moon) and the blindness of the shadow (Pluto). A deep understanding of Pluto reveals added layers of meaning to the composure and issues of the Moon. By working with Pluto, the emotional work of the Moon is not only accelerated, it becomes empowered.

The essential difference between the material that composes the Moon and the contents in the Plutonian shadow is one of *identification*. The Moon is hardened material that composes a sense of self. Though the Moon usually has content of which a person isn't necessarily proud (for instance, being lazy, combative or shallow), these qualities are understood and accepted as parts of the self. In contrast, Pluto points to psychic material that is disowned. Many of us do not accept that serial killers, child molesters, pathological liars, religious crusaders or the mentally ill are in any way sacred reflections of the self. Of course, very few people are these things, but that is beside the point. Part of awakening is to connect with *all* of life (Sun), not just hunker down in the personality/ego (Moon) in separation. As we are all microcosms of the universe itself, we can find the seeds of *everything* inside, including what is dark and depraved. When we recognize that we have those shadowy parts within, we no longer project them out and set up oppositional relationships with life. Instead, we more fully understand that the shadow stems from unconsciousness, which is universal.

Pluto was discovered in 1930, only 85 years ago, illustrating how disconnected we have historically been from the shadow. Psychology proliferated with the discovery of Pluto, and the integration of Pluto in astrological practice is one of the greatest advancements in 20th Century astrology. Now we can place the phenomenon of Pluto within the framework of awakening and emphasize its connection with the spiritual (rather than the historical personality) angle or conception of the Moon.

Whereas some approaches look at Pluto as "the soul," here we see it in terms of the shadow contents from which the ego is separated. The Sun is the light of soul realization, and it lights up the unconsciousness (Moon) to get access to the Underworld (Pluto). To quote Rumi: "The wound is the place where the light enters you." We tend to get hurt or wounded when we participate fully with life, and this actually triggers the awakening process. If we stay safe and contracted, no light can enter, and we don't awaken.

Light and dark are often seen in a dualistic way, each playing an important role. Day is not better than night, and summer is not better than winter. Light and dark are a polarity at the relative level, and there is truth in both. However, the transpersonal view is another perspective. Light overcomes darkness; it's not an equal relationship. To quote St. Francis of Assissi: "All the darkness in the world cannot extinguish the light of a single candle." Though it is paradoxical, we are learning to understand two levels of reality, the relative (Mercury) and the transpersonal (Uranus), which have completely different scopes. Light and dark are equal from one perspective, and yet they are not from another!

The process of spiritual awakening is to bring light into the dark. When we turn on a light in a room, it overcomes the darkness every time. Similarly, the more spiritual awareness is brought into the unconscious, the more movement is accelerated in the liberating channel. There is also the manifesting channel—movement towards separation and, therefore, darkness. That is a topic for a future volume of this series. For now, we explore liberation by resolving our Plutonian darkness.

Pluto and the Twelve Major Archetypes

We will look at how Pluto connects with each of the twelve major archetypal themes within the system. Once again, we know that planets (what), signs (how) and houses (where) are very different. To keep this analysis concise, I have discussed them together in broad strokes. As we get into charts, we will further specify and focus on the more subtle nuances between planet, sign and house.

Working with the shadow has the potential to bring us profound and gripping moments of spiritual breakthrough. The key is to keep in mind that Plutonian material originates from unconscious navigation, and it therefore always begins in darkness, where there is blindness. Pluto concerns extremes and transformation; the brighter potentials are substantial when the process of awakening is engaged. Through conscious engagement, Pluto not only helps the individual heal but also can potentially serve our collective empowered evolution. What results is a newfound global contract of shared power instead of Plutocratic and hierarchical control.

1 – Aries, Mars: The combination of Pluto's unrelenting intensity with the archetype of the warrior can be extreme. This combination is the epitome of passion, and the darker side can be most wounding. In the shadow can be remnants of force, aggression, hostility, rage, anger or violence. Previous destructive or painful Plutonian experiences grow to become consciously impactful and constructive. Another major area is sexuality, and

there can be all sorts of issues including repression, darker impulses, or experiences that are deemed "unacceptable." This combination doesn't always point to a karmic history of rape or some other form of sexual pathology, but that can be possible.

Upon the embrace of the Plutonian material, there is a potential transformation into ecstasy, realized passion, and remarkable intensity, which shakes us to our core and renews a commitment to life. The awakened version is fearless. After going through psychological battle with these "demons," what is one going to be afraid of? In fact, the person would be willing to die in the name of being a spiritual warrior. The personal will (Mars) becomes an instrument for evolution. People with this placement may become adept at surgery and other dramatic and painful procedures, martial arts or athletics. There is boundless leadership potential here, a fearless charge into the unknown.

2 – Taurus, Venus: Psychic scars around security, body issues, money, inner peace, and comfort may compromise trust in life. There can be deep suspicion that the shoe is going to drop...because it already has! Working through insecurity or fear is the program. Methods to develop physical stamina or emotional self-sufficiency allow for greater poise and endurance. The task is to learn to be with the self and allow the body to release its guarded energy. When the impacts of hurtful experiences are integrated, one reaches peace (Venus). Instead of being overpowered by Plutonian material, one rises to greater power. The external world is no longer approached as being filled with destabilizing forces.

Issues around safety and security transform, and a new value system emerges around resources, money and commodities. Rather than having these things serving the ego, there can be efforts to make them more meaningful for spiritual growth. One example is investing in projects that can change the world, with perhaps a focus on environmental or natural resource issues. As the person becomes more connected and in harmony with the self, he or she champions a peaceable and beautiful relationship between humans and nature.

3 – Gemini, Mercury: Deep egoic wounding in intellectual, communication, perception and learning areas. There could be emotional turmoil related to the teachings received or deep insecurities about one's intelligence. There may be untrue and abusive ideas about the self that inhibit well-being. The spiritual work is to question one's mind and see that it is rooted in prior pain. After this brain cleansing, one has a renewed perspective on the self and the world. The mind develops the sharpness of a razor, the insight becomes increasingly penetrating, and layers of depth are continually better understood.

Like the psychopomp who travels between worlds, Pluto in connection with the third archetype is able to venture into psychic depths, then communicate and disperse the energy. Mercury is the communicator and teacher, and Pluto informs this role with messages that become increasingly challenging to spark evolution—a psychologist or truth teller who unflinchingly speaks out for change. The conscious possibility is to develop into some sort of storyteller, writer or messenger who makes an unforgettable impact on others, and possibly influence the trajectory of our collective evolution.

4 – Cancer, Moon: The principle area here is love, which plays out internally and within family contexts. There are often challenging dynamics around nurturance issues. Self-love tends to initially rate very low. If this is not addressed, it will play out interpersonally in painful ways until it is transformed. There has likely been a significant amount of emotional self-abuse that can be alleviated through personal accountability rather than a blame game with others. When this maturation takes place, new and meaningful connections emerge to reflect this growth. Also, a renewed relationship with the archetype of family brings

197

resolution. This can be done by connecting with the birth family in a transformed way, creating one's own family, or both.

Pluto's connection to the fourth archetype is arguably the most psychologically charged combination in all of astrology. The unprocessed psychic material is in need of catharsis and release. The transformation from an egoic to a spiritual identification models and supports similar development in others.

5 – Leo, Sun: As Pluto relates to darkness and this archetype deals with light, there is a most dynamic process. Initially, the radiance of life can be compromised, resulting in a sense of dread or negativity about the world. Is the world inherently hospitable? Are things going to be all right? The ego may perceive forces out there that can overpower goodness, and the individual may feel meaningless and unimportant. There can be narcissistic wounding, which can play out with depression or overcompensation with grandiosity. The healthy way forward is to renew a commitment to life—to emerge triumphantly and create, express, and find newfound joy in living. This combination potentially becomes exuberant and dazzling.

Those with Pluto combined with the fifth archetype potentially radiate an energy that many will find discomforting. The life path may traverse over proverbial landmines of conflict, which these natives progressively learn to manage constructively. The gift is to engage in such processes, to hold power consciously, and bring a renewed presence to life. What potentially emerges is a newfound innocence and joy, a celebration of life that is more whole and wise.

6 – Virgo, Mercury: Withering judgments, criticality and self-abusive tendencies compromise effectiveness and potentially lead to health issues (physical, emotional or mental). At the extreme (Pluto), Virgo and the sixth archetype can identify as a slave or as downtrodden, feeling worthless and inept, deserving of some form of punishment. Another version is simply a refusal

to mature and be accountable to the self and others. There can be a blind spot or distortion around effort, which can manifest as extreme workaholic tendencies or laziness. These people are learning to apply themselves wholeheartedly, attain greater balance, and learn how to work with the shadow constructively — in the self, and then also to assist others. Through healthy and effective routines, they are in the trenches of spiritual evolution.

The development of new methods and technologies helps the world similarly transform pain into power. There is a technological wizardry available here, the implementation of ways and means to assist clinicians and practitioners with new tools. With Pluto involved, these projects or techniques can be used in a variety of ways to work productively for our collective survival.

7 – Libra, Venus: Is the universe fair and just? Why do "bad" things happen to "good" people? Pluto's connection with the seventh archetype can be a collapse of trust, life thrown out of balance because of suspicion or thoughts of impending doom. This becomes projected, which may result in relationships similarly veering into unbalanced and potentially dark scenarios. Upon integration with the underlying psychology, the solution is discovered. We create a more just world by connecting openly with one another, truly loving everyone as the self because (at the soul level) they are.

Pluto and the seventh archetype socializes power to be shared. People with this combination tend to enter dynamics in which all sides can reorient to what is *really* going on, mainly an energetic transaction to bring spiritual wholeness. The potential is for conflict management, to work through all of the issues and barriers that keep us apart.

8 – Scorpio, Pluto: Interpersonal wounding (control, power dynamics), abuse of some kind (emotional, psychological, physical, sexual, etc.) has left a profound mark that is deeply

buried, shrouded in hurt, fear or pain. In the Underworld might be passionate urges that have been deemed inappropriate or wrong in some way. There could be a profound need for control with questions about its origins and management. The curriculum is to enter the psychological labyrinth and get to the bottom of these issues. Then the proverbial phoenix rises from the ashes with conscious empowerment. Connections become ecstatic, and unbounded intimacy fills the heart.

Pluto extends to our collective and transpersonal evolution. This combination is the one that addresses the shadowy underbelly of our current global predicament. We have to address issues of global overpopulation, which may threaten our resources and result in famine, disease or human rights violations. Those with this signature are making the tough decisions, and acting boldly, for our collective survival.

9 – Sagittarius, Jupiter: Associated with religion and belief systems, the ninth archetype often pretends to know everything. Pluto corrects this fallacy by blowing the doors off of certainty. This combination rips us from the illusion of limited understanding and invites us to the heights of greater spiritual knowledge. There is some form of dark, misguided navigation in the soul history. Growth involves a renewed life path with increased perspective, meaning and spiritual mission. Those with this signature may assertively confront dogma in all of its guises and challenge the collective to rethink all belief systems. They become impassioned champions of evolutionary (Pluto) expansion (Jupiter).

There might be an initial mistrust or psychic overwhelm about the policies that govern this planet—how man has tarnished and hurt Gaia with errant and unconscious agendas and misguided aims. The spiritual work now is to live the most conscious path that clarifies broader solutions. Confronting the darker philosophies and religions, and assisting them in operating consciously, helps the planet heal.

10 – Capricorn, Saturn: Here can be found Plutocratic themes of corruption, control of resources, elitism, power-grabbing and other Machiavellian dynamics that institutionalize darkness at a structural level. Those with this signature may have been oppressed or oppressors, which are two sides of the same coin. The dark Saturn/Capricorn steps on throats on its climb up the mountain. Healing involves lifting others to the top.

Conscious use of authority and confronting any type of authority figure who lags in the shadow are essential. This combination potentially sculpts a complete social/cultural makeover that exterminates the vestiges of abuse and the domination mentality. There can be an unyielding determination to promote our collective advancement through fierceness instead of fear.

11 – Aquarius, Uranus: This signature can indicate the subjugation of the freedom impulse, a deep wound around seizing novel and thrilling possibilities, or a profound fear of the future. There can be conformity to group think, or the chart owner can be swallowed by collective pressures that limit individuation. Deep in the psyche may be the idea that the world is going to Hell and there's nothing we can do about it. There can be a deadening of feeling, a detached and listless zombie walk through life. Upon the personal retrieval of optimism and trust in life, a collective contribution becomes available.

Empowered advocacy of evolution is the conscious expression. The work is to create a collective village of unlimited possibilities for all. There is the regeneration of community into shared and progressive global power. The development of technologies and other futuristic projects; demonstrations, movements and causes transform the collective landscape. The end result is to transform the world itself to reflect the "mind" within which we are enveloped.

12 – Pisces, Neptune: A painful lack of acceptance and compassion for the self has left psychic scars. There can be immense sadness, dejection, disillusionment or other unresolved emotion in the shadow. Some may experience an existential crisis, of the world itself being wounding or harmful. There is little recognition or awareness that the world is a reflection of self, which is transformed through more consciously engaging the dreaming process.

Through the application of unconditional love, perception shifts to reveal an endless waterfall of grace, meaning, and spiritual uplift within everything. The personal closet of unconscious pain is cleared out, and a broader orientation emerges. Through spiritual practices (such as the Tibeten *tonglen*), an emotional connection with all sentient beings is strengthened. The potential is to lessen global suffering through altruism, love and the acceptance of unconsciousness in all of its forms.

Plutonian Chart Examples

David Berkowitz

Below is the chart of David Berkowitz, aka "Son of Sam," the notorious serial killer who terrorized New York City in the 1970s. He has an Aquarius Moon in the third house, indicating an attunement to intellectual possibilities and maybe a personal story about being brilliant. The Moon is trine Jupiter in Gemini in the seventh, suggesting the need to communicate and share his thoughts with others. The Moon is also square Venus in Aries in the sixth, so there is frustration about being received by others and some fiery intensity around it.

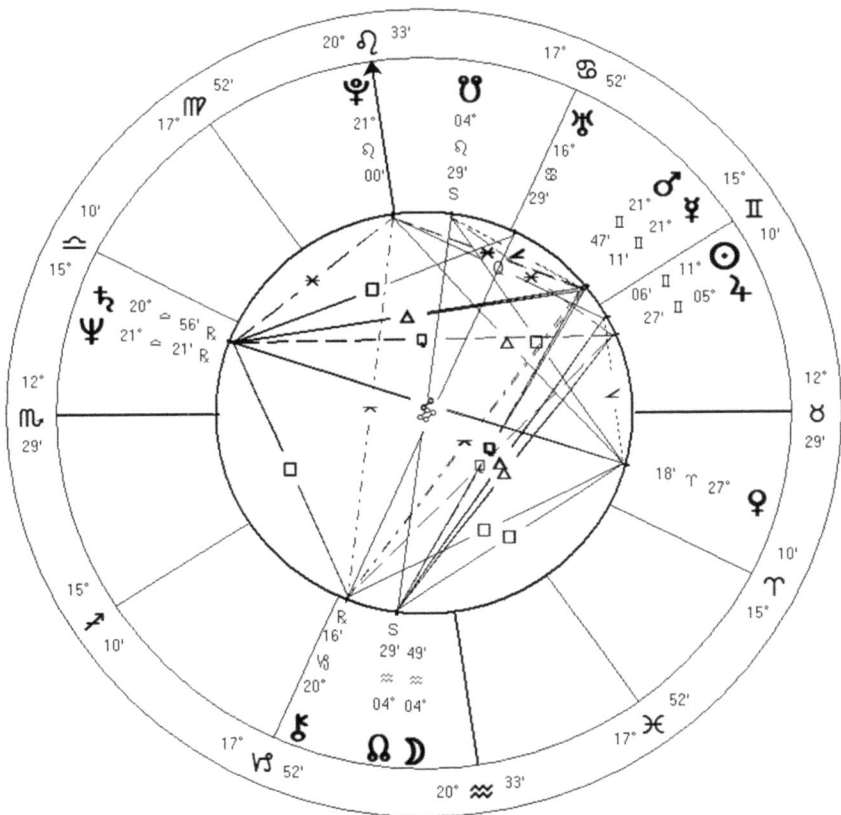

The South Node is in Leo in the ninth, which correlates with karmic issues around being appreciated in educational settings, which is further echoed by the Sun in Gemini in the interpersonal seventh house. Berkowitz is upset with others for not recognizing his capabilities, and the Moon's defense in Aquarius is to detach from the emotions and hope for better outcomes tomorrow. As a result, his intensity is pushed into the shadow.

Pluto is found in Leo right on the Midheaven. Among its many aspects, the sextile to Mercury repeats the theme of intellectual issues, and the trine to Venus brings in the social

203

dimension. Residence in Leo in the tenth has to do with stature and recognition. As Pluto is deeply unconscious and can act pathologically, Berkowitz is willing to do anything to be recognized. If the brighter possibility is unattainable, then the darker version is the distortion. Pluto is also sextile Mars in Gemini in the eighth, which goes along with indiscriminate (Gemini) violence (eighth), also connected to communication and learning issues. It's as if he is going to teach the world a lesson: "You'd better respect and listen to me!" Berkowitz did achieve recognition, and infamy is the darker polarity of fame (Pluto in Leo). It's quite evident that the Moon issues play out in shadowy ways through Pluto.

J. Edgar Hoover

The FBI director had a Pisces Moon in the second house, which suggests some discomfort with the self and a yearning to realize greater acceptance and serenity within. The inner disquiet and distancing from self-nourishment led to a karmic pattern of analysis and investigation (Virgo South Node) of interpersonal and intimate processes (eighth house). Mercury (dispositor of the South Node) in the twelfth suggests secrecy with this analysis, while Jupiter in Gemini in the sixth (square the nodes) amounts to a good deal of data (Gemini) collection (sixth). The North Node in Pisces in the second shows an intention to be able to arrive at greater comfort and ease in himself.

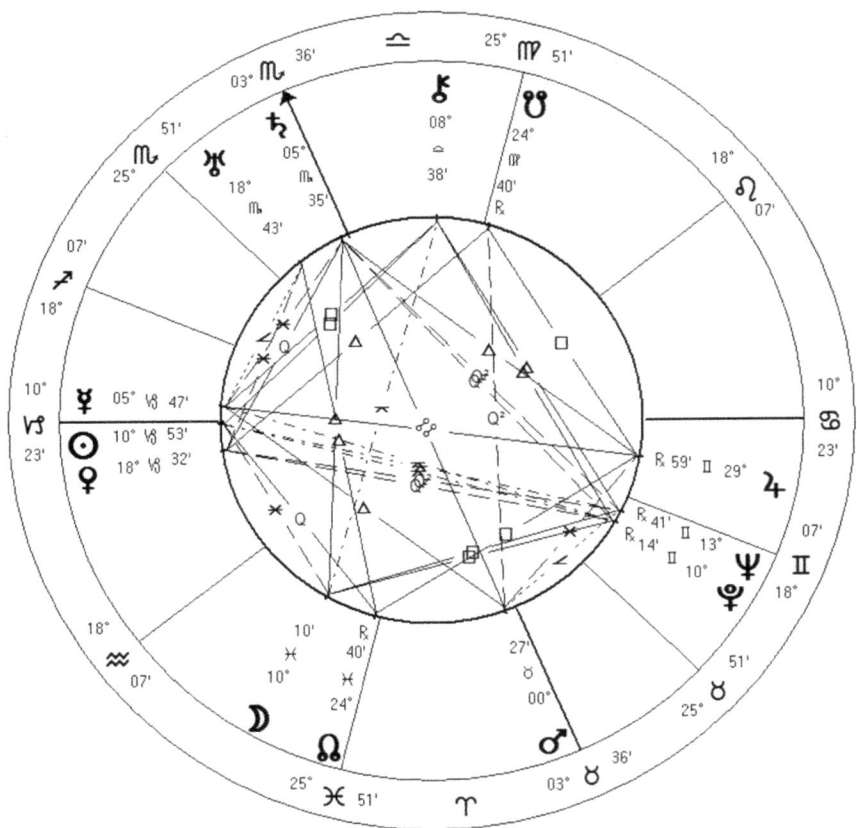

As for Pluto, it is tightly square the Pisces Moon from Gemini in the fifth house. In the shadow is immense curiosity (Gemini) about the taboo (Pluto) and a need to participate with it innocently (fifth house), even with fantasy, and without limitations (Pluto conjunct Neptune). This material has been "unacceptable," disowned, and projected onto others. Hoover kept his sexuality secretive and was known to publicly hold the conservative line. He was especially concerned about subversion and sought to control "radicals." He amassed a databank on private sexual behavior of public officials, providing him with leverage if needed. From a position of great authority, Hoover

205

assumed the role of the top cop to enforce what is thought to be "appropriate" behavior.

At the transpersonal level, the world is a reflection of the self. We can understand Hoover's meticulous investigation of those who step "out of line" as a policing of his own desires. With a Scorpio Midheaven, his shadow is played out in his vocation. Because of his prominent position, this shadow had an enormous reach and impact on the world. Ultimately, Hoover has sparked dialogue about broader acceptance of sexual curiosities and all types of behaviors. Instead of policing such things, we now are learning to celebrate them, and laws are now changing to accept gay marriage and there is greater tolerance of transgender issues. The collective Plutonian shadow around sexuality is being transformed.

The Chart Skeleton

Finally! We put all the pieces discussed so far together in a workable format to approach charts. The "chart skeleton" organizes the fundamental structure of evolutionary growth and is depicted below.

(Uranus, Neptune)

Sun

South Node   Moon   North Node

Pluto

At the top are Uranus and Neptune—the matrix of energetic interconnection (Uranus) and the dreaming process (Neptune) that fills it. These energies involve intentions and desires for incarnation at the transpersonal level. They inform the skeleton from "above," the organization of the co-creative dream space which envelops us. The skeleton deals with the reconciliation of the personal story at the egoic level.

There is a resemblance to the human body. Above is the heavens (Uranus, Neptune), and the Underworld (Pluto) is below. In the middle is the Moon, our heart and biology, the emotional system of the separate self. This is the centerpiece, and the Moon is the central energy in which we enter the human journey on its path towards greater wholeness. After thoroughly understanding a person's inner mechanics (needs, issues, defense mechanisms, unfinished work), we look to the Moon's nodes. Analogous to the arms of the skeleton, the nodes are positioned to the left and right of the Moon. Arms assist us in tackling our work—getting stuff done—and the nodes concern working on our spiritual curriculum.

Underneath the Moon and the nodes is Pluto, which would be analogous to the lower chakra areas. Here resides power, the sexual/regenerative function, and processes of waste removal. Pluto is where we push material down into the bowels of unconsciousness, and/or it can be the deepening into our power when this material is embraced. To do so, we have to go into our shadow and learn to take ownership of it.

The Sun is positioned at the crown, where the aura of awareness radiates out. There is an ascending movement upon strengthening the pieces below—more access to the clarity of awareness and the ability to be present when we attend to our emotions and spiritual work. Also, the Sun has access to the connectedness (Uranus) and dreaming processes (Neptune) above—soul (Sun) co-creates reality through intention. Also, the unconsciousness of the Moon radiates out through the Sun for us to become aware of our unconsciousness and learn to integrate with it.

As for charts, *everything* that has to do with the Moon (seed), the nodes of the Moon (gardening), Pluto (underground) and the Sun (flower) becomes part of the skeleton. So we look at sign and house positions, all aspects to other planets, and dispositors. As we'll see, this includes many parts of the chart, and it can sometimes get quite complex.

What about the other planets? The inner planets are the tools of the separate self. Each of us has a mind (Mercury), an orientation to the sensual and social realms (Venus) and the ability to exercise our desire and free will (Mars). These functions are *supportive* of the core process of spiritual evolution. Jupiter and Saturn have a social and collective scope, how a person discovers a life path and tangibly contributes to society. These planets have much to do with how the core energies extend into the world, but they are not the primal energies of "where we live" in ourselves at a psychospiritual level. Below are a couple chart examples.

Neil Armstrong

Armstrong had a Sagittarius Moon loosely conjunct Saturn in Capricorn in the eighth house, square Venus in Virgo in the fifth, trine Mercury/Neptune in Virgo in the fourth and sextile/trine the nodal axis. He was resolving emotional dependency (eighth house) on others' support—previously conditioned to live a life path (Sagittarius Moon) in adherence to a conventional value system.

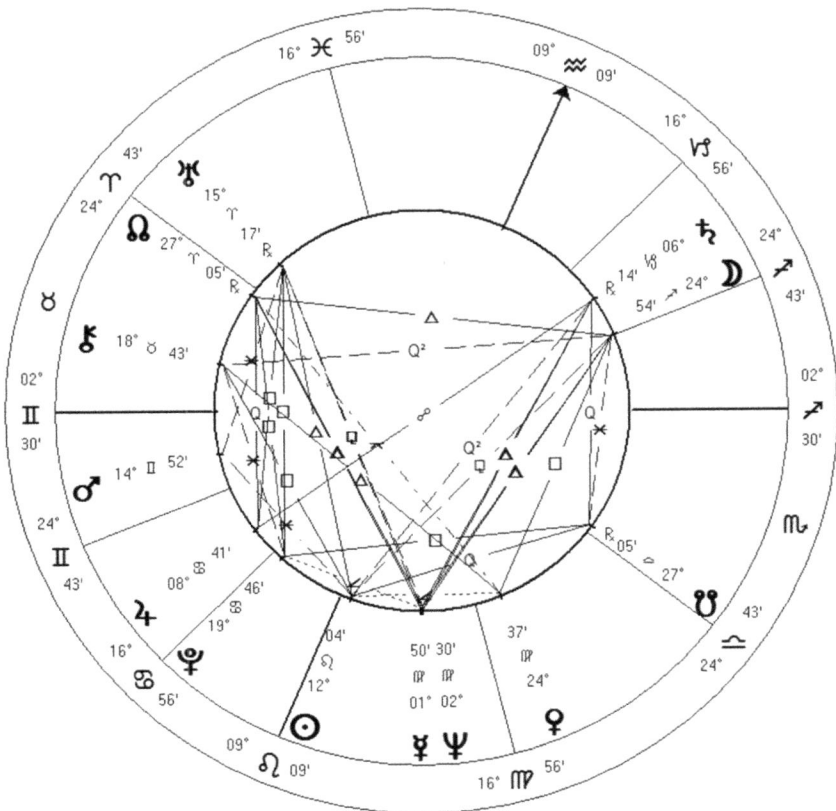

There is an unfinished need (Moon) for broader adventure and perspective (Sagittarius), as well as a need to claim his own stature and achievement (Saturn in Capricorn). The prior acceptance of more formal ways of connecting (Moon conjunct Saturn in the eighth) is in conflict (square) with a desire to develop greater spontaneity (Venus in Virgo in the fifth). Armstrong also came into this lifetime with bold visions and ideas for fantastic discovery (Moon trine Mercury/Neptune).

The South Node in Libra in the sixth house indicates behavior patterns of following (Libra) the rules (sixth), being compliant with tasks and having a socialized, deferential

209

disposition. As the dispositor of the South Node, Venus suggests that his own sense of spontaneity (fifth house) has been compromised by his work ethic (Virgo), and now the task (Virgo) is to be himself (fifth) and have more fiery (fifth house) experiences. Indeed, Venus is quincunx the Aries North Node in the eleventh house, seeking to join (Venus) with broader collective (eleventh) expansion. Neil was becoming a leader/pioneer (Aries) out in the world (eleventh) to build on the karmic pattern of diligence, preparation and modesty.

The North Node dispositor is Mars in Gemini in the first house, indicating an intention for bold leadership and using what he's learned (Gemini) in more exciting ways. Mars is sextile Uranus in Aries—more support for breakthrough pioneering experiences. Mars is also sextile Armstrong's Leo Sun—his path of awakening was to claim greater visibility and presence, to shine his unique light brighter. He accomplishes this by developing courage and a steadfast allegiance to self (Uranus in Aries).

Pluto in Cancer squares the nodes from the third house, suggesting psychological pressure around study and learning, being heavily influenced to achieve and taking this very personally. In the shadow is emotional insecurity about being smart enough. The Moon is Pluto's dispositor, which connects back to the eighth house area of others' power. Armstrong comes from a deep humility to do things the "right" way, and this has led to an inner (Cancer) questioning (third) of his abilities. The work is to achieve greater intellectual empowerment, which then becomes channeled into the pioneering North Node intentions.

The Sun is in the fourth house, showing an intention to deepen into himself, to find love within (fourth house), healing the prior pattern of seeking love interpersonally (eighth-house Moon). Then, he becomes an innovator (Sun trine Uranus) on the broader world stage (eleventh house), being the first (Aries) to step forward in a new way. Most fascinating, his adventurous

Sagittarius Moon is trine the Aries North Node—and of course, it was the Moon itself where Armstrong explored. The Moon is waxing (building) and bright (visible), lit up by the charismatic Leo Sun to fuel his mission (Sagittarius).

Most interesting is the Sun's quintile to the South Node. Deep inside (fourth house), Armstrong had wanted to realize greater visibility and attention, but the karmic tendency was to remain hidden. The quintile, like Uranus, can be unrealized potential that requires breakthrough to claim. That is exactly what Armstrong accomplished in becoming a celebrity (Leo).

Marilyn Monroe

The fabled movie star had an Aquarius Moon in the seventh house conjunct Jupiter, indicating an unresolved need to have buoyant, larger-than-life experiences in relationships. The need is in sharp conflict with the chart's most central aspect (featuring the dispositors of both nodes), the square from the Moon to Saturn in Scorpio in the fourth. Heavy, stern and quite likely abusive (Scorpio) forces in the home have harmed Monroe's heart. The deeper layer is some inner challenge around self-love (fourth), which plays out within nurturing and family contexts in the home. The Moon is also opposite Neptune in Leo in the first, suggesting a yearning for a lighter and more loving relationship with herself. As the first house conveys the native's persona and approach, Monroe adapted a style geared to attract positivity, becoming a sex symbol adored by many. Leo is prone to externalize in this way; the spiritual work is to find love and acceptance within, then to radiate this out generously to inspire others.

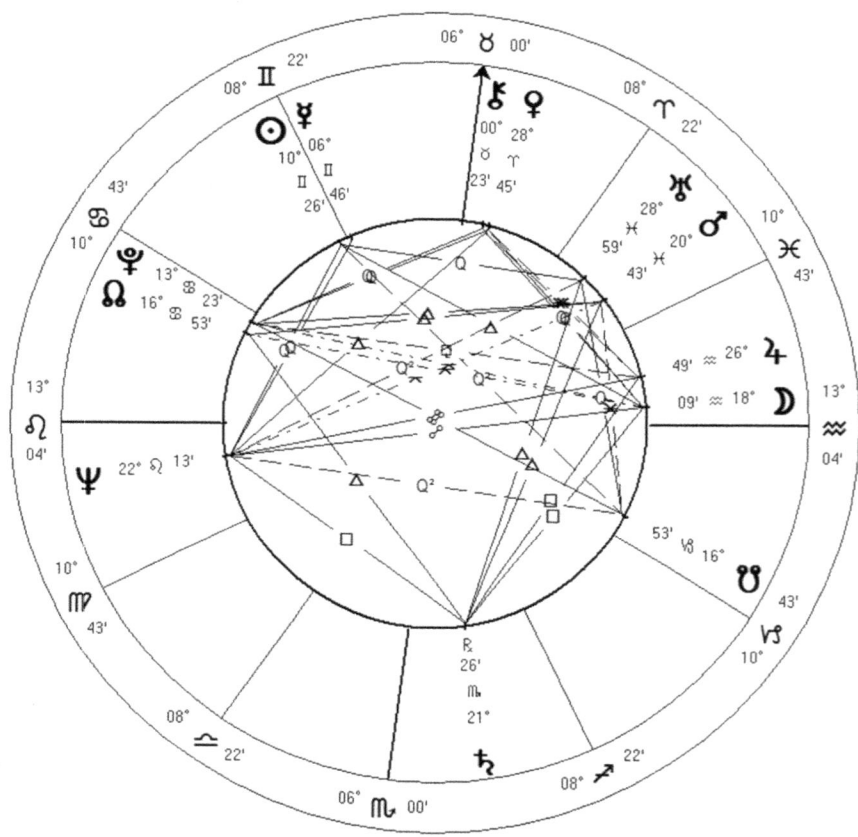

The South Node is in Capricorn in the sixth house, implying a karmic pattern of tirelessly trying to do everything right and in accordance with the rules. There is subservience (sixth) to traditional/patriarchal demands (dark Capricorn). As the dispositor, the fourth-house Saturn conveys that this has played out with power dynamics (Scorpio) in the home. (Indeed, Marilyn had a most tumultuous/abusive relationship with her father.) Further repeating the theme of deferring to others is Mars in Pisces in the eighth sextile the South Node.

Opposing the South Node is Pluto in Cancer in the twelfth, indicative of powerful (Pluto), emotionally painful (Cancer) forces antagonizing her, which led to surrender, loss and existential crisis (twelfth). Both Neptune in Leo and the Gemini Sun make biquintiles to the South Node, suggesting that the carefree and spirited Monroe could be more realized upon greater resolution of the painful (South Node) patterns.

The North Node in Cancer conjunct Pluto in the twelfth is a clear prescription to move into her emotional process, love herself unconditionally and release the past. The Aquarius Moon is the dispositor, suggesting the intention is to break down the defense mechanism of detachment (Aquarius) and the need to look for love in others (seventh). Then she could realize the unmet need for the buoyant and expansive relationship needs she coveted.

The Sun is in Gemini in the eleventh house, quintile both Uranus in Pisces in the eighth and Neptune in Leo in the first. The path of awakening is the development of greater perspective, ingenuity and public visibility. The emotional work involved with the Moon and nodes would need greater completion. Then, the quintiles from the outer planets involve further reaches of discovery in spiritual, playful, and intimate ways, exactly what her Moon had been craving. In fact, the Sun is also trine her Aquarian Moon, adding energy and illumination to the unresolved needs for breakthrough. Also, the Moon is bright (visible) and waning (dispersing), consistent with sharing one's light with the world. Monroe did reinvent herself (from Norma Jeane Mortenson), but the shadow components of her Pluto led to an early loss, and she never did resolve her despair.

Chapter 8
Chart Factors

The "chart skeleton" is composed of the major pieces and holds the structure of evolutionary advancement. In this chapter, we'll address some of the other factors that surround that structure and address additional questions that help to create a coherent whole from the parts. How should the chart be cast? How do we connect the various pieces? What should we emphasize, and what is more peripheral? How can we attain wholeness and really grasp the inherent message? We will explore understanding bits (a planet in a sign residing in a house) and linking them together. More on houses and the dispositors' roles will be introduced. We'll also touch on declination, retrogrades, weights of chart factors and a few other issues.

Casting the Chart

There are as many ways to cast a chart as there are astrologers. We have a variety of house systems and different schools of thought regarding what points should appear. Since there is no widespread consensus, it is easy to get into debates. The intention here is to offer what works, and why, for the *Awakening* approach. I can speak only from my own experience, and I respect other viewpoints. It has been a focus of mine to research the following chart casting issues. I can assure you that my conclusions have come from much scrutiny and have been informed by experiences in the counseling room with actual chart owners and their life events. The reader is encouraged to follow his or her guidance and see what feels right.

House System

Let's tackle the thorny issue of house system first. Placidus is the most popular system and the one I used for many years. I was then challenged to research Porphyry by a few friends and colleagues to see what I found. This prompted me to do substantial research on the house system issue, and I did ultimately switch to Porphyry. It has appeal because of its simplicity. Porphyry divides the quadrants created by the angles (MC/Nadir and Asc/Dsc) by 3. The 3 houses in each quadrant are the same size. Since astrology is built on simple geometry, having a simple geometric formula does provide consistency.

In contrast, Placidus is based on movement through time—the duration it takes for the Ascendant degree to reach the Midheaven becomes trisected to form the intermediate house cusps. That sounds simple, but there can be complicated mathematical formulations involved, and critics contend that it breaks down in the more extreme latitudes. We know that the house layout is a relation to space, not time. Therefore, Porphyry enjoys more theoretical consistency in this regard.

The question, though, is whether it works. Porphyry has been fully implemented into my counseling room since 2006, and I have counseled hundreds of clients who have some background in astrology and use another house system (usually Placidus but also Koch and others). The response has been validating. There aren't usually too many differences; perhaps a planet or two move from one house to another. On multiple occasions, clients have informed me that my interpretation of the differences resonates more with their personal experience, and many have said that they, too, would switch systems. Even some who are very attached to another system admit that Porphyry is worth further research and consideration.

In addition, I've researched planetary transits over the intermediate (non-angular) house cusps—not only with clients, but also news events, celebrity biographies, friends and family...any subject with accurate birth data. Again, the results were striking and affirming.

This is not to say that other house systems don't have legitimacy. I agree with the view that different house systems may be looking at different facets of our experience, so we gravitate to the system that is consistent with what we want to examine. For this psycho-spiritual evolutionary approach, Porphyry has very clearly emerged as the most useful. Of course, we all see what we want to see, and there is a self-confirming bias to which we are all subject. However, *my bias was to confirm Placidus*, and it took much evidence to convince me to change.

As discussed elsewhere in this text, houses by their nature are fluid areas of experience. The relative distance to the angles, which orients us to the external world, does not change with different systems. Therefore, we can see the planets as occupying some place in the evolutionary motion that circles around the wheel. When a planet is towards an end of one house, the natural movement is to the next. The point is that we shouldn't anchor any planet too firmly in a house, but look at the entire layout in terms of cyclical motion. It's a tricky issue—house placements are valid, and they are also part of a broader cycle of moving through space.

True or Mean Node

The next issue is whether to use the true or mean node. The true node indicates the nodes' exact position, while the mean is a statistical calculation. I use the true node because it makes sense to go by what nature reveals instead of leveling nuance in favor of mathematical formulations. Spirit is far more advanced than we are and is not making "mistakes" with the spastic-like wobble of the true nodal positions. In fact, this apparent wildness allows for greater uniqueness, which defines our human experience. In contrast, the mean node eliminates this uniqueness to provide a smoother illustration to how the nodes move through the zodiac. Is it really our job to "correct" what is naturally found using mathematics?

Since the true and mean nodes don't vary all that much, one system *usually* places the nodes in the same signs and houses as the other. While changing house systems often changes planet placements, there are few examples in which clients who use the mean node saw significant differences. However, I have encountered several situations where the sign does in fact change. Furthermore, even a degree matters significantly when we look at progressions, solar arcs, and other phenomena that move very slowly. In my own experience and research, the true node does appear to be true. Again, the feedback from actual resonance with clients has been affirming. In fact, some of the biggest breakthroughs and revelations I have witnessed resulted from understanding a different sign polarity with the nodes. The true node makes more sense to this astrologer, not just theoretically, but also in practice.

Parallax Moon

Another factor in casting charts is the use of the parallax Moon. The positions of the planets are generated by their spatial relationship to Earth. Since the distances from Earth are so extreme, the location on Earth does not affect calculations — except for the Moon, which is significantly closer. So the parallax Moon is calculated *from the actual birthplace* instead of from the center of the Earth (where no one is born). There is no reason not to have the precise Moon placement. I encourage everyone to upgrade to an astrology program that includes this function.

As with the true/mean node, I have experienced several examples now in my practice where the Moon sign shifted because of a parallax Moon correction. Each time, the client has agreed that the "new" placement is more resonant and, subsequently, has attained greater self-knowledge. Since the Moon is so important in this approach, it's critical to have the correct sign placement.

Tropical Zodiac

The final note is regarding the tropical zodiac. Critics argue that this system varies from the actual placements of the observable planets, so the sidereal zodiac is more consistent with nature. Though this is technically true, there is another factor to consider.

The planets are very far away from us (Pluto, on average, is over three billion miles away). Now look around at the closeness of your immediate environment where we project our energetic attunement into life. Consciousness is calibrated to nature around us. At the equinox, we *experience* day and night as equal. We are diurnal beings, and our biorhythms become attuned to our experience of light and dark. We are in harmony with the changing of the seasons.

The tropical zodiac makes the adjustment to be consistent with our immediate environment. At the moment of the vernal equinox, the Sun is at 0 degrees Aries. So readers can rest assured that the tropical zodiac is not something disconnected from reality (a criticism), but actually *orients us closer to nature*. We exist on planet Earth, not on the planets and stars that are millions and billions of miles away. Accepting the tropical zodiac goes along with accepting the idea of relativity—our frame of reference determines our experience of the world. Theory aside, I have found the tropical zodiac to be uncannily accurate and completely reliable.

Points to Display

Modern astrology software provides an endless array of options as to what may appear on a chart. Aside from the regular cast of planetary characters, the newer discoveries of Eris, Sedna, Orca and other objects in the Kuiper Belt are fertile for deeper exploration. There are thousands of asteroids, the Part of Fortune, Vertex, Black Moon Lilith, planetary nodes and more! We can also be aware of planetary midpoints, planetary aspects to angles and house cusps, and where prenatal eclipses fall. Astrology is truly endless; none of us can master it all, as there is just so much.

I have found that including too many points on a chart creates clutter and dilutes what is most central. Trying to include and master a large amount of data is a tall order. This creates quite a dilemma because these other energies and points *are* relevant. I have studied many of them, and I'm continually amazed and impressed at how sophisticated and nuanced astrology can be. However, the issue is losing sight of the forest for the trees.

In the charts in this book, I have chosen to include the ten major planets and Chiron, which is comfortable and workable. With the addition of more points to address, integrating everything gets progressively harder. As one develops mastery, more can be included. In fact, each of us has a unique attunement to the system, with different skill sets and soul intentions for our growth and potential contribution. It makes perfect sense that we would gravitate to areas of personal interest. For instance, someone interested in medical issues may include the asteroid Hygiea, while those specifically focusing on environmental issues may have Sedna as a key player in their approach.

Personally, I work with the four major asteroids and the Black Moon Lilith. Though I didn't include those energies throughout this text in favor of keeping the discussions simpler, below are some brief ideas about them for you to research further.

The scope of the asteroids is given context by their orbital placement between Mars and Jupiter. Mars concerns our behavior choices, while Jupiter enters social/cultural areas. The asteroids can be seen in terms of the *roles* we choose to play in the broader world.

Ceres (grain goddess) correlates with nurturance issues. The name shares the same root as cereal, and has to do with what feeds us. Whereas the Moon encapsulates biological survival and happiness needs, Ceres concerns how love and nurturance play out socially. Ceres/Demeter had her daughter, Persephone, abducted by Pluto and taken to the Underworld. Being a parent is a fragile arrangement. Wanting continuity of love is human, and we may become anxious or upset should this not be constant. Ceres in the chart describes the soul's historical patterning around how maternal (and, more broadly, parental) bonding has played out. The asteroid represents an emotional energy — the bright side relates to unconditional personal love, while the darker version may point to pain, suffering, upset and anxiety should this not be present.

Athena is the warrior priestess, the empowered feminine. The daughter of Jupiter/Zeus, she is publicly focused on collective and worldly issues, wanting to make an impact. Strategic and savvy, with many interests, she balances patriarchal tendencies in the corridors of power. Initially, Athena needs to learn how power is managed. The younger, immature or unconscious side to this energy is complicit with those with more status, similar to a political intern. As she matures, Athena becomes empowered in her own right and asserts her own agenda. Prominent Athenas can be found in the charts of many feminists (male or female) or others who take initiative to right the imbalances of patriarchy.

Vesta is the sacred flame residing in each of us. We all have a burning desire inside to craft something meaningful. Earthy in nature, this energy is about devoting oneself to the development of a particular skill, craft or practice. The Vestal Virgins took vows of chastity and were excused from other obligations to develop sacred practices and rituals. Vesta concerns focus and humility, how we honor what is being cultivated from inside. The unconscious version is disconnected from others and neurotic about performance. It may point to issues around celibacy, removal and taking piousness too far.

Juno is a romantic energy specifically relating to how we partner with a beloved. Whereas Venus is more broadly social, Juno has to do with marriage and other romantic connections. It pertains to the agreed-upon terms of connecting, how intimacy is managed, jealousy, and the power dynamics between partners. Juno/Hera was the wife of Zeus, who was famous for his infidelity. The dark Juno can give power away or be envious, hurtful and scornful. The brighter side holds the warmth, contentment and beauty of a loving partnership.

There are many interpretations of the Black Moon Lilith. In my research, I have found a strong correlation with Kundalini energy, the regenerative power of our instinctual and libidinal force. If you follow its motion using the true apogee (instead of mean), you will notice quick movements and frequent shifting of direction—similar to how a snake slithers. (It turns retrograde and direct very often and covers the same degrees of the zodiac many times.) I believe the Black Moon Lilith pertains to the transmutation of sexual energy from profane to sacred. The unconscious side points to repressed sexual issues, while the bright side holds the resolution of such issues and the experience of ecstatic union and integration. Whereas Scorpio has to do with intimacy and bonding broadly, the Black Moon Lilith specifically relates to working directly with intimate energy. Unlike the asteroids mentioned above, this energy does not concern roles, but *process*.

Bits

When we first look at a chart, we see a number of symbols around a wheel. Eventually our perception morphs into a profound understanding of past life dynamics, the nature of the unconscious, the path of awakening, and much more. It's quite incredible, actually. Let's examine how symbols can be turned into portals that reveal our spiritual depth.

As discussed before, the chart skeleton is the structure in which we can approach the chart's evolutionary themes. We begin with understanding the spiritual childhood (Moon) and its shadow (Pluto), and then we make our way through the spiritual lessons (nodes) and the path of awakening (Sun). Within this framework, we find a variety of planetary connections. For instance, the Moon may be square Saturn, or Venus may be the dispositor of the South Node and opposite Jupiter. We can look at each part in itself, then grasp the interconnectedness of the chart.

It would be too laborious (and even tangential) to address all of the possible combinations that compose an astrological "bit"—a planet in a sign residing in a house. Instead, we will explore these bits from a broader perspective, which can then be applied to specific chart situations.

A bit describes a wide variety of energetic potentials available to the chart owner. Planets are energy (what), signs are developmental programs and modify the energy in particular ways (how), and houses are the areas in which life plays out (where). It is helpful to approach a bit in that sequence—grasping the energy, modifying it by sign and applying it to the house.

First, we address how the energy of a planet connects with the program of a sign. It is essential to reinforce again that planets don't have preferences for certain signs, no more so than words prefer to be spoken in English rather than Japanese. (The judgments that are a part of the astrology tradition have to do with our socially constructed values about perceived advantage, which is detailed in *Volume 1*.) In this approach, all of the combinations of planet and sign are indispensable for evolution, and every chart reflects the ideal and perfect energetic "wiring" for the life journey.

To enter a planet–sign combination, the application of keywords can initially point the beginner in the right direction. For example, Jupiter in Taurus keywords might be "finding meaning (Jupiter) in nature (Taurus)" or "motivated (Jupiter) by finances (Taurus)." Once the beginner is in the ballpark, his or her right-brain faculties (imagination, intuition, creativity) become instrumental in truly getting the deeper meaning. Historically, this tends to be underplayed or discouraged because of the mindset that subjectivity can lead us astray. However, too much emphasis on either the left or right brain creates an imbalance.

There are a variety of ways to approach the chart with imagination. We might close our eyes, meditate on the bit and see what happens. When I tune into this combination (Jupiter in Taurus), the following images appear in my mind's eye: a lumberjack hard at work, valuing the gift of the trees; a wall street investor excited about a new venture; a couch potato indulging in leisure time; or a geologist taking a soil sample and surveying the land. There are thousands of other possibilities too! We can emotionally feel the value being placed on what is tangible. These images are not literal suggestions about what the client should become. They capture the *essence* of the planet–sign combination, which then can "marinate" in your consciousness. Whatever mental pictures, sensations and "knowings" emerge become increasingly instructive with practice. *We learn to understand the archetypal patterns at an additional level of depth.* Let's explore some more images with other examples:

Venus in Cancer: lovers cuddling on a sofa, a family enjoying Thanksgiving, hugging a close friend, working from home, a clingy child.

Uranus in Capricorn: Inside trader, wrecking ball hitting a building, a picket line, breakthrough invention getting a patent, the first day on a new job.

Mars in Gemini: an auctioneer, a ballet dancer, a dexterous swashbuckler, an editor marking a paper, a thief running down the street, a sports statistician.

Moon in Sagittarius: a boat of immigrants landing at Ellis Island, children on an adventure, religious home schooling, a hitchhiker, drinking water at a desert oasis, road signs.

Mercury in Aquarius: an antenna getting hit by lightning, a confused dyslexic student, yelling fire in a theater, an astrology software technician, the Freedom of Information Act.

Neptune in Aries: a martyr lighting him/herself on fire, the illusory "man behind the curtain," firing bullets of love, a selfless leader, a headless zombie.

Pluto in Libra: an exploding see-saw, divorce court, prolonged eye contact, the black market, healing estrangement, new lovers revealing truths.

House Application

The houses further refine the archetypal possibilities of a bit into specific trends of manifestation; they are *areas* of experience. We can think of the cycle of the houses as twelve different mirrors. Each one reflects the associated archetype—one (Aries, Mars) through twelve (Pisces, Neptune)—into the world. The following examples pair a sign with a house to see what facets of that sign become activated and externalized. (Later, we'll bring in the planets.)

Sagittarius in the first: Instead of the philosophical side, the first house emphasizes action. This combination is directed towards its aims, a behavioral disposition driven by mission.

Libra in the second: Although Libra is usually seen in interpersonal ways, other facets of the sign are accentuated in the second house, which is an area of self-alignment. Here, Libra is about learning to value one's own beauty, to strengthen self-worth in order to connect with others.

Cancer in the third: In this house of learning, the lesson becomes the development of emotional intelligence and the communication of feelings.

Aries in the fourth: Not outwardly assertive in this inward realm, Aries learns protection, self-defense and the cultivation of inner power.

Scorpio in the fifth: The eighth sign becomes light and expressive, as seen on Halloween. The program is to reveal and share darkness and passions unselfconsciously and bond joyfully.

Aquarius in the sixth: Here innovation becomes practical, the development of technologies or ways to work with progressive ideas. It's not about communities or systems but techniques and applications that have earthy utility.

Pisces in the seventh: Instead of transcendence, the seventh house brings a social component to Pisces. The program is to see the sacred reflection of self in others and experience the mutuality of unconditional love.

Capricorn in the eighth: In this house of power, the side of Capricorn interested in control becomes accentuated. The program is to share power, to deepen through commitment.

Taurus in the ninth: Reliability and pragmatics are brought to issues of life direction. The lesson is to be secure with the belief system and feel comfortable with one's path.

Gemini in the tenth: Learning takes on public roles and vocational outlets. The native may learn to represent him- or herself as an authority of knowledge: teacher, communicator, storyteller, or author.

Virgo in the eleventh: This combination may bring assistance and solutions to communal realms, improving matters on a global scale, and doing hands-on projects that promote collective evolution.

Leo in the twelfth: Leo placed here is not theatrical or visible, but warmth is found through meditative or contemplative practice—connecting with nature, feeling the vitality of Spirit.

Complete Bits

Now we'll add planets to do examples of complete bits, i.e., a planet in a sign and house. First we'll discuss a planet in a sign, and then relate it to the context of a house.

Saturn in Aries in the seventh house: The sober energy of discipline and maturation (Saturn), applied to the spiritual program of courage (Aries), is a call to personally focus and commit to one's self-development. Images that arise include a hermit standing alone on a mountaintop, an athlete spending hours training, a wise warrior mentoring impetuous youth, a lid placed on boiling water. There is a tempering of passions, refining them to reach another level of expression. The intention is taking on substantial challenges, learning to focus energy on personal goals.

In the seventh house, we connect with others. Saturn in Aries in this interpersonal realm socializes this serious intention into personal commitments. Not exclusively about romantic relationships (though that is often a part of it), the seventh involves one-to-one interactions. This placement is a program of connecting with others (seventh) with fierce (Aries) dedication

227

(Saturn). When the going gets tough (Saturn), the native ratchets up commitment to work through adversity and conflict (Aries) to arrive at more bonded togetherness.

Venus in Gemini in the sixth house: Relational energy (Venus) becomes spritely and communicative (Gemini), an interest in open-minded discovery and expanding personal contacts. Images include a butterfly moving from flower to flower, enjoying a crossword puzzle, kernels of corn popping, and the diversity of romantic possibilities. Venus in Gemini is innocent and willing to try new things, fascinated by the options that life offers.

Placed in the work-oriented sixth house, skill development, mentoring/apprenticeship relations, learning, tutoring and schooling is highlighted. It might play out with conducting workshops, areas of instruction or an engagement in lively and informative pursuits. Working with others to write songs or poetry or other creative sharing is possible. This bit concerns social and intellectual collaboration.

Jupiter in Aquarius in the second house: Life direction (Jupiter) is individuating and broadening into new possibilities (Aquarius). More progressive philosophies are being sought, radical open-mindedness cultivated. Images include a rocket taking off into space, a zany professor with a twinkle in his eye, a spectacular thunderstorm, a motorcycle jumping over cars. This is a thrilling, though initially unstable, combination about taking a big bite out of life and discovering (Jupiter) new (Aquarius) meaning.

In the self-oriented second house, the chart owner is learning to become more secure and confident living with such vigor. In fact, when an authentic life path is solidified (second house) and the person becomes more daring, there is potential for such bravado to literally pay off. Any material abundance achieved is a reflection of the inner alignment with a more progressive truth. This bit is a challenge to "go for it" — to live freely in a non-conditioned way.

Mercury in Capricorn in the fifth house: The messenger (Mercury) becomes focused and serious in achievement-oriented Capricorn. A premium is placed on clarity and precision, communicating from wisdom. Images include a press secretary, an operating manual, a comedian with a dry sense of humor, writing a "great work," crossing items off a to-do list. This is a hands-on Mercury, organized and effective, seeking excellence.

The fifth house brings out expressiveness, spontaneity and creativity. Mercury in Capricorn becomes more open and directive — a songwriter, author, or any type of profession based on intellectual creativity. Learning to speak up with greater authority is the task.

Sun in Taurus in the tenth house: The life energy (Sun) is becoming more stable and resourceful. Development involves greater self-reliance and toughness. Images include robust grapes growing in a vineyard, smiling while counting money, eating a gourmet meal, Buddha sitting in the sun, a sculpture garden. The path of awakening (Sun) potentially becomes rich, embodied and natural.

In the public tenth house, a Taurus Sun is learning to represent poise and steadiness through firm management; an awakened (Sun) use of money/resources (Taurus) from a position of authority. How can the chart owner promote abundance and blossoming for all?

Moon in Leo in the ninth: Emotions are naturally expressed, and there is a need for approval or attention. One is resolving the need to be loved externally and to connect with Spirit within. Images include baby animals, a young student with arm raised, a family vacation, posing in front of a mirror, a prince or princess roaming about a castle.

In the ninth house, there is likely adherence and conformity to a conditioned belief system. The work is to mature beyond this and discover (ninth) what truly brings warmth and meaning. Living a truly fulfilling life path brings emotional happiness.

Neptune in Scorpio in the twelfth: There is a deep longing (Neptune) for profound intimacy (Scorpio), perhaps a spiritual history of being hurt or let down. The work is to arrive at greater unconditional love and compassion within, then to have that experienced in relations. Images include crying in the dark, a séance, Shakespearean tragedy, a sexual healer, Halloween make-up, a hunger strike.

Placed in the twelfth house, unsettling psychic contents have been put in the "closet," and now the work is to connect with them. Any deep longing and pain is ideally released, the emotional system becomes refreshed. The transformation is a renewed trust of life. One makes peace with the universe itself and has greater understanding and acceptance of prior woundedness. Ultimately, the realization of co-creating through consciousness brings the inspiration to dream again.

Mars in Virgo in the third house: This combination represents action directed into projects, and the will is towards betterment, precision and expertise. Images include acupuncture, a focused welder, a brain surgeon doing an operation, a shovel striking an X on the ground.

The third house brings this precision into learning areas, showing specialization in certain niches. It also might manifest as clear and direct speech patterns. The spiritual lesson is to get to the point of inquiry, thoroughly explore the territory and communicate what is researched.

Uranus in Cancer in the eighth: The planet of breakthrough is in the program of feeling, further awakening the heart. Images include resuscitating an unconscious person, an earthquake shaking a house, hugging a stranger, an astrological counselor, an illegal alien.

In the process-oriented eighth house, the combination plays out with the revelation of emotional truths, arriving at new, more heartfelt ways to connect. Prior emotional estrangement is healed, and empathy for others strengthens.

Pluto in Sagittarius in the fourth: Deep spiritual growth occurs through the transformation of limiting and wounding ideology. Belief systems have been characterized by darkness. The lesson is to now "crusade" for conscious evolution. Images include a plane flying into a building, a butterfly emerging from a cocoon and taking flight, a galloping horse ablaze, a prisoner breaking out, the vast expanse of the starry sky.

With this combination situated in the fourth house, the work becomes internal and often plays out in family and/or homeland issues. Ultimately one discovers an emotional truth that motivates life. The fourth house makes the normally outward Sagittarian focus much more personal and emotional.

Connecting Bits

The next step is to connect bits together. Through the various aspects, planetary energies mutually inform one another, and ideally synthesize to create something new. The task is coming together to perform this integration instead of coming apart. Usually, when we are less developed, more insecure and not as aware, there is a tendency to identify with one side of a planetary pair in aspect and project the other. Ultimately, this projection enables us to learn about the other side from the other's reflection.

There are endless combinations and permutations of how planetary bits combine to create something novel. In more simplified approaches to astrology (as in Sun signs), people are jammed into twelve boxes. When we actually get into how the system functions, no two people look even remotely the same. Every chart has many planets in aspect, a variety of energetic dialogues. There is no cookbook formula to describe all of the possibilities, which are endless. A solid grasp of the basics is needed; then our task is to bring in the synthesizing scope of right-brain thinking. To get us started, there are a few questions to address:

What is the purpose of the dialogue?
What is the brightest available expression?
How can the connection collaborate unconsciously?
How can the connection serve the overall movement of personal evolution as seen with the chart? (This is not applicable to the examples below.)

The first example is Mercury in Scorpio in the seventh house trine Saturn in Pisces in the eleventh. The mind may initially be influenced by others' thinking and is learning to communicate its own voice, to be unafraid to delve deep and speak truths. Probing and psychologically attuned to inter-personal processes, the shadow may be lying or stinging others with hurtful language. An image that arises is lovers making prolonged eye contact after sharing personal revelations.

Saturn in Pisces in the eleventh may initially surrender (Pisces) to mainstream sensibilities (Saturn) in culture and society (eleventh). There may be a yearning to have public participation be spiritually nourishing, and some resignation when it's not. Maturation (Saturn) involves social connecting (eleventh) with more loving (Pisces) allies, with an eye toward creating conscious community. An image is a spiritual gathering held in a city.

Integration: Saturn lends a serious edge to Mercury, making its scope more professional and studious, bolstering interest in research. Pisces adds an emphasis on spiritual development, which complements the psychological scope of Scorpio. Mercury brings ideas, focus and intimate interpersonal processes up to the collective arena (eleventh).

The purpose of the dialogue is to mature the mind, to accomplish something professionally that may help improve matters on the planet. The brightest expression is intellectual mastery of concepts that promote spiritual development both interpersonally and collectively. Managed unconsciously, it may be punitive and restrict truth-telling. The adherence to social norms may quell dialogue, and an overly serious manner may inhibit depth.

Another example is the Sun in Gemini in the twelfth opposing Neptune in Sagittarius in the sixth.

A Gemini Sun in the twelfth is awakening into a greater understanding of Spirit by engaging in contemplative experiences and learning about consciousness. Then the life force is able to be an inspired and imaginative messenger. Challenges are dispersing energy, confusion, existential crisis regarding faith or over-intellectualizing experience.

Neptune in Sagittarius in the sixth house is learning to engage in contemplative skills, and perhaps even to develop into some form of practitioner or instructor. On the way to this mature promise, there may be a lack of clarity about life direction, prior tendencies to give one's power to those perceived to be more competent, or some insecurity about being adept.

Integration: As the twelfth house and Neptune go together, there is an obvious overlap regarding spiritual development. Furthermore, the Sun and Neptune also convey the processes of awakening (Sun) and greater fluency working with levels of consciousness (Neptune). The Sun can give energy to light the way for Neptune in Sagittarius excursions. The more proficient the chart owner becomes with learning spiritual practice (sixth house), the more the Gemini Sun understands the workings of Spirit.

The purpose of the dialogue is to understand and experience spiritual phenomena and to teach this knowledge. The brightest possibility is being a selfless messenger of wisdom, assisting others in working through unconscious tendencies. However, if the chart owner is managing this interchange unconsciously, there can be confusion and distortions, leading to ill-advised guidance for the self and others. The challenge of Neptune/Sun is a poorly formed sense of self and trouble showing up in life.

A final example is the Moon in Capricorn in the second, square Jupiter in Aries in the fifth. The Moon is becoming more secure in itself to realize unfulfilled needs for accomplishment. There might be guardedness or inhibition based on historical insecurity or conditioning to be reserved and appropriate.

Jupiter in Aries in the fifth is developing greater self-expression in fiery and spontaneous ways. Finding greater purpose through unbridled self-alignment and spirited play is the intention. This carefree spirit is initially quelled by the Moon's reserve. The challenge could be overcompensation of the freedom impulse in unwise ways or perpetuation of the inability to exercise that freedom.

Integration: Leadership potential is realized through confidence and simply going for it. The chart owner uncompromisingly, and expressively, asserts the self in newfound ways. Joy about working on career pursuits progressively emerges as the chosen vocation brings meaning and connection to soul intent.

The purpose of the planetary dialogue is to discover and lead a life path and career that are emotionally resonant. A darker version is a rigidity stemming from unquestioned assumptions of how the path "should" be travelled. Decisions can be forced and aims misdirected by leftover unconsciousness around social conditioning.

More on Houses and Dispositors

As discussed in Chapter 2, the houses convey our connection to the space around us. They relate to our conception of the external world and how we move within it. Like a compass, the chart is a navigational tool. The four angles are most instructive as to how we orient to the major arenas of life, while the other houses build from what is established. Analogous to the equinoxes and solstices, the angles are cardinal—not more important, but more immediate or central in life—and set the tone for the season to come.

The Ascendant conveys the orientation of the personal will, while the Midheaven is how one approaches public life. The Descendant suggests the approach to relationships, while the Nadir relates to issues in the home. Often overshadowed, it is the dispositors of these house cusps that energize the houses in question. Approximately one out of every twelve people has the same rising sign, though everyone has a unique situation with its dispositor. The condition of this planet plays a focal role, as it clarifies the chart owner's behavior tendencies. Its house placement suggests an area that motivates the life.

What about "empty" houses? When using only the ten major planets, we are bound to have at least two houses that are not occupied by a planet. The likelihood of empty houses changes as other points (beyond the major planets) are incorporated. The novice astrologer may have some confusion about how to handle empty houses, and clients often ask about them.

Everyone has energy in all areas of life. If a person does not have a planet in the fourth house, he or she is not resigned to a lifetime of homelessness, nor is someone lacking planets in the tenth perpetually unemployed. Also, residence inside a house does not confine a planet to that realm of life. Someone with a twelfth-house Sun participates in life away from dreams, spiritual practice or places of removal.

The planet that serves as the dispositor of a house provides information about that house. Its entire profile or condition is dispersed into the house it disposits. Since most planets are in aspect to a few other planets, these aspected planets, too, are part of the mix. There is ongoing debate as to whether to use ancient or modern dispositors, and the *Awakening* approach strongly advocates the latter. In fact, they are essential for supporting growth beyond the patriarchal value system from which we are awakening, and (in my experience) they work much better.

Although these planets are frequently called "rulers" or "lords," the term "dispositor" is preferred here because these other terms suggest that a planet might be controlling a sign or house. Planets, signs and houses are *associated* archetypally, without a sense of hierarchy or domination. Planetary energy does play the role of catalyst, which is then modified by sign and plays out in a house—all of these parts go together. There are twelve major archetypes in astrology, and planets (what), signs (how) and houses (where) are components of these archetypes; none of these functions is more important or dominant over the others.

It's best to see the chart holistically—everything is a part of one cohesive psyche. Therefore, we bring the self to every area of experience. The appearance of a planet inside a house indicates a particular focus on this realm. There is spiritual work to attend to in this area, but houses are not clearly defined areas as we experience in the world around us. There is great overlap as to what experience would fit into a house. For instance, a person talking to someone at work is simultaneously involved with tenth- and seventh-house matters, and perhaps others too. It is best not to be too rigid about house placements but instead to see them as a way the psyche projects energy onto the external world.

Weighting Chart Factors

Quite often in astrological discourse, there is a tendency to weight chart factors—a practice similar to how scientists and researchers approach their crafts. There are a variety of ways to discern or judge the condition or merits a chart portrays. In fact, many computer programs provide charts and graphs depicting astrological data. "Cookbook Astrology" is a term used for astrology books that provide a recipe to understand a chart. You just have to look something up and apply it. All of this is the province of Mercurial left-brain focus, the dominant way we have been trained to learn.

The left brain is valid, but it's only half the story—a *horizontal* analysis that flattens depth in favor of data. These types of analyses do not take into consideration factors of emotion, spiritual lessons and evolutionary growth. What is left out of the equation is the chart owner's consciousness! Ideally, we can attain a sound understanding of the basics, determine what the parts mean, and build to incorporating right-brain processes to achieve greater meaning and synthesis.

Depth is found with the Moon, our watery biological connection with life. We can grasp the fundamental humanness of the Moon profile as the origin of the ego dream. Our subjectivity becomes projected through our solar radiance to create and shape our patterns. In this approach, beginning with the Moon is suggested, as we all begin as spiritual children on the road to maturation. Chart factors can be seen through this filter.

The awakening approach integrates the *vertical* dimension of the evolution of consciousness—movement through the liberating channel described earlier. A person is co-creating along with these energies. The chart is like a "car," and the chart owner is the "driver," who may or may not be adept at driving (analogous to being conscious). Therefore, less emphasis is placed on weighting chart factors or assigning points, as this flattens depth and consciousness.

Declination

Along the lines of including depth, another issue to address is declination—the distance of the planets north or south of the Earth's ecliptic. As commonly used, the natal chart is a two-dimensional depiction of the Solar System at the time of birth, so this variable is excluded. As astrology modernizes and incorporates other dimensions, declination is a most fertile area of inquiry, and many are looking into it. Most computer programs will provide information on a planet's declination, and some brief introductory remarks follow.

The apparent motion of the Sun around the Earth (geocentric perspective) has a range of declination. At the summer solstice, it is about 23 degrees north, while at the winter solstice, 23 degrees south. At the two equinoxes, it is equal to the ecliptic. It travels north to south and repeats the cycle, making a pattern that resembles a sine wave. All of the planets occupy some position north or south of the ecliptic, and sometimes they extend greater than the 23-degree range that contains the Sun. When this occurs, the planet is said to be "out of bounds." Such a planet is discussed as having qualities similar to those associated with Uranus's being beyond the Saturnian boundary—freer, non-conditioned, more individualistic but less stable or reliable.

When two planets share the same declination, say, 11 north, they are "parallel" to each other. A planet at 11 north is considered "contraparallel" to one at 11 south. These planets have a connection—quite similar to being in aspect to each other.

Exploring these relationships provides rich material for a more comprehensive understanding of planetary dialogues.

It would be too much to fully address and implement this variable throughout this book. However, the next planned volume will have a section dedicated to declination. In the meantime, the reader is encouraged to explore this variable, which is increasingly being recognized for its importance. It really does bring astrology to another dimension, and it's a fascinating area of inquiry.

Retrograde Planets

Most charts have retrograde planets. As all of the planets circle around the Sun in the same direction, retrograde motion is a phenomenon purely from the vantage point on Earth. On our host planet, we are enrolled in the process of spiritual growth. When planets appear to be moving retrograde, they are retracing certain degrees of the zodiac—we have the opportunity to go over and integrate spiritual lessons deeply. The planets that appear retrograde in the natal chart are performing this synthesis throughout life.

Initially there may be challenges with the retrograde planet, some kind of inhibition or issue around optimal usage and expression. Finding a more solid inner connection with the energy is necessary. It is often helpful to withdraw from external support or guidance with the planet to achieve this reorientation. There may be ongoing difficulty with external conditions unless and until this process reaches some level of inner cohesiveness. Many experience a continual repetition or *return* of issues until this is learned. Then there is a deeper, more intuitive focus with the planet, and newfound skills become available.

The Sun and Moon never appear retrograde from the vantage point on Earth. All of the other planets do. I have found that retrograde inner and social planets are most relevant; these are discussed below.

Mercury is retrograde 19% of the time and has received the most attention. Often looked at in egoic ways as something irritating, the spiritual lesson is to tighten up Mercury phenomena (communication, intellectual matters, details, editing, how things work). Sometimes there are breakdowns, flights are delayed or contracts stall. None of this is "bad"—it *helps us* in the long run. With retrogrades, we review, rethink, retool, refashion, etc. The spiritual purpose is to be diligent, thorough, deliberate and focused. Those with Mercury retrograde in the natal chart are learning to rely on the self for precision and expertise.

Venus is retrograde about 7% of the time—the least commonly found in a chart. Instead of the usual orientation to the external world (environment, others), there can be some degree of initial inhibition, a blockage in feeling directness or flow. There might be the feeling of being "different" in some way or a belief that others don't understand. All of this is helpful to retract the petition that the external world *should* provide support. People with Venus retrograde are learning to befriend the inner self and use it as a resource. With more developed strength and confidence, the external world reflects back plenty of connection. If not, then interpersonal struggles may persist until this is achieved.

Mars is retrograde almost 10% of the time. Usually the most direct, driven and assertive, Mars retrograde may be restrained. There can be restriction or frustration in displaying empowerment. Some people with Mars retrograde have difficulty expressing anger or sexuality. One or both are held within and simmer until they reach a boiling point. The spiritual opportunity is to mature an internal drive that is unshakable in its resolve. Leadership potential is very possible with this combination, but it will require dedication, self-reliance and discipline.

Jupiter is retrograde 30% of the time. There can be issues with teachings, organized religions, others' philosophies and conditioned learnings. The chart owner is learning to find a meaningful truth within. Upon greater internal orientation with the proverbial quest for answers, life becomes strongly rooted to a sense of mission. Challenges include rigidity, fanaticism, or living an errant path if this internal truth is not discovered.

Saturn is retrograde 36% of the time. As Saturn involves integrity and structure, some with this placement have initial struggles simply showing up in the world. They may shy away from responsibility and take a protective stance. Also, there may be discomfort with one's own sense of authority and, therefore, issues with others' management of it. Upon maturation, greater authority is found within, which serves as the foundation for making a solid career contribution.

The outer planets are retrograde almost half of the time and therefore do not portray the same unique and personal scenarios of the quicker-moving ones. Also, transpersonal in scope, the nature of the outer planet energies is less about conditions in the mundane world. I have not found the direction of outer planets to have major significance, and therefore, this section does not address them.

Synthesis: The Chart Gestalt

The chart skeleton will always involve many planets. It's a handy way to enter the chart by exploring the most central energies of the spiritual curriculum. Outside of the Sun, Moon, nodes and Pluto (and connected factors), other planets are relevant supporting players. So...where to go next? The answer usually reveals itself. There tends to be an inherent logic or story to the chart that is understood through the skeleton. Since there are not too many planets not connected to the skeleton, where to go next really isn't such a big issue. Ultimately, each bit is understood, and the aspects that connect the planets bring the bits together.

Everything on the chart is addressed. The planetary dialogues are seen as the energetic "wiring," and the house layout describes how they become dispersed into the world. Over time, the chart can be seen in its unity. The dictionary defines gestalt as "an organized whole that is perceived as more than the sum of its parts." This is the gold standard—the chart owner has one consciousness.

The breakdown is more left brain, while attaining synthesis is more the province of the right brain. We *feel* the nature of the soul condition. When I truly understand a chart at this level, I want to give the chart owner a hug. Emotion kicks in—there is compassion for the unconsciousness that created the karma, and also a heartfelt championing of the more awake path. The gifts and challenges are all understood for what they are, and there is absolutely no judgment toward the chart owner.

Astrology books can never fully capture the process of synthesis, as it occurs "above the chart," that is, within the astrologer's consciousness. It may sound like a tall order to synthesize so many chart factors, but not to worry. In fact, it is helpful not to be too analytical. Through imagery and intuition, we can arrive at a deeper knowing. We just "get it," and it's abundantly clear. One might ask, "Who says that our right-brain knowing is accurate?" This is where we get metaphysical.

The astrologer has a spiritual connection with the client. At the soul level, there is an agreement to convey the knowledge through the chart. Synchronicity brings astrologer and client together to relay the information. The more the astrologer is pursuing a path of growth, health and awareness, the more the heart is engaged with the soul of the client. The symbols of the astrology chart are a portal into the transpersonal where astrologer and client meet. More on this will be discussed in the counseling section.

As with any other skill or craft, mastering astrology simply takes time and practice. I recommend that every student look at hundreds, if not thousands, of charts. Over time, the basics become so familiar that synthesis naturally emerges. The approach spelled out in this book targets the most central and relevant factors as a starting point; then the rest of the analysis naturally flows. To follow the analogy further, the skeleton is the structure for the entire "body."

Chapter 9
Collective and Transpersonal Scope

The lessons that are part of the personal curriculum extend to the broader social and cultural milieu. In fact, from the transpersonal viewpoint, the external world is a reflection of self. Therefore, engagement with the world plays out our lessons and potentially brings us completion. As we mature, we progressively make a broader mark in the world.

Indeed, we are all teaching what we are learning, but this doesn't necessarily have to do with assuming conventional roles in society. There are a variety of ways in which we make an impact, some visible and prominent, others personal or contemplative. In this chapter we'll be looking at the collective (Jupiter, Saturn) and transpersonal (Uranus, Neptune) energies that detail how we extend outwards into life to share the gifts we are cultivating. (Pluto was addressed in Chapter 7.)

Actualizing Jupiter

Contrary to its historical designation of being "benefic," here we understand that there is a range to Jupiter (as with everything in astrology) from unconscious to awake. The dark side of Jupiter fuels religious fanatics, immature decisions, misguided aims, pomposity, entitlement and many other potential problems. All of this can be transformed as a person becomes more conscious.

Jupiter informs a life direction, a meaningful way to live within the limits (Saturn) of the "real" world. Education and religion have historically played the roles of informing this path, but we are also influenced by family, culture, history or peers. All of the directives that aim to mold us are filtered to arrive at one's personal life philosophy. We all, even atheists, believe in something. The assimilation of all of this information and these influences potentially clarifies a sense of purpose, even a *mission*.

To reach the conscious potential, the scope of Jupiter must extend beyond Saturn. If the governing philosophy stays within separation consciousness, then egoic or personality agendas tend to reign. The motivation to excel is understood *within* the mundane world. With Saturn as the most outer planet for most of recorded history, the mundane world has historically been the scope.

Today we know that Jupiter orbits within the transpersonal energies of the outer planets. Therefore, all philosophy, religion or broader understanding can be held within the broader framework of oneness, interconnection and the multi-dimensional scope of the transpersonal. However, the intermediary is Saturn, the reality principle, which will be addressed in the next section. For now, let's look at Jupiter in connection with the twelve major archetypes in terms of its spiritual dimensions.

1 – Aries, Mars: Jupiter combines with the first archetype to fire the will with self-direction. Claiming one's own path, truth and assertive expression are being further developed. Though the hazard is some degree of recklessness or prematurity in claiming expertise, the learning is through trial and error, being able to go for it. Leadership capabilities are possible; the question is whether there is courage and faith in oneself to claim them. The potential is to be a personal vehicle driven by spiritual purpose.

2 – Taurus, Venus: Solid convictions are being formulated. The growth is towards self-sufficiency, anchored in the life path. Ideally, one's purpose stems from this inner foundation and a commitment to live one's truth. The expansion of only material

interests is the egoic distortion, while the spiritual intention is to enlarge the capacity of self-worth. Then there is trust and confidence in the self to actualize spiritual intent.

3 – Gemini, Mercury: The potential is dazzling intellectual advancement, an infectious desire for knowledge. As Jupiter relates to higher education, this is the mark of the teacher. The mind is on the proverbial quest, the endless adventure of learning. With this combination, the chart owner is literally teaching what has been learned. Getting caught in reason or endless speculation is matured by greater perspective. The most awake version synthesizes large-scale philosophical understanding with smaller world details to develop novel ideas.

4 – Cancer, Moon: The journey of self-discovery, a voyage into the heart and one's heritage provides an emotional foundation to make one's mark. Family is often the area in which there is conditioning around a belief system. By cultivating the deepest truth inside, layers of conditioning are put into perspective. Then there may be something to teach the family, either that of origin or one created as an adult. This combination encourages an emotionally charged investment in the prosperity of the human race itself.

5 – Leo, Sun: The largest planet combined with the Sun (a star) is perhaps the most magnanimous in all of astrology. Living large is the program, with plenty of self-indulgent egoic traps along the way (narcissism, hedonism, etc.). Ultimately, it serves spiritual development to learn how to shine consciously and become inspirational with one's radiance. There can be pronounced theatrical, creative (or just lively) energy that warms the hearts of others; an invitation to make the human drama more enjoyable.

6 – Virgo, Mercury: Integration is found through meaningful work that makes a difference in peoples' lives—any type of coaching, facilitation or instruction for personal

development. In addition to areas of health and well-being, the research and analytical side of the sixth archetype can also be expanded to make inroads into technological development. Becoming a master or mentor at a well-honed skill or craft that supports personal and/or collective evolution is the promise. The challenge is to expand the scope of Virgo beyond its mundane focus to connect it with the larger picture.

7 – Libra, Venus: High culture and engaging socialization that brings people together in joint purpose is the potential. Finding like-minded partners and celebrating togetherness is part of the life path. There may be a tendency for social conformity in hopes for workable collaboration. Upon greater maturation, differences are handled with a diplomatic touch. Finding mutual, life-enhancing exchanges brings one's spirit and purpose forward. The potential is to find common ground with universal principles that unite us.

8 – Scorpio, Pluto: An unflinching exploration into the important negotiations and processes that support psycho-spiritual integration, this combination finds meaning in the dark. Whereas Scorpio/Pluto territory can be unseemly to the ego at times, Jupiter relishes the journey into such territory. In fact, it is understood as the fertilizer for newfound growth. The hazard is a fixation or preoccupation with taboo (sexuality, psychology, wounding, death), which darkens the life path and may unwittingly put forth an errant agenda. The promise is to have these very areas more consciously included in our lives.

9 – Sagittarius, Jupiter: In its home archetype, Jupiter is single-minded in its pursuit of an informed life philosophy. Continually on the proverbial quest, this highly spirited energy finds purpose through a broad range of experiences. Often cross-cultural in scope, there is a global reach and desire to branch out. The unconscious version may harden into narrow convictions and missionary zeal. The potential is to become learned and wise

about the ways of the world and to model this to inspire others. Rallying around universal principles is the promise.

10 – Capricorn, Saturn: The expansive energy of Jupiter potentially enlarges, and provides greater purpose, to the dominant organization of society. The intention is to create a meaningful career and use positions of influence to structure a spiritually conscious vision. With an ambitious intention, there's also a sizable pitfall. If the path of awakening is not being pursued, then this combination can be exploitative, corrupt or self-serving in public roles. Ultimately, being a player in corridors of power is the spiritual curriculum, regardless of how it is navigated.

11- Aquarius, Uranus: The eleventh archetype combines with Jupiter to produce excitement about novelty, reform, transpersonal philosophy or leaps into the unknown. A highly experimental pairing, there is a marked intention to reinvent the life path to be less conditioned. Trying out various possibilities is part of the program—to engage in the proverbial journey, not to be fixated on the destination. In the fervor of such jazzy and inventive energy, one can make reckless, ungrounded or overly speculative decisions that result in disconnection or perplexity. If this should unfold, then that is part of the experiment and is rich for learning.

12 – Pisces, Neptune: Jupiterian journeying potentially leads to the transcendent. Fashioning a mystical philosophy backed by contemplative experience is the curriculum. A most lofty partnership, the challenge is losing sight of the "real" world. However, what is experienced and integrated can be brought back to earthy arenas to inspire and refresh. Confusion about the metaphysical gradually transforms through opening, and opening further. The twelfth archetype adds an emotional component, and the quest extends to our collective heart.

Managing Saturn

Saturn conveys the boundary of consensus reality. In terms of our spiritual development, it suggests the boundary of what has been consciously integrated in the psyche. As the perimeter between the familiar and the unknown, Saturn involves social and cultural conditioning, the forces that shape an individual to be an effective and contributing member of society. We tend to become pulled into an earthy orientation of self-preservation and cooperation.

Historically, a small percentage of people have been able to individuate beyond consensus reality. Also, most generally do not see the external world as their own consciousness, a concept hardly ever considered or discussed, never mind taught. In fact, it sounds crazy to consciousness at Levels 4 or 5 (where most people are). Most do not identify as being energy (Sun) or see through the illusion of separation. Relatively few are consciously working with the dreamlike nature of existence. In short, Saturn has castrated us! Most people are positioned within the Saturnian soul cage trying to make the best of it at the egoic level.

Realistically, we have to initially look at Saturn as controlling, even inhibiting, spiritual growth. Remember that the outer planets have only been discovered recently in the evolutionary unfolding, so the roots of our spiritual situation have been overseen by Saturn as the final authority for eons. We are now at the time when we are awakening beyond, but the weight of our collective history must be acknowledged.

The reigning power structure has been rooted in tradition, tends to be overseen by men, and wants to perpetuate its control. Patriarchy is discussed at length in Volume 1 of this series. Saturn in the chart portrays how the chart owner has dealt with (often with strong conditioning) patriarchal forces. Upon maturation and ownership of Saturn (instead of projecting onto authority), we claim mastery and help change society. *The planet Saturn conveys how we might develop into our spiritual adulthood.* Below are some ways it connects with each of the twelve archetypes.

1 – Aries, Mars: There can be an initial restriction of free will and choices, autonomy or instinctual expression. Some have been conditioned to exert their behavior in ways that support convention or tradition. The task is to take back power and be a force unto oneself. Evolution involves personal mastery of behavior choices and a declaration of independence. When we are willing to go it alone, we discover the self. Then we arise to greater leadership and help change the world.

2 – Taurus, Venus: Overcoming fear of depleting resources, security issues or financial stress increases self-sufficiency. There can be a strong motivation, often an urgency, to succeed. At first, conventional routes are generally taken, with a heightened value placed on possessions as a barometer for status. Mastery of one's own internal self-worth now serves as a springboard for a solid vocation. The self becomes one's rock of reliability, and the world is approached with newfound poise.

3 – Gemini, Mercury: The hardening into rational, logical and socially acceptable intellectual positions is being questioned. The trap is believing that the smarter or more academically successful one is, the more potential advantage one has in the world. Mastery comes through thinking for oneself and developing the personal stature to share one's own ideas. There can be a powerful contribution in writing, communication or teaching—the development into intellectual authority that is no longer conformist.

4 – Cancer, Moon: Conventional domestic arrangements tend to provide a constancy of nurturance. Maturation involves the integration of greater depth or heart in the home, and this starts within. Initially, there may be an inner toughness, the self-

admonition to "grow up" and "deal with it," leading to the deflection or minimization of feelings. Any tendency to inhibit sensitivity or love is being turned around to make that the priority. The work is to grow *into* the self. Then a moving and heartfelt vocation is a natural fit.

5 – Leo, Sun: The suppression of personal expression may be a historical pattern. Sometimes external authorities tell us to be "appropriate," and too much sharing is seen as unnecessary or unwanted. A lack of value may be placed on creativity and leisure in favor of buckling down to achieve results. Further evolution entails the cultivation of joy and greater participation with life. The promise is maturation into immense power and charisma, to radiate one's stature and bring light to the broader world.

6 – Virgo, Mercury: Historically, a premium has been placed on productivity, effectiveness, and discipline that has been heavily influenced by authorities. A strong work ethic may be driven by stern, restrictive judgments about performance. Spiritual maturation involves a dedication to a skill or craft stemming from an *inner* authority. One becomes a conscious mentor, expert or specialist who supports, rather than inhibits, others. Done consciously, there is expertise in the area of personal growth, health or assisting the earth realm in functioning smoothly.

7 – Libra, Venus: There are often traditional partnering patterns, conformity to social norms, and the expectation to trust the judicial/political system and established legal order. The price for social inclusion is some degree of losing the self. Now the work is to show others self-mastery and maturity, to collaborate and strengthen interpersonal bonds. One is able to choose the terms of engagement and decide what is fair and just. Then there is greater wisdom to be applied into social, cultural and judicial spheres.

8 – Scorpio, Pluto: Some initial suppression of shadow material has led to muting the intensity of meaningful connection.

Learning not to be "difficult" can result in inhibiting necessary emotional releases and psychological processing. The work is to attend to this terrain and thereby reach greater intimacy with others. The regeneration of the bonding instinct brings fulfillment. In some cases, having a vocation in psychological, intimate, or other Scorpionic fields is a way to master this placement. Instead of fearing power, one becomes it.

9 – Sagittarius, Jupiter: There can be a karmic history of rigidity or narrowness in the spiritual path. The adherence to overly conservative or limiting ideology has squeezed the scope of discovery. The task is to take concerted efforts to broaden one's horizons, to take charge of the reigning belief system. Asserting one's authority on moral, philosophical or religious issues in conscious ways becomes instructive and inspiring to others.

10 – Capricorn, Saturn: Acceptance of mainstream or conventional values with vocational issues may bring success, but ultimately this may be a soul cage. Spiritual growth involves the cultivation of personal strength to direct matters from an inner resolve. Then public roles are approached with solidity and integrity. Career becomes an area of personal honor, and a masterful contribution to evolution is formulated and delivered.

11 – Aquarius, Uranus: Freedom has likely been restricted in some way in the soul history. There might be a lid placed on alternative paradigms, metaphysical pursuits or more liberated social connecting. Now the work is to muster the energy to master such areas. Revolutionizing the career to be more progressive, humanitarian and/or global in scope brings greater self-respect. This combination puts pressure on established systems and frameworks to modernize. People with this placement often hold positions as reformers who usher in the future.

12 – Pisces, Neptune: Spiritual skepticism or disillusionment has hampered a trust of life and broader vision. Contemplative work helps uplift consciousness and inspires more

creative ways to contribute to our collective evolution. Some even ascend to positions of leadership in spiritual arenas. The possibility is to give form and structure to the content of one's dreams. Grounding the transpersonal in some way is the trek up the proverbial mountain.

The Outer Planets

The outer planets play a significant role in developing a transpersonal astrology, for they are the transpersonal planets. The issue is that very few people are managing these energies at the clearest level, as who is truly awake? However, we all do have access to them and steadily develop into their promise as we go. It's best not to think of being awake, or not, in a dichotomous way. Rather, it's a developmental process, similar to a light on a dimmer switch that gradually gets brighter.

Saturn is the gateway to the outer planets and we must cross that threshold with maturity. How many of us really accept reality...all of it? The ticket beyond the relative world is to completely work within its limitations. First and foremost, this includes the acceptance of death—exactly what the ego is perpetually strategizing to avoid. We also have to accept our struggles, challenges and blockages and master any sense of being overwhelmed—basically heal the darker tendencies of our Saturn. Finally, we have to work at the brighter components of Saturn, to develop our most noble contribution.

The more we engage the program of Saturn, the more we access what is beyond. Most any younger person is not going to have the clearest connection with the transpersonal planets because we have to go through the process of maturation—after all, Saturn is the Elder. We continually get flashes and invitations from these energies, but integration with them does take time, practice and concerted spiritual development.

For those who are growing towards the transpersonal, the outer planets convey our "super powers." They are the energies that do not have to comply with the mundane world, the laws of classical physics or linear time. They are spiritual gifts for us to bring in once we get ourselves out of the way. Everything from enhanced intuition (or psychic ability), to incredible physical dexterity, to all types of ingenuity are available. There are as many types of super powers as there are astrological factors! We all have access to astonishing capabilities—the key to remember is that we are only vessels for these gifts. If we succumb to the egoic takeover and believe that we are special, then we are prone to distort them and even use them darkly. Let's look at the spiritual potentials for Uranus and Neptune connected to each of the twelve archetypes.

Uranian Breakthrough

The revolutionary planet brings the gift of *genius*, which connects with the various archetypes to produce extraordinary talent in a myriad of ways. Uranus potentially brings in attributes and skills that have yet to be realized in our evolutionary unfolding. Also, trans-Saturnian phenomena do not have to conform to our notions of what is construed as "reality." So this planet brings in the astounding and incredible, which make us rethink what is possible. Below is a brief summary of how this perplexing yet brilliant energy might manifest. My book, *Uranus: The Constant of Change*, gives hundreds of actual examples and is a good resource for further reading.

1 – Aries, Mars: From initial fear or hesitation, development takes place in the realms of action, physical assertion and leadership. Frequently found in the charts of record-breaking athletes, martial artists, warriors and those involved with innovating military technology, fearlessness is being learned. Though the darker version is destructive, the potential is

255

to revolutionize the individual's ability to truly be a force of change in the world. These natives are learning to put the self on the line for progress and advancement. Though physical strength may be a part of this, the broader purpose is the cultivation of personal power to change the world.

2 – Taurus, Venus: Overcoming insecurity, anxiety or issues of self-worth turns to greater comfort, even pleasure, about claiming one's uniqueness. The internal base of operations becomes solidified in a new way. From there, some form of ingenuity emerges. Whether in art, projects or money-making endeavors, there is renewed creativity. A hallmark is innovative technique, such as modifying a guitar to be electric or bringing in unorthodox materials to physical art. What is valued changes dramatically. The conscious side is complete acceptance of the world, which stems from a stronger value of self.

3 – Gemini, Mercury: The personal mind becomes liberated from prior confines to connect with the transpersonal. The potential is a direct line into the complexity and sophistication of nature's intelligence. Receiving information as a subtle "knowing," the mind processes very quickly and tends to be several moves ahead of others. Novel connections, seeing life from other perspectives, and giving voice to unheard-of possibilities are part of the program. The downside is intellectual restlessness leading to anxiety, unsettledness and other ungrounded conditions. Nevertheless, there is access to genius, with the understanding that the separate self serves as a vessel for it.

4 – Cancer, Moon: The potential is emotional liberation. The personal story is becoming redefined. Initially there may be some degree of shock or trauma in the deepest feelings. The transition is to release this concretized energy and physically embody this jazzy energy of reform. Many with this combination come into the present lifetime unresolved, even restless, about

self-reinvention. Upon deeper love of the self, the foundation is set for broader awakening. Another component of Uranus with the fourth archetype is to connect with family in a new way; with the family of origin, or through the creation of their own. Either way, these bonds can be reinvented to include a broader (more non-attached) metaphysical scope instead of just feeling obligated to be a certain way to preserve a family myth.

5 – Leo, Sun: A fifth-archetype placement suggests a redefinition of how the life energy is understood and radiated. Instead of personality and ego, we can embody the transpersonal like a character in a play. Rather than feeling removed (Uranus) from participation, the chart owner has the potential to become lively and dazzling with surprising and clever uses. Through awakening into selflessness, use of the life force advances evolution in unforeseen ways. Taking personal credit for such creativity is the selfish route. While the darker version is narcissistic, even potentially destructive, the brighter possibility warms the world in exciting, even theatrical, ways.

6 – Virgo, Mercury: The combination in astrology most relevant to the development of technology. With mutable earth, the Uranian matrix of innovation is grounded into countless forms, including electronics and all sorts of gadgets. There is the potential for inventiveness with mentorship and skill development, as well as innovations in health care, nutrition or other ways of supporting well-being. In the process of becoming some form of practitioner, these natives may have issues with their own self-improvement. Resolving any neurosis, self-flagellation or unhealthy routines paves the way for teaching what is being learned. The revolution is from helplessness to exquisite abilities in problem-solving.

7 – Libra, Venus: Issues of fairness or equality are part of the work. Relationships may have previously lacked grace or tact or been impeded in some way. There could be experiences in the

soul history that felt unjust or unfair. Now the breakthrough potential is within social realms, both personal and collective, balancing the scales. The promise is to rally social movements, heal estrangements and create more awake interconnections. People with this exchange help redefine relationships, making them more metaphysically attuned and less co-dependent. They might stimulate awareness that everyone is a reflection of the self. Uranus with the seventh archetype uproots conventional ways of approaching others so we can more authentically come together.

8 – Scorpio, Pluto: Before spiritual growth accelerates, there may be some trauma or psychological challenges that have been pushed down because of their wild nature. Now the motion is to liberate any unpredictable or wounded energy and learn to manage it in newfound ways. Intimacy and sexuality, the more intense and emotional ways we connect, are primed to revolutionize through a more sacred, tantric or spiritual embrace. Areas of alchemy, hypnosis or shamanism are part of the scope here. In order to rise to such challenges, one must not blame anyone or anything for internal upset. Taking full responsibility for the ego dream allows the power of this combination to manifest in productive ways. If not, then wildness will perpetuate.

9 – Sagittarius, Jupiter: The potential is unbounded perspective, a panoramic view into the nature of life. There can be talent at deriving far-ranging philosophies, discoveries and understandings that may reform religion, higher education or belief systems. These natives can be very optimistic about human potential and become excellent inspirational "cheerleaders" for growth and breakthrough. There is also a strong correlation with adventure, air and space travel, and spiritual seeking of any sort. The unconscious version is to walk an errant path and unwittingly misguide others. It can sour into pompous and ornery ways, creating alienation and mistrust.

10 – Capricorn, Saturn: Structuring the transpersonal, bringing future possibilities into manifestation and changing the organization of culture and society is the program. Updating traditions to be relevant for modern life, these individuals often act as insiders in the corridors of power for reform. Many of them go through dramatic changes with career and end up inventing new ones by implementing advances and technologies. More than any other combination, they literally *work* with Uranian energy and give it form. The challenge is the destruction of what is actually useful from the past or the implementation of reforms in a roughshod way. It takes a lot of effort and discipline to tame (Saturn) the wild (Uranus).

11 – Aquarius, Uranus: In its home sign, the Uranian expression is undiluted. The previous spiritual challenges may have included anonymity, a lack of venturing to the transpersonal or unfulfilled revolutionary intent. Now, after personal maturation is furthered, the focus is on collective advancement. Areas include culture, social organization, technology, progressive causes or any movements geared to bring in the future. A challenge is getting started and being in the present. With such a forward-looking signature, it's easy to remain impotent and speculative. Great ideas need humans to bring them to life.

12 – Pisces, Neptune: Consciousness itself is the area of accelerated growth. Any prior trepidation or confusion about contemplative or meditative experiences is being addressed. Initially there may be deep grief or existential malaise about existence, which is pushed away from awareness. Upon integration with this material, greater wholeness leads to spiritual development. What becomes available is unbounded journeying and visioning, deep immersion into mystical processes (both in the inner and outer worlds). Those with this combination are

becoming conscious dreamers, ones with inspirational messages to share with humanity.

Neptunian Vision

Neptune inspires whatever it touches to be full of love, grace, vision, creativity and imagination. It infuses the other archetypes with a sense of magic and mystique, a quality that we can't quite put a finger on but moves us nonetheless. As the dreaming process itself, Neptune's connection to the relative realm invites us to dream into existence. We are bridging dimensions, consciously piercing through the veil of separation. Below are some thoughts on how Neptune connects with each of the twelve archetypes in ways that inspire and uplift.

1 – Aries, Mars: There is potentially an extraordinary aptitude with movement. Tai Chi, Qi Gong or other practices that bring Spirit into expression are included. One becomes a spiritual (Neptune) warrior (Aries, Mars), fearless by acting through divine guidance. Whereas the unconsciousness of the first archetype is instinctual, acting in service to preservation, this combination elevates behavior to be in service to soul intent. The potential is to act intuitively in ways that heal unconscious patterns. Managed unconsciously, there is a lack of behavioral focus or manipulation patterns with others.

2 – Taurus, Venus: Neptune's relation with the second archetype potentially grounds beauty in form—the creation of sublime art and creative works that bring us to other realms. There can be a serene mindfulness, the calm embodiment of grace, gentleness and subtlety. In connection with the earth element, Neptune reminds us that all tangible things are temporary manifestations of metaphysical processes. We can learn to be non-attached to money, possessions and the various fleeting delights of the sensual world. The challenge here is making tangible things

false gods—worshipping the manifest world and giving power away to it.

3 – Gemini, Mercury: Here, the mind learns to perceive the beauty of nature with heightened clarity. Synthesizing the right brain (Neptune) with the left (Mercury) creates a holistic approach—intuition and a subtleness of perspective rather than judgment or over-analysis. The potential is to be some version of a spiritual (Neptune) teacher (Mercury), a messenger for a more awake state of being. Many of these individuals become very learned in spiritual studies and have a knack for inspiring others. Challenges and pitfalls include confusion, distortion and ungrounded speculations that take us away from reality.

4 – Cancer, Moon: Unconditional love is the theme here. Within each of us is a tender need to feel reconnected with Spirit, to experience a sense of redemption after being lost in the initial throes of unconsciousness. Upon this reunification, the vessel of the separate self becomes infused and refreshed. The past is healed and accepted, and deeper spiritual gifts are made more available. The potential is to dream more lucidly—both the nighttime dreams and the projection of consciousness into the world in the waking state. The challenge is the inability to love the self and the perpetual state of painful longing.

5 – Leo, Sun: This combination relates to the idea of spiritual awakening itself. How can our life energy and presence radiate selfless, loving and inspired energy? Similar to Uranus/Sun, there is a redefinition of the human experience as being spiritual instead of egoic. The difference is that Neptune is pure feeling, with access to profoundly loving energy to channel. The potential is to be some form of healer or creative visionary. The unconscious version is injecting ego into the mix. This can take form as a messianic complex, narcissistic tendencies or identity confusion. As growth proceeds and egoic needs are

gradually transcended, one becomes centered and radiant in the soul self.

6 – Virgo, Mercury: At first glance, this may appear to be a mismatch—the most ethereal planet and the most earthy, detailed archetype. However, Neptune's sign forms a polarity (Pisces opposes Virgo), which is able to focus attention on spiritual development. What are the exercises and techniques that help us spiritually mature? How do we raise our consciousness? While taking concrete measures to grow is the promise, the challenge is the dissipation of energy, procrastination and other behaviors that do not promote development.

7 – Libra, Venus: Romantic ideals are found here—in both personal connection and the culture at large. How can we create the most enlightened ways to connect? There can be a delicacy in human relations—forgiveness, compassion, and experiencing the self in other at a more emotional level. A profoundly touching and sensitive disposition can also lead to giving power away, unrealistic ideals of how we "should" be, and the cultural norms that demand acquiescence. The promise here is similar to the sentiment of *Namaste*, experiencing divinity in each other.

8 – Scorpio, Pluto: Sacred intimacy, bonding and sexuality—the deepest interpenetration of consciousness is the evolutionary curriculum. With Neptune, we expand beyond the ego/personality system into the alchemical Scorpionic/Plutonian waters. Experiences considered genuinely "shamanic" fit here. Within these layers, deep healing, purgation and transformation are possible. However, with Scorpio/Pluto we find the shadow, and Neptune can get lost in it. There can be darker, distorted forms of spirituality that are predatory, manipulative and wounding for all involved. Transpersonal in focus, this is an advanced program. It would correlate to Level 8 in the model of consciousness being used in this book. To move in that direction,

we surrender (Neptune) to the realities of our shadow without any defense, humbly facing all of ourselves.

9 – Sagittarius, Jupiter: Neptune's connection with the ninth archetype equates to a panoramic spiritual vision, intuiting and discovering the universal truths that compose existence. An emphasis on experience (Neptune) that broadens our outlook (Sagittarius), spiritual seeking and adventure is ample. Through both external and internal journeys, the ineffable reach of consciousness becomes clearer. The spiritual philosopher who sees the big picture has the task of teaching wisdom. The unconscious version is prematurely claiming expertise about spiritual matters and unwittingly propagating half-truths and distortions.

10 – Capricorn, Saturn: The tenth archetype concretizes Neptune's vision into society. The interchange refreshes traditions and stagnant modes of operating to be more conscious. Prior alienation or disenchantment about the world transforms into an inspired work ethic to be part of the solution. The gift is profound forgiveness, the acceptance of the past with humility and grace. These individuals have the patience and persistence to infuse the mundane world with unconditional love. Ideally, they occupy public roles and careers that further spiritual evolution. A challenge is surrendering (Neptune) to protocol and established ways (Saturn), or reducing the complexities of the transpersonal to make it marketable.

11 – Aquarius, Uranus: How can community, culture and society itself exist as an interconnected and conscious being? The promise is to assist the trajectory of collective evolution through inspired technology, conscious activism, and advocacy for universal spiritual principles that unite us. Every individual must learn to do his or her own spiritual individuation (Aquarius) to make this a reality. The challenge is the "not my responsibility"

263

syndrome—being anonymous and detached about collective matters and thinking that one person cannot make a difference.

12 – Pisces, Neptune: The connection Neptune has with its home archetype emphasizes both the promise and the challenges, depending on the consciousness involved. The brighter side involves heightened empathy for the unconsciousness of humanity. When individuals raise the vibration from just personality to include soul, the collective consciousness changes. Every act of love and compassion has an impact on the world. In the end, we are all one. The challenge is the ongoing disillusionment and grief about feeling disconnected from this unity. Giving up, despair and even harmful escapist tendencies may result.

Part 2 — Counseling

Chapter 10
Being an Astrological Counselor

Part 1 of this book is written mostly in the style of a textbook, with an informational tone, in order to relay the concepts in an orderly fashion. Part 2 is presented more conversationally, as a discussion of how to work with the ideas. Much of the content in Part 1 is explained further and also applied to the counseling situation.

We'll address many of the issues involved with being an astrological counselor: how to present information with clients, framing the spiritual work, discussing sensitive topics, and supporting their path. We'll discuss counseling itself, both the potential and limitations. There are many issues and concerns which come up when practicing astrology, and this section will seek to answer them.

I imagine that a segment of people reading this book may be looking to develop skill in astrology, but not necessarily wanting to serve as an astrological counselor. I think this section is valuable (and important) for them nonetheless. It brings a more personal and human understanding to spiritual growth while also deepening and expanding the material presented. Furthermore, there will be many interesting ideas for one's own process of working with astrological material.

We are at the beginning of a new threshold of astrological counseling, one that is truly transpersonal in scope. Though there have been many spiritually-oriented astrology books written, there aren't too many out there that specifically address how to work with people in the context of spiritual awakening. I am thrilled and honored to share my bag of tricks here. It has been an amazing journey developing this unique way of assisting people to grow, and what follows is truly my life's passion. Counseling has been the path of my soul, and this is a culmination of what has developed.

Becoming an Astrological Counselor

Any career choice is a big decision. Choosing to do something marginalized and even ridiculed by some segments of society makes the decision to be an astrologer even more challenging. In my case (and many others) there was a process of individuation, almost like a rite of passage. I dropped out of a Ph.D. program in mainstream psychology to study Transpersonal Counseling Psychology at Naropa University (then called Naropa Institute) and attained a Master's Degree. Initially, this was not a popular decision with my family or peers. In this more alternative academic setting I was able to incorporate astrology into my studies, including doing my thesis on using astrology as a counseling tool. Simultaneously I participated in the Steven Forrest Apprenticeship Program for five years. When I graduated from Naropa I decided to be an astrological counselor, also a choice which raised some concerns for others.

Choosing to be an astrologer instead of getting a doctorate was the best professional decision I ever made. I get to be myself and do something extraordinary which touches peoples' lives. Though gratifying, those who become astrologers agree to accept a fair amount of projection in a variety of ways—almost like the price of admission. Developing inner strength and a non-attached attitude enables one to accept this price. There are many who are unwilling to put themselves out there in such a way.

Moving beyond the confines of mainstream sensibilities (Saturn) can be liberating, but a less conventional career path has its challenges. There are only a small handful of accredited schools which have anything to do with astrology. I have never heard of any insurance plan which would pay for sessions. Also, there currently are no universal standards to be an astrologer. Most people become certified by a large umbrella group (such as NCGR or ISAR) or through a variety of other programs (through non-accredited schools, apprenticeship programs). Many astrologers are completely self-taught.

It's important to distinguish between an "astrologer" and what I'm referring to as a "counseling astrologer." Historically, the role of astrologer was to provide information—like the court astrologer for the king. If astrology is used to simply convey information, this wouldn't be too much different than the weatherman giving a forecast. There would be no need for counseling credentials or skills. However, if there is more involved than merely providing information, then counseling training and credentials should be strongly considered.

Using the model of spiritual development detailed in this book, historically astrology (and much of society) has been at Level 4. The world is seen and approached in cause and effect ways. Mundane concerns dominate and there isn't much to process. Level 5 consciousness became more widespread in the 20th Century and the proliferation of psychological or humanistic astrology is the parallel. To me, psychological training and/or credentials makes sense for doing psychological work. Astrology is a tool which illuminates the unconscious, which is extremely sensitive territory. Clients can be triggered. There are many degrees of skillfulness in working with what possibly may emerge in a session. I have been told numerous times that a single astrological consult touched on deeper issues than years of therapy.

The field of astrology is currently facing the growing pains of advancing from Level 4. As consciousness evolves, there is more complexity, depth and nuance to how life is organized and approached. With this greater individuation, too much regulation creates conformity to certain underlying principles and standards. It's appropriate for an astrologer operating at Level 5 (and beyond) to be versed in astrological basics, but to also have some type of training in counseling because they are serving as a counselor.

Counseling is not therapy. The essential difference is that therapy is working directly with the material in an experiential way. Some astrologers specialize in this—for instance, those who do past-life regression work or any other deep processes based on the chart. Some astrologers do intensive couples therapy similar to that of a marriage therapist. The astrology is in the background, informing the astrological therapist, and the sessions resemble a more conventional therapeutic setting.

In contrast, the astrological counseling described in this book is not therapy. It's counseling someone about their life path based on the intentions of the chart. Referring the client to other professionals for ongoing therapy is always an option. As discussed in the following chapters, I give a variety of suggestions for how to work with the issues in the chart, but the work itself is not performed during the consultation.

For Level 5 and beyond, the shift from seeing a session as a "reading" to a "consultation" is very helpful. A "reading" is declarative, one-sided and has an air of infallibility: "This is what the chart says." The mindset at Level 4 can negate free will and novel, co-creative responses from the client. A "reading" positions the astrologer as delivering information about what the universe has in store for a person. I have heard many conventional astrologers say that they are "telling" the client what to expect.

As discussed earlier, science informs us that we are not existing in a predictable machine, but in something more like a multi-dimensional dream laboratory. Therefore, assuming the astrologer knows what will unfold puts additional pressure on the client, giving the suggestion that they "should" behave in a certain way. A "consultation" conveys that the astrologer is not an oracle with all of the answers. It's an open-ended invitation for greater process and discussion of the lessons.

To me, the success of a counseling astrologer is contingent on two factors—practice and life experience. After the basics are fully grasped, one's relationship with astrology seems to endlessly deepen based on how much one's consciousness connects with it. Like any other skill or craft, spending a lot of time becoming progressively familiar with how astrology plays out in real life is instructive. Studying a lot of charts is a part of this, but also seeing astrology in the world too. Upon seeing a cityscape, Capricorn may come to mind. Watching the movie *Gladiator*, the Mars/Aries archetype bursts into life. Life is the canvas. Learning to see the manifestation of astrology clicks everything into place.

Life experience informs the astrologer. It's helpful to have experience in relationships if you are going to address them. Being aware of how belief systems can be wounding assists in understanding someone's ninth house Pluto. For the approach spelled out in this book, one's own spiritual development is essential. Simply stated, "walking one's talk" makes the spiritual astrologer more credible and impactful.

Some Logistics

I strongly recommend providing a recording of the session to all clients. There is a voluminous amount of information to be captured. Also, this relieves the pressure for the client to take good notes. Often, clients choose to take notes in addition to the recording, which is their prerogative.

I use a simple voice recorder which is capable of converting the session into an MP3 file that can be emailed to the client. Occasionally a client requests that the session be provided to them on a CD, which is doable on most media players. To record phone sessions, I use a little gadget (initially purchased from the now defunct *Radio Shack*) which plugs directly into the phone line. Regardless of whether the client chooses to have astrology jargon as part of the experience, I provide them with a copy of their natal astrology chart, along with transits and progressions, if those are being addressed. (More on those topics will be covered in a future *Astrology of Awakening* volume.)

There can be a fair amount of administrative work involved. Being a professional astrologer potentially involves creating and maintaining a website, publishing a newsletter, advertising, networking, public speaking (possibly), and organizing the business (including tracking expenses, paying taxes, etc.). At the onset, there is a lot of focus on generating clientele. After some time, one's practice develops momentum. Clients return, refer others and there is less emphasis on trying to "make it." Also, starting out can be filled with financial anxiety if one is choosing to be self-employed. Many times it's necessary to initially have another job to stabilize income. Health insurance is also a concern.

I worked part-time on the weekends for many years while doing astrology during the week. Something amazing happened—when I quit the job, my practice took off! As discussed elsewhere in this book, when we follow the intentions of our charts, the universe tends to meet us. Freeing up my schedule (and psyche) to welcome more clients resulted in them showing up.

Preparation time is another task. When I first started doing consultations, I put in around 90 minutes to two hours of preparation time for every session. This gradually decreased as the years went by and today it is far less. The approach spelled out in these pages is now second-nature to me. Just like any skill or craft, practice and repetition really helps. Today, my preparation time is about 15 to 20 minutes, which I often do while eating breakfast or lunch.

Another task is scheduling—I've been surprised by how challenging this can be. Everyone has a different schedule, and there are also differences with time zones that must be negotiated for phone and Skype clients. Instead of asking a client what works best for them, I provide them with a list of options to choose from. Being fairly flexible, I am willing to work evenings or weekends to accommodate people. Some astrologers hire personal assistants for scheduling and administrative work.

What Is An Astrological Counselor Actually Doing?

There are many approaches to astrology in addition to counseling. Developing a mission statement or clarifying one's intentions helps focus the work. Here are some thoughts about my process with this important question.

To me, the principle task of an astrological counselor is to assist a client's awareness of the soul intentions described in the chart. The job is to be supportive rather than directive. By delivering information which resonates, clients feel witnessed and understood. Much of the session can involve bringing to consciousness what the client already knows and feels at a subtle level, helping to accelerate momentum on their path.

The supportive posture can be derailed by some common distortions. On the part of the astrologer, there can be the "expert syndrome" which unwittingly becomes instructive and opinionated. It's crucial to empower the client to arrive at their own decisions by simply laying out the information for them to process (more on this later). The client may see their role as needing to defer to the authority of the astrologer. Quite frequently there is a pull or request for the astrologer to enter the directive (rather than supportive) role. In more conventional forms of astrology, this is expected. It is thought that the astrologer has all of the answers. Today, with this co-creative approach, we can see the chart as asking questions and support the client to arrive at their own answers.

The philosophical underpinnings of the overall approach can be stated overtly to the clients. I might say, "This approach is not fortune-telling or predictive, I have no idea what will happen in your life. You are in a co-creative relationship with your chart, so outcomes are completely up to you. Think of it like the weather. The weatherman may correctly reveal the temperatures for the next several days, chances for precipitation and the like, but can never say how you will choose, or should choose, to exist within these conditions. Just because it's 90 degrees on a summer day does not mean you should go swimming. Likewise, everything in your chart is an energetic invitation. My job is to point out the territory and potentials, the cosmic weather, and together we can discuss what may be most appropriate for your unique path. The astrology chart is general—just a bunch of symbols on a page. The details of how best to navigate possibilities is found inside your heart."

In this approach, the astrological counselor has no agenda for the client whatsoever. It's none of the astrologer's business whether the client grows or not. Having an agenda for the client can be very stressful to receive. Many clients have some anxiousness about being seen, which can be compounded by any perceived judgment from the astrologer. Rather than unconsciously stressing the client out, the exact opposite is our intention.

The goal is to normalize and humanize spiritual development, to actually relieve stress by portraying a broader trajectory of evolution. The client understands that any place in this unfolding is totally fine and beautiful. We aren't expected to have the lessons and issues aced on Day One, or Year 30 or 40 for that matter. The chart is to be navigated *throughout* the lifetime, the lessons to be progressively engaged. Wherever the client is in the process is completely OK. I have routinely experienced how self-abusive and judgmental clients (and people in general) can be towards themselves. Much of the astrologer's job can be to support people in accepting who they are.

What's Love Got To Do With It?

In my view, the role of the astrological counselor is to love the client. Of course, this is not romantic love, but love at the soul level—*unconditionally caring for their maturation*. An astrologer can be completely accepting of a client's spiritual situation and assertively advocate for their growth. We metaphorically or energetically put an arm around the client, like a good friend on the path. A non-judgmental accepting disposition is supportive, to give frequent messages about the universality of spiritual lessons, and how human it is for us to struggle.

As detailed in Part 1 of this book, the core of this approach is based on securing an internal loving foundation as the platform for spiritual awakening. The same can be said for the approach in the counseling room. As will be discussed, the beginning of the session concerns this important step. Ideally, a bond between astrologer and client is established in this way.

In all of my experience with astrology (reading books, having discussions, attending lectures or conferences), I don't believe I have ever come across any emphasis (or even discussion) about the importance of self-love. Furthermore, I have found that unconditional self-love is a rare commodity on this planet. Since most of us do not provide this to ourselves, it is unconsciously ignored, and therefore not the usual orientation in an astrological approach. A distinction of this approach is to courageously make love (particularly self-love) the orientation. Love becomes the motivation for how the astrologer connects with the client, as well as the central lesson to support within the client.

Use of Astrology Terminology

Before I get started with any client, I gauge whether or not to bring in astrology terminology. This often occurs when the appointment is being scheduled, by email or phone. If not, it's the first thing that I ask them. "What is your background in astrology? Do you have comfort with the language, or do you have interest in learning it?" For some, any astrology jargon is going to confuse and even bewilder, while others can't get enough. Usually, this issue is easily resolved; someone either has a background in astrology or they don't. When a person has little or no astrological background, it can be brought in, or not, depending on *their* preference.

Sometimes a client is unsure if they want astrology terms included and might say, "Let's do what you feel is best." I explain that it's not the astrologer's preference, it's what's most accessible and helpful for them. Still, some unsure clients may not know what to say and look to the astrologer to run the show. I have found it best to operate by the policy of including astrology jargon *only when it's requested*.

There are three main ways that astrology terms can be part of the session: "Large," "Small" or "None" (and these options can be offered to the client). Large is the full inclusion for those who have a background and are comfortable with the language. The challenge is often to negotiate different perspectives and emphases, as the *Awakening* approach tends to be somewhat unique. Large is also appropriate for those eager to learn more and see the consultation as a way to do that. I tell the client that astrology terms will be mentioned like they're in parenthesis at the beginning of a paragraph, and everything will be sufficiently

276

explained. In a sense, there is some degree of tutoring the client using their own chart. The client understands that the session is recorded and they can go back and listen at their leisure. It's important to print out a chart with a legend that clarifies all of the symbols.

The Small option mentions the basics (Sun, Moon, ASC and anything else which seems most relevant), for those who request it. There is enough terminology to keep the session in the mystique of an astrological experience, yet not so much that you lose the client with a lot of unfamiliar words. Again, the astrology is mentioned like it's in parenthesis at the start of a paragraph, and everything is thoroughly explained. The discussion of the lessons and issues is usually so rich and compelling, *much of the session occurs away from the chart*. As for the astrology piece, the client may take away a deeper understanding of why they are a Pisces Sun or just how strong the pull of their Aries Moon is. They don't need to hear about their Pluto/Jupiter quincunx, and it's not a good use of time to explain exactly what the nodes are. The point of the session is counseling, not teaching—so conveying the richness of the chart (the Large option) is not the focus.

There are many times when clients have no background or interest in astrology whatsoever and it is agreed to give it to them straight. Though astrologers like to use jargon, I find this type of consult to be very liberating. With the Small and Large options, the astrologer may need to be sensitive about not confusing clients. The None option allows the focus to be completely on the meaning of the chart and the conversation tends to be more direct. Some may say that this isn't really an astrology consult because astrology is not discussed. I would argue that the exclusion of astrology makes the consultation far more effective than imposing it on someone who is not interested. The key is to meet the client where they are. Each of these types of sessions are fun to do, and in the final analysis, the same fundamental approach is applied.

The Importance of Language

In addition to managing jargon, there are some other issues pertinent to language which need to be addressed. Every client has a unique relationship with language including word preferences and many potential triggers. We may unwittingly say a word the client misinterprets or despises, and thereby lose rapport. Also, if communication is not completely clear or relatable, the potential impact of the session is compromised.

If the client mentions any dislike or discomfort with the words being used, it is helpful to address it immediately. For example, in describing the Scorpio archetype, there are many words which potentially describe its entire spectrum. In trying to capture the range, a client may be turned off, or even insulted, by some of the shadow possibilities based on the vocabulary used (none of the unconscious side is particularly flattering)! No matter how sensitively and diplomatically the information is presented, it can be triggering. I might say, "Astrology is an archetypal system and speaks in broad themes. It's my job to interpret and convey the gist of these themes. There are many different words, even languages, which can be used. It can be helpful to listen from this broader, more thematic, level instead of focusing too much on the nuances of the vocabulary I happen to use. I'm using language to try to get in the ballpark." When a client seems to dislike a particular word, and is caught on it, I find a substitute which fits better with their experience. As always, a disposition of openness to the client's experience is most helpful.

There are many ways to present astrological material, so the skillful use of language becomes an art. Another linguistic issue is style. Some people tend to be serious and formal, while others might be more whimsical and witty. Creating a professional container for the session brings trust and focus.

Within that structure, there is plenty of room to connect in the most relatable and human ways.

There are endless possibilities for how to present issues, themes or questions for the client's growth. How can we animate the themes to really *land* and make the most impact? Part of the astrologer's toolbox is life experience. We all see through the lens of our experience and this is not necessarily something to limit in order to follow some guideline of objectivity. Instead, the richness of our wisdom is what truly connects. Let's use a few examples of how astrological material might be presented in a way that really hits home.

Venus in Pisces in the eighth house: An astrologer might say, "Having deep spiritual connection is something you value. Sharing resources brings intimacy. You can be very idealistic about love, so make sure not to give your power away." All of this is true and will likely bring an affirmative response. However, it may not be *moving* to the client. To animate and go deeper, we can paint a picture of this Venus. "There's a part of you that may want to banish time and other concerns, to be in the moment of sacred contact. I can imagine you staring into a lover's eyes in candlelight without needing to talk, playing with the edges between self and other. There's a deepening through contemplative exercises, perhaps along the lines of tantric practices or other ways to raise intensity in mutually loving ways. This Venus wants to be immersed in meaningful contact, surrendering to intimate processes. With this strong need to deeply connect, one hazard might be surrendering to the wishes of others instead of experiencing mutuality."

For Uranus in Virgo in the third house an accurate description is, "You are very interested in how things work, a methodical intelligence that is both innovative and practical." A more resonant animation might be something like, "What an inventive mind! There's clockwork precision, yet great intuition. I imagine you with focused attention and having 'Eureka' moments—intellectual fireworks, new discoveries—your mind is potentially Einsteinian when you apply yourself. I bet if you wanted to make a new technology you could. How much are you willing to invest in your brilliance?"

Mars in Scorpio in the ninth house, "You are dedicated to living a life connected with your passions. Energy is directed into higher learning, adventures and a self-directed philosophy." More animated: "This Mars is like a warrior with eyes wide adorned with war paint. Have you ever seen the movie *Braveheart*? That's you, fiercely charging ahead. Part of you is willing to die for what you believe in. This warrior has a very sharp dagger which can cut to the point. Just make sure you are fighting the right battles. As you develop your courage, you become an unflinching catalyst for truth, a fighter for what you know in your gut is right."

The movie reference was mentioned to make the next point: *Know your audience.* The consultation is very different for an adolescent compared to an elder. Someone in their 80s is likely not going to get references to the current pop culture, while a youngster has significantly less life experience to draw from. Mentioning a movie which won the Best Picture award is a lot safer than a more obscure choice. However, it still may not be part of the client's experience, so it's best to be very discerning about what to bring in. I find that *painting pictures* with words, bringing in imagery, metaphor and creativity brings the session to life. References to songs, movies, famous people or current events in the news can be used effectively if done tactfully and with knowledge of the audience.

The last issue with language is being aware of the session's flow. Some clients choose to say very little, while others seem to want to dominate. The counseling astrologer can delicately and respectfully invite reticent clients to share more, while also not pressuring, and accepting their choice. Overly verbose clients may need limits set, and this can be done tastefully. I frequently ask open ended questions which invite clients to share their experience of the session. I try not to give a monologue, while also making sure to direct the session. Pausing and asking, "Does that make sense?" is an easy way to check in and establish flow. At the beginning of the session I let the client know, "This is a dialogue, not a presentation. You are welcome to share what is up and together we'll create the session." More about conducting the session is in the following chapter.

Chapter 11
Conducting the Session

In this chapter I'll be commenting on the various segments of the session as they play out. Though each session is unique, what follows is a rough guide to how this approach takes form in the counseling room. The aim of this chapter is to discuss a session from a broad perspective rather than the nuances of every individual factor of the chart. I'll be addressing many of the issues which tend to emerge and also suggesting ways to manage the various phases of the session. I want to invite the reader to see the experience of counseling as an *art*, and to support the organization of astrological material to make the greatest impact. I encourage you to find your own unique way, just as I have done. There are many ways to be an "artist," so bring in your own creativity and intuition.

Different Phases

Though every counseling session is unique, this approach has four phases which unfold sequentially. Each has its own flavor and builds from the phases which come before.

The first phase is the Introduction. In some ways, this is the most challenging as rapport is established and the tone of the session becomes set. With the astrologer/client relationship solidified, the next phase is Deepening. Here, the bulk of the spiritual work is discussed—a review of the "spiritual childhood," and the karmic patterns connected to it. The discussion centers on the personality/egoic level and its resolution. Next is Emergence. The trajectory now enters possibilities, an excitement about the blossoming into the soul self. There's a broader discussion of the transpersonal and the championing of growth. Finally, the last phase is Conclusion, wrapping it all up.

A good analogy for a session's motion can be found in the sport of diving. The Introduction is like getting on the platform. Deepening is jumping into the water, going to the depths. Emergence is coming up towards air, and the Conclusion is drying off, completing the experience.

Introduction

Prior to the session, there is correspondence to set it up, questions are asked and answered, and some familiarity is established. Now, it's time for it to start. The first issue is: how to begin?

Some astrologers might say some words or a prayer, pull Tarot cards or other divination tools, or do some type of ritual. I tend not to do these things because it may appear "flaky" to some people, turn the focus away from astrology, or potentially cause discomfort. If there's any risk at all for alienation, then best to err on the pragmatic side. If you want to do something intentional, sitting in a moment of silence is a great option, which is generally not considered to be too "out there." I invite my clients to take a breath and arrive, and it usually lasts from 15 seconds to a minute.

For phone consultations I choose not to do this because the silence tends to be more uncertain, even confusing. The client might be on the other end of the phone puzzled, waiting for the session to start. In-person sessions have cues and a closer energetic connection which makes this more amenable. For phone consultations, I simply ask, "Are you ready for our time today?"

Instead of being directive at the start, I make it clear that we are going to create the session together. I welcome the client into the session by inviting any questions and asking what they wish to attain during the consultation. This signals the desire to serve their needs, and also gives the astrologer some insight into the level of consciousness in which the client is most oriented. Answers may include something about self-gain (Level 4), maturation (5), healing (6) or spiritual alignment and non-egoic concerns for evolution (7). Whatever developmental level a client appears to be in is respected, even loved. Also, we really have no idea, and our assumptions may be off. The point is to try one's best to meet a client where they are. Hearing directly from them is crucial, always being open to their experience. Any consult will address both egoic and transpersonal issues, but having knowledge of the client is helpful in presenting information and discussing issues in ways they can receive.

Getting on the same page is the primary task at the start. Whether the astrologer likes it or not, there is a ton of misinformation about this field, many expectations and projections. There can be wide-eyed wonder, skepticism, fortune-telling demands or attributing something other-worldly to the astrologer. There are as many different approaches to astrology as there are astrologers, so clients have a wide variety of ideas as to what may unfold.

I let the client know exactly where I am coming from in simple and straightforward language. I give (what I've termed) my "opening spiel," which tends to put the client at ease and able to anticipate what will unfold. It goes something like this: "This approach is about spiritual growth. As part of the human experience, we all develop from child to adult. Similarly, we are all growing from a spiritual childhood to greater maturation. This plays out over many lifetimes, so reincarnation is assumed. Are you open to that?" (Since the client population is self-selecting, this is often just a formality. Occasionally, someone may indicate uncertainty but also an openness to continue. Never has anyone said "that doesn't work for me" and chose to terminate before beginning.)

"Ok, great. So, we all used to be even less conscious and mature than we are now!" (I find that bringing in some humility and humor is disarming and creates trust.) This is totally fine and part of the universal course of spiritual development. During our time, we'll first journey back to what is still unresolved and unprocessed from your spiritual childhood, then move towards what the intentions are for further growth in the present incarnation when this is addressed. My job is to be a messenger in the most non-judgmental and compassionate way I know how. Does that work for you?" Generally, there is a nod of the head or a response like, "makes sense to me," and we get into the session.

Deepening

The mystical poet Rumi is quoted as writing: "The very center of your heart is where life begins. The most beautiful place on earth." The deepening part of the consult addresses where we "begin" in the evolutionary journey and we dive into it. As discussed in Part 1, I always start with the Moon and there are two major reasons why. First, it sets up the developmental trajectory from spiritual childhood to adulthood. The second reason is a bit more strategic, basically to get the client's respect and establish rapport. Focusing on the internal depths typified by the Moon, the client feels seen and understood for who they really are. As the Moon points to habitual ways of operating and survival/happiness issues, it cuts to their very core, and you get their attention by naming it.

I often use the line, "How human of you!" to empathize and connect with their fundamental humanity as revealed by their Moon. Another favorite, "You were doing the very best you knew how." And an old stand-by is, "We are all emerging from unconsciousness, this is just your version of it." As mentioned in Part 1, we can imagine how anyone's Moon profile might play out in the context of elementary school. We can picture them as youthful, vulnerable, impressionable and trying to cope with life. We can affirm the needs and strategies of their lunar coping mechanism as beautiful and necessary. Again, the discussion is of the entire lunar profile (sign, house, aspects) in a cohesive way. The aim is to really capture their emotional unconscious, which can have a tremendous impact.

Many clients carry some degree of suspicion regarding whether the astrologer actually has skill and if the session will resonate. Not only is this dispelled by starting with the Moon, the tables are turned. Positive, affirming and loving statements about who they really are inside let them know that they have found a strong friend and ally who will assertively advocate for their growth and spiritual health. In this opening segment of Deepening, the astrologer energetically puts an arm around the client by completely validating the legitimacy of their fundamental humanness.

Self-Love

The Moon involves many things, but at its core, it has to do with love. When we have a solid internal foundation of love, we are positioned for broader expansion and awakening. Without it, we are unconsciously searching for love as it pertains to our very survival. From a spiritual viewpoint, we are interacting with ourselves in all of our experiences. Therefore, it's no one's "job" to provide this love for us. Rather, it's found within and reflected back, just like a movie screen reflects the film (and the Moon reflects the Sun).

Since we all start out vulnerable, insecure and needy as infants and children, the human condition is typified by the resolution of nurturing issues. Approaching the issue of love can be uncomfortable for some. I find it best to cut to the chase and keep the flow of the session direct. I say, "Can I ask you an incredibly personal question?" I have their attention. You could hear a pin drop. They don't know what's coming, and most would never expect where I'm about to go. "I want to ask you about self-love, which I define as 'unconditional regard, acceptance and care for the self.' Think of your childhood, and on average, where might you have been on a self-love scale, from 1 to 10? Please don't think about it too much — what's the first number that comes to mind?"

Inevitably, many people do tend to think about it a lot! Sometimes people ask for a specific age to focus on and I suggest to be more general about childhood and adolescence. Some people say that it's too hard to give a number in fear of inaccuracy, or that it fluctuated a lot. If there's difficulty answering, I encourage them to just give *the best possible guess* if they have to choose, I restate that we're looking for the *average*, and to approach the exercise very simply without much thought. Most people do end up arriving at a number. I let them know that this is a way to understand their spiritual condition, how and why their path has played out in the way it has. It helps give context to the themes and lessons depicted in the chart.

After asking hundreds people this question over the years, the results have been striking. In fact, I have even bolstered my focus on this issue because it's so revealing (and chilling)! When asking about the developmental years, approximately 70% of people select a number between 4 and 7 on the scale, and about 25% choose 1 to 3. So, 95% of people are 7 or below! At most, 5% report 8 or 9, and no one has said 10. (Occasionally someone says, "zero" or a negative number. I do not ask them to fit a number into the scale – it's clear where they stand and I don't harp on it.) The pervasiveness of low numbers portrays that unconditional self-love (10) is universally lacking in early stages of development. Its paucity is the root of karmic challenges, and exactly what we need to heal to awaken.

When a number is given, I thank the client for their honesty and tell them that they are in the same boat as everyone else. Revealing this information can be a big step for many people—it's rare to think of the self in such terms. To humanize the situation, and create deeper rapport, I might say, "Hey, you were ahead of me. I was about a 2!" This self-disclosure puts the client at ease while also dismantling any "expert" projections.

Sometimes clients are quite impacted by the discussion of self-love—many have never discussed the issue at all. I sometimes mention my findings on the matter and people tend to be moved by what I share. I might point out that the Moon orbits the Earth, symbolic that we come to this planet to be surrounded by the energy of love until we fully let it in. "The way I see it, this is love school." Many seem fascinated by this idea and their interest in the session is piqued even more.

Another facet of this discussion is examining the underlying reasons why the number is not 10. I often ask them if they have a sense of the inner dynamics which led to their self-rating. Though there are many possible reasons, a unifying theme has emerged in my experience. In some way, people seem to think that they "should" be different than who they are, or be "better" in some way. The underlying mindset is that they weren't fully worthy of unconditional love, driven by some negative story about the self. Most people disclose that there is an inner critic which informs them of their shortcomings.

There are a few things here to address. First, I might mention that the inner critic has an important job, mainly to see to our self-improvement. However, the inner critic tends not to be an expert on spiritual development. I remind them of what we discussed at the beginning—all of us are growing from unconsciousness to being more awake. Then, I may lovingly challenge them in this way. "Would you go into a school, point your finger at a first grader and say, 'What is wrong with you? Why don't you have a Ph.D. or a full-time job?' That is what you may have been doing if you insisted as a youngster that you should've been better or more advanced than where you were. Would you agree that there is nothing *wrong* whatsoever with being in first grade? Would you agree that there's nothing wrong with being at any developmental level?" After clients concur that it's OK to be anywhere in one's development, I invite them to apply that to the self. "Which makes more sense? Spirit created a natural evolutionary movement that life goes through, and all of the stages are completely beautiful and fine? Or that the beginning stages are not OK, and we basically start out "bad" or "wrong" in some way?"

Negative self-talk is the core of much suffering and may also inhibit spiritual growth. "I have a suggestion. How about replacing 'bad' with 'unconscious?' Whatever you think was bad, wrong, or 'should' have been better, is simply the extension of not being enlightened yet. This is where we all start out, in the darkness of unconsciousness, just like a baby who has no advanced intellect or awareness of the environment and can't even feed itself. You agree that none of this is bad, right? So, accepting your own unconsciousness is what this is about. I have some suggestions of how to work with this if you are interested." (These will be detailed in the next chapter.)

The other way to work with this is to challenge the link between love and the necessity to earn it, i.e., feeling "worthy." Here's an approach to confront it: "From what you shared, it sounds like you need to perform in order to receive love—or at least, that's the way it felt to you. Now, think of the Moon in the sky which holds the energy of love. We are constantly in energetic connection to it, same with all of the planetary energies—in fact, we can't get away from them! Do the trees need to do anything to earn the sustenance of the Sun? Perhaps it's not that we need to do anything to experience love. Rather, it might be that *we have to get our blockages out of the way*. The greatest obstacle we put in the way is our minds, especially self-judgment. To me, anything less than a 10 on the self-love scale is an unnecessary and painful distortion of the natural state. Is it possible that the universe is unconditionally loving and you have forgotten?"

Attachment to Non-Attachment

The lunar profile elucidates the nature of the ego dream, which clarifies *why* we have the charts we have. Connecting the other dynamics of the chart to this inner core brings perspective to the entire chart. For instance, the condition of the South Node, Pluto or Saturn can be understood as having origins within the inner self. "Remember how important it was for your Capricorn Moon to have structure? Your eighth house Saturn suggests a deep commitment towards others which stems from that need. There's a strong karmic pattern of bonding because of it."

As the consult develops, the pieces most pertinent for growing into "spiritual adulthood" (Sun, North Node and dispositor, outer planets, etc.) are gradually brought in. These too can be seen as assisting the Moon in getting its unfulfilled needs met. As the consult follows a developmental trajectory, the conversation about the Moon changes dramatically. At the conclusion, a portrayal of the person living the chart consciously is depicted. The Moon is happy and fulfilled, the work taken on is achieved. Then, something quite unexpected happens...*the attachments of the Moon lose their hold*. We get what we want, but we're no longer so needy of it. As we mature, lunar needs become less urgent, similar to a twelve-year-old boy who really thought he wanted to be the next Elvis.

291

Recall the evolutionary motion described in Chapter 1. We initially start out oriented to ego (Levels 1-3), we enter the world to contribute our spiritual work (4-6), then we mature to embody the soul self (7-9). The trajectory of the consultation mimics this motion. We are enrolled in the liberating channel of spiritual growth. (Recall, there is a complementary "manifesting" channel. However, any client is certain to be resolving the spiritual childhood to attain maturation, so this focus is warranted. In a future volume of this series, heliocentric astrology and manifestation will be addressed, which is another type of consultation.)

As we learn to embody and live the more awakened self, Moon material becomes a "give away," something important to contribute to the world and others *selflessly* (in contrast to the prior personal urgency). The maturation of the Moon involves the letting go of attachments. The solidified lunar material coming into the present life has *dissolved*. No longer do future incarnations need to work through it. I like to say, "This is what your freedom looks like." At the beginning of the consult, the client's lunar profile is validated, loved and taken very seriously as the work to address in the lifetime. At the end, we can look at the Moon in an endearing way, seeing its sweet innocence. Sometimes clients and I have a good laugh at how their prior needs used to seem so important.

The Karmic Lessons

After the Moon is fully addressed, the nodes of the Moon are the logical place to go next. Both nodes are ultimately discussed, along with all attendant factors (planets which disposit the nodes, and those in aspect to the axis). A direct link between the condition of the ego dream (Moon) and the resulting spiritual lessons and dramas (nodes) is made. *Discovering this link is key to unlocking the emotional origins of our karmic patterns*. Through practice and experience, making this connection becomes easier. The more I have been able to work in this way, the more resonant my consultations have become. I see it as the next great frontier in evolutionary astrology. Let's do a hypothetical example here.

A chart might feature a Sagittarius Moon in the eleventh house, South Node in Cancer in the seventh house, and North Node in Capricorn in the first. I might say to a client, "So, in your spiritual childhood, this pattern of adhering to certain directives (Sagittarius) reinforced by groupthink and cultural conditioning (eleventh house), led to some relationship karma you are now addressing (seventh house South Node). Initially, safety is found in numbers, and having community can be very supportive. However, the social norms of whatever congregations (eleventh house) where you sought love and security influenced you to care for the needs (Cancer) of the partner (seventh house) and follow their lead. One possibility is being a woman in a more traditional marital arrangement."

Recalling the client's status on the self-love scale provides perspective. "With a rating of 5 on the self-love scale, it was natural to follow this pattern because you were trying your best to follow the rules to be loved, a completely human and understandable choice. However, this didn't allow you the autonomy (first house North Node) to develop your own ambition (Capricorn). The way to balance the karmic books is to do exactly that—there's a big intention here for you to now create strong boundaries with others in order for you to work on career pursuits. The higher you get on the self-love scale, the more this becomes possible, as you are no longer unconsciously trying to earn love from others, you find it within."

In the discussion of past life dynamics, some clients are looking for specifics. Past life regression techniques aimed to illuminate this material are increasing in popularity, including among astrologers. Entering the chart in an experiential way can be most revealing and potentially healing. My focus is astrological counseling, rather than wearing the hat of a healer, but others may want to work with consciousness directly.

If clients inquire about details of their past lives, my response is, "All I have is this piece of paper with a bunch of symbols. These symbols are like portals into the broader archetypal realm which holds many possibilities. I have access to past life themes at this metaphysical level, but as you can see, there are no specifics."

We can have certainty of what the spiritual issues are. In this example: dependency, giving power away, always looking to support others, behaving in ways to earn love. Biographical details are speculative, and too much emphasis on these possibilities is often tangential. I maintain focus on the broader lessons and refer the client out for more specificity.

The South Node profile is the window to how prior lives were actually navigated and what forces were at play. It's important to keep in mind that there is something to "clean up" because the patterns stemmed from unconsciousness (Moon). Just as the Moon involves attachments, the behavior patterns are also quite reflexive and familiar. They are often very recognizable in the biography. In fact, I haven't had the experience where the client didn't validate the behavior tendencies and patterns depicted with the South Node profile. Often, it becomes quite emotional for the client to discuss them, especially when it's revealed that these tendencies have been a merry-go-round in the soul history. Further awakening lifts one from the repetition.

In my experience, it has been quite common for clients with any degree of background in the field of evolutionary astrology to see the South Node as something to "move away" from. As discussed earlier, I very strongly disagree with this notion. In fact, I make it a major point to frame the South Node in the most conscious light as something that is being developed. In this example I might say, "Your soul has been interested in having loving (Cancer) partnerships (seventh house). The less conscious version involved dependency patterns. Now, with a deeper reservoir of self-love (Cancer), don't you want to have true connection and equality (seventh house) with others? Your freedom involves no longer having to earn it, or to petition others to provide it. You are not moving away from relationships— rather a movement from an egoic to a spiritual paradigm *within* them." I explain that the South Node pattern is like a work of art they are in the process of completing. Why "move away" from what you have been working on for lifetimes?

Championing Growth

The discussion of the North Node can be like a spiritual cheerleading session. I call the North Node "the point of karmic reconciliation," and assertively describe its invitation for further development. As it's something we are progressively cultivating, it's appropriate to describe its most conscious expression. For the Capricorn North Node in the first house, I might say: "To balance the patterns of dependency, greater autonomy is the edge. You are terrific at serving others, now what about *your* aims? Instead of identifying as weak, this lifetime involves the development of toughness, setting boundaries, being self-aligned. When this is more developed, career and public issues become more of the focus. Is there a part of you that wants to do your own thing? Claiming that is the program. Then, you will actually have more balanced and loving relationships because you will be much more in your wholeness."

Frequently, there's some kind of "That's not me" reaction, or "Wouldn't that be nice, but I don't see it happening" response. I may counter with, "Right, it hasn't been your way of operating, that's why it's the intention to develop. Spending time working on your own career (or whatever the spirit of the North Node is in a chart), can gather momentum and progressively build to be a great strength for you. As it's such a central intention for this lifetime, you actually have a set of amazing gifts to claim here. When we follow the soul's intentions, we align with the universe and many surprises tend to unfold." I might challenge them. "You've earned it haven't you?", "This is your birth right, how your soul intends for you to reconcile your karma." Still, there might be resistance to a new way of operating, filled with what I call "convenient excuses" which is addressed in the following chapter. Sometimes I bring in this line: "I had a dear friend named Kelly Lee Phipps who has now passed away. He used to say something like, 'If you argue for your limitations, you get to keep them. If you advocate for your possibilities, you get to create them.'"

On one hand, the North Node can feel inaccessible—and on the other, it also is prone to *overcompensation*. In the Vedic tradition it is called Rahu, the dragon's head. Sometimes people latch on to the spirit of the North Node (and attendant factors), with naïve enthusiasm. Like a hungry dragon, it can gobble everything up in its path without mindfulness or grace. In this example, the chart owner may shun relationships altogether (first house) and lead with cold stoicism (Capricorn). Ultimately, this is not rewarding, so *balancing* with the South Node is the remedy.

The South Node (Ketu) is the dragon's behind. Many people want to get away from what comes out of the behind. Hence, the idea to "move away" from it, which may actually be an egoic strategy of avoiding responsibility for prior patterns. An alternative is to do the entire Nodal Axis *consciously*. What comes out of the dragon's behind can be used as fertilizer for new growth, and the integration of the North Node "feeds" the process.

The dispositor of the North Node carries the intentions further and plays a crucial role. I call it the "planet of spiritual gold" because of its energetic activation of spiritual growth. It is often a planet that is initially not very well integrated into the psyche as, like the North Node, it's a stretch to develop into. It's important to review it along the spectrum of dark to bright. We can have empathy for its initial challenges, then discuss its growth and centrality in reconciling the karma. Therefore, the conversation about it follows this evolutionary trajectory.

Spiritual gold means that this planet has great potential value at the soul level. It has qualities, attributes and new discoveries that specifically address the prior challenges of the karmic past. Its development (and everything it's connected with), brings a sense of completion and also a beautiful gift to the world. "We all teach what we are learning," I tell clients in relation to this planet. Once again, the idea is that the world is a reflection of the self. As we heal and grow, we naturally extend our newfound wholeness and empowerment outward in some way. This connects the evolution at the soul level with the relative, thereby bridging worlds.

In our example, perhaps Saturn (dispositor of the first house Capricorn North Node) is in Pisces in the third house. "From this position of greater strength and healthy self-alignment, there seems to be an intention to study, and maybe even develop into a teacher of spirituality in some way. Previously, there may have been great challenges in sculpting a spiritually nourishing (Pisces) contribution (Saturn), and now that is the great work. I'm curious, what comes up with this idea of developing a more solid spiritual perspective and communicating it in some way?" Asking open-ended questions engages the client with their chart. Addressing the North Node and its dispositor can be a lengthy conversation about how best to partner with the intentions. It's important not to rush through this part of the session. Almost always, the client will be activated—something inside awakened that may not have been discussed with this focus. Many clients may already be working on their North Node profile, and this emphasis drives it home and can be extremely affirming.

Addressing the Shadow

The most personal and psychologically-charged material is found with Pluto. I choose to bring it in after some rapport is established. Though it may be logical to address the shadow (Pluto) after discussing the emotional body (Moon), too much too soon in the consult can be overwhelming. The Nodal discussion tends to be very evocative and exciting, and the client potentially feels validated, and often amazed, by the unfolding of the session. The time is as ripe as any to get to the root.

I address Pluto in terms of *power*, which takes many forms. In the tenth or eleventh house it has to do with professional or public empowerment, in the social houses (fifth through eighth), the negotiation of power with others, and in the first house, how power is embodied, etc. The sign and aspects color and inform more of the dynamic.

To enter this sensitive terrain, I employ what I call my "human disclaimer" which normalizes the material. "Part of the price of being human is that we all have a built-in defense system in order to function. We are able to push 'unacceptable' or disturbing material into the depths of the unconscious, often called the 'shadow.' Bringing light to the shadow allows us to become more whole and furthers the process of awakening. Let's look at your version of this."

As discussed in Chapter 7, this approach relates Pluto to the Moon. In opening up the discussion, we may recall the lunar survival instincts mentioned at the start. Similar to relating the

Moon to the karmic patterns depicted in the South Node, we can also discover its connection with the shadow.

For our example, let's place Pluto in Virgo in the ninth house square Jupiter in Gemini in the sixth. "So, the initial strategy was to find safety in numbers, affiliating with like-minded allies in collective purpose. Sure enough, your chart suggests that the shadow is found in areas of broader understandings and belief systems (ninth house), which have been disempowering to you (dark Virgo). My sense is that there was a significant cost in absorbing a lot of teachings which you may not have fully agreed with. In this lifetime, a death and rebirth (Pluto) around your governing life philosophy is the intention. It's completely appropriate to be methodical and discerning (bright Virgo) about the principles you base your life on. What's your reaction to me saying that the chart is depicting a theme of being misguided (Sagittarius Moon, ninth house Pluto), which contributed to issues of emotional satisfaction in your relationships? I know that can be challenging to hear."

Pluto's square to Jupiter: "Interestingly, your chart suggests that you have an enormously open mind (Jupiter in Gemini) which has been wounded, taken down to the proverbial Underworld. Now the task is to ardently develop (sixth house) your curious disposition, perhaps even to facilitate or teach others to quench their thirst for knowledge. We all teach what we are learning, and you have a special aptitude with open-minded analysis. The most conscious expression is to contribute to our collective body of knowledge and help make sense of this existence. Isn't that what you wanted all along?"

The discussion of Pluto can be lengthy in some consultations. It is the deepest part of the chart, the proverbial egoic "bowels." It is a delicate balance to honor it without getting bogged down in it. I have found that the degree of focus on Pluto changes from client to client. Some are simply more wounded than others, and some are more willing to go there. If a client does not want to discuss deeply personal dynamics, I do not push it. However, I give some general remarks about their Pluto for them to digest.

At this point, the lunar dynamics have been discussed, including the karmic patterns (Nodal Axis) and shadow (Pluto). *Spiritual awakening involves the brightest expression of the Moon*, so weaving back to its needs brings wholeness. "Finding a new crowd (eleventh) is quite healing for you. Connecting with new associates, movements or endeavors which are future-oriented (conscious eleventh house), and based on a transformed world view (Pluto in the ninth) would be quite satisfying, I imagine. In fact, an initial motivation was to discover this (Sagittarius Moon), but the whole thing played out unconsciously as a reflection of where you used to be. As you become more spiritually mature, you reengage with the same themes, just from a position of more consciousness." This creates a natural segue to the Sun.

Emergence: Into the Light

Most anyone knows their Sun sign and expects it to be addressed in an astrology consultation. It can be surprising that it's put on the back burner for a healthy chunk of the session! However, it's quite worth the payoff. Reviewing the past provides the awareness as to *why* they have the Sun profile (not just sign placement) they do. With the karmic context established, the discussion of the Sun is the centerpiece of the session, just as the Sun is the center of the Solar System.

The Sun is the energy of presence, and supporting the flowering into the eternal now is an important part of the consultation. Like a flower, the Sun requires water (love) and plenty of warmth (fire/energy) for it to grow. The client is encouraged to maximize the position on the self-love scale for the "watering." To promote warmth/fire, bolstering one's action in accordance with the Sun profile increases its power. The more we "do" the Sun, the more alive we feel and connected to soul intent.

For instance, if a person has the Sun conjunct Mars in Aries, then encouraging exercise, expressions of leadership and courage will make them feel vital. In contrast, a twelfth house Pisces Sun would be supported through retreat, contemplative practice or visionary exercises. A Virgo Sun conjunct Venus might feel vitality and well-being doing crafts or mentoring. A fifth house Gemini Sun in aspect to Neptune may feel charged by creative writing or other types of inspired communication.

Just like a seed progressively develops towards bearing its fruit, the discussion of the Sun is also understood as a lengthy process of evolution. After all, the Sun pertains to enlightenment! As we move along the spectrum from dark to light, being realistic about the darker pitfalls along the path is necessary. Initially, most anyone is identified in ego instead of soul. Therefore, the Sun is reduced to ego and the darker facets of the Sun profile become pronounced, which is especially evident in the younger years. A client can see how the life force was managed less consciously then and how those experiences actually serve development. Sometimes clients give themselves a hard time about this mismanagement, and a response is to inform them it's just part of the curriculum, we are learning self-acceptance. In order to mature, we can love (water) the past, and accept the expression of our unconsciousness. Then our gifts can ripen.

Most (if not all) people know their Sun sign, but expanding the solar identity beyond this simplification assists greater self-awareness. Whatever planet (or planets) seem most connected to the Sun are essential to emphasize. In fact, these are the "fruits" which can be developed. We are energy (planets) and sign placements *modify* energy into a particular evolutionary program and style. Planetary energies potentially become brighter and more dazzling, unique expressions of Spirit which the chart owner has the joy to brilliantly express. A client may walk away with the knowledge of being a "Plutonian", "Jupiterian" or "Venusian", or some combination of energies which are most connected with the Sun.

The house placement of the Sun is an area where we naturally shine. However, the Sun is very likely to make aspects to other planets (in other houses), and connecting its energy to these areas is essential. Also, whatever house has Leo on the cusp is disposited by the Sun, so it naturally disperses its energy here too. Furthermore, everything revolves around the Sun and reflects its light. Its role is always central, connected to everything in the chart as the person's inherent life force. Too much focus on the house placement reduces its scope, but it is an area to encourage focus and development.

It's important to distinguish the developmental differences between the Sun and the North Node. The North Node (and its dispositor) are what we can more fully develop to *reconcile the past,* balance the karmic books, and give a gift along the lines of that curriculum. In contrast, *the Sun is a gift that Spirit gives to each of us.* As we awaken, we realize that we are borrowing our solar energy and it's really not us at all! We are conduits for this enlightened energy to move through us. We accept the gift and radiantly share and display it to warm others and light the world. However, to open the gift we must resolve the past and its unconsciousness to receive it. What becomes available is sublime, as there is potentially no end to the *wattage* of our developing enlightenment. We can gloriously paint the picture of the client's awakened self, to see everything connected with the Sun in its brightest expression. In the situation of a Leo North Node, the Sun is the dispositor. Therefore, it plays both roles and can be looked at from these different angles.

Partnering with Soul: The Transpersonal Discussion

The Sun is our soul connection with all of life and plays a mediating role in our spiritual maturation. It links the egoic/personality self (Moon) with the Oneness of the universe. Through the projection of awareness, we are able to meet the self in the world to play out our dramas and engage our lessons. We ultimately find that the little self and the big Self are the same— we are made in the image of our creative source energy and reflect it.

At this point in the consultation, it's now appropriate to support a more conscious partnering with soul. In my experience, very few people have a sound understanding of how to do this, while this astrological paradigm tends to be new to almost everyone. Therefore, some explanation is warranted. Though this part of the consultation is philosophical (and a bit of teaching), it becomes directly related to the client's chart. I have asked many clients if the information is useful to receive and have heard overwhelming support for it. The discussion goes something like this:

"Most people are only aware of the personality level. I'd like to discuss what it could be like to live at the soul level, are you open to that? Great. Imagine the Sun in the sky, how it radiates its light onto everything. Look around right now. Everything you perceive is being lit up by the Sun's light, right? Ok, you're the Sun, a Taurus Sun (or whatever sign they are, this helps bring it home). You radiate out your consciousness, your lessons, tendencies, biases, emotions, unresolved karmic issues, basically your astrology chart, onto life—just like a movie projector onto a screen. You are creating your own experience based on the quality of your consciousness, so you're interacting with your own *version* of a red car, a dog, or the President. Right now, you are interacting with your version of Eric Meyers, which is constructed by your impressions and theories of who you think I am. We all do this, all the time. It's like a movie, and you are the writer, director and starring actor in your drama.

"Other people are the characters in your movie and play roles consistent with the dynamics and issues spelled out in your chart. They help you become more aware of your unconsciousness. Just like the Moon reflects the light of the Sun, other people reflect back your light. The implications of this are profound: Remember how you used to be a 5 (or whatever number they reported) on the self-love scale? Life was pretty tough then wasn't it? What was reflected back was not always so loving. *You were interacting with yourself.* It's fine, this is what we all do. It's just the process of awakening. So now, we can recognize that we are doing this, and the entire world shifts. If and when you become higher on the scale, you will create a new reality. You have to love and accept that you used to be less conscious, basically forgive yourself, and everyone else too, because they were you. You "hired" these people to catalyze your issues so you can work through them, to *help* you free the energies which have been buried. An astrology chart shows the state of your emotional unconscious on your birthday, way back in (state the year of their birth). Whatever painful experiences you went through were created by your soul (Sun, present moment) to help liberate you. Now there's a choice: you can recognize the self in the reflections of others and grow, or stay rooted in separation consciousness and blame your issues on everybody else. One signal of issues coming to resolution is not only forgiving others, but having *gratitude* for how they helped you learn and be more conscious.

"When we retract the petition that other people love us, we are free. All they do is reflect who we are. Would you expect the characters on a movie screen to love you? It's an illusion, just a reflection! Sure, the personality level is still valid, the ego does experience loving bonds with others, but we're talking about the soul or metaphysical level. The key is to find love internally, at the source. So, there's a slogan that runs my life I'd like to share with you, and you are welcome to make it your own, if you'd like: 'I don't need you (meaning anyone outside of me) to love me, that's my job.' The more I integrate this truth, the more liberated I feel."

At this point I like to pause to make sure it's being understood. I ask for questions and repeat points if necessary. I hear all of what the client would like to say. When this interlude concludes, I go to the next part.

"Other people are interacting with themselves *through* you. You're the (state their name) character in *their* movie, and you might play such roles as daughter, wife, employee, mechanic, astrologer or anything else. All of it is projected onto you, which has nothing to do with you, and it's none of your business either. Have you ever had the experience of being super nice with great intentions and someone else thinks of you negatively? See, they are interacting with themselves and blaming it on you! The implications here are profound. First, there is no possible way you can ever *mess up* for another person. Whatever you do will fit into their movie in ways consistent with their consciousness and the lessons of their chart. Just like you see in a theatrical movie, the main character always goes through challenges and adversity to come of age. So, we don't have to protect other people from the spiritual curriculum they 'signed up' for. Everything you do assists their growth."

Sometimes a client may say something like, "Wait, you're saying if I killed someone, that's exactly what they need?" The answer is, "Not exactly. It's not in your nature to behave in such a way, so the question is irrelevant. We are dealing with *reality* here, not hypotheticals. The issue is for you to be free to live your authentic truth, and I don't think that is part of it. If someone has a problem with you, or gets hurt by you, then they actually have a problem with themselves and are playing out their hurt through you. It's not your job to deprive them of potentially working through it. Freedom arrives when you don't take it personally, which a solid foundation of self-love provides. If you get an emotional charge through your interactions, then school is in session for you! Something unconscious is ready to be more fully loved. As you mature, you will no longer get triggered so much. Instead, you will deepen compassion for yourself and everyone else through every interaction."

I ask again if the idea makes sense, which it usually does. As it's such an important part of spiritual growth, I do not jump to the next part of the consult until the client seems ready. I get back into astrology by linking the solar projection to their chart, and discuss their own unique radiance, how their soul self has specific qualities.

The House Layout & Other Factors

The basic structure of Moon, Nodes, Pluto and Sun creates an excellent format to frame the central components of the spiritual journey to greater awakening. At this point, the consultation is about two-thirds complete, with roughly that percentage of the chart (sometimes more) discussed. What's left is the house layout and bringing in the other planets not directly a part of the chart skeleton.

Planetary residency in houses is included in the discussion so far. For instance, the Sun profile involves its sign, aspects to other planets as well as its house placement. For a consult with a large amount of astrology terms, there is continual referencing of houses and the planets which reside in them. For the "Small" consult, houses are seldom mentioned, except for the Ascendant (and often the Midheaven) because it is so popular and something to take away from the experience.

Bringing in the Ascendant after the chart skeleton is strategic for two reasons. First, it avoids the conflation of the Ascendant with the planets. As discussed in earlier chapters, the planets are energy, the actual substances which compose the psyche. Houses are how space is approached. After we thoroughly understand our energetic (planetary) nature, we can discuss how it's dispersed in our daily navigation. When the Ascendant is discussed, I also include referencing its dispositor as this planet energizes the first house. The view of the Ascendant is of *direction* or *orientation* (instead of consciousness or identity, which is the province of the planets) for the spiritual work to *play out*.

Sometimes a client has heard that they *are* a Virgo due to having the Ascendant there. In these cases I remind them that the life energy is the Sun, the centrality of our being. The planets are the various facets of our other energetic functioning (Mercury-mind, Mars-passion, etc.). Then, energy can be *directed* into a craft or specialization (in this case, Virgo), to move in the world as an instructor or mentor (Virgo). If they agree with reincarnation, then I mention that consciousness exists apart from being on the physical earth plane. The Ascendant is an orientation to the horizon from a specific place on the Earth's surface. When we die, we move on, no longer are we wedded to the four directions from a spot on this planet. Therefore, the Ascendant is like a mask we *temporarily wear*—not our fundamental identity.

I frame the discussion of the Ascendant in terms of partnering the archetype with one's behavior (as the first house is thematically associated with Mars/Aries). Stylistic in nature, I discuss how the sign's qualities are perfect for the evolutionary work being discussed. With a thorough understanding of the evolutionary situation, we can always discover the brilliance of having a particular Ascendant to navigate through life.

Often underplayed, I find the Midheaven (MC) to be a very significant point to discuss. Like the Ascendant, I describe how the MC is an *orientation*, here, to public life. Its dispositor is central in providing the detailed information to take it further. On the charts I cast using my software, there is an arrow at the top which points to the sign on the MC like its saying, "Do this archetype professionally!" I agree that the MC profile is the "cosmic job description," and many seek astrological counsel to more fully grasp their role. The MC and its dispositor, as well as Saturn, and any planets in Capricorn, provide a wealth of information about public life.

Another major area is relationship. As with self-orientation and career, this is usually addressed during the unfolding of the chart skeleton. We can eyeball the nature of the seventh house to see the orientation and issues concerning interpersonal exchanges. Again, the consultation is a masterful blending of information presented cogently to the client throughout the session. I do not recommend too rigid a format. Relationship issues are certain to emerge at some point. In discussing the house layout, it can be mentioned and reinforced if necessary.

The fourth house is a bit different. Since the Moon is where the consult begins (in this approach), the nature of the fourth house is important to keep in mind. This area portrays how lunar issues initially play out in the early home. The sign on the cusp, its dispositor, and any planets held within are very instructive. Recall that the Moon is the actual concretized energy of the separate self, whereas the fourth house conveys how family and emotional issues take shape in the present lifetime.

The angular houses are only a third of the chart. All of the houses have signs on the cusp and planets which serve as dispositors. Each area is understood for its uniqueness and analysis and discussion is not limited to the angular houses.

However, angular houses are more immediate—clients do tend to be more focused on the central areas of self, family, relationship and career—hence, the historical focus with these realms. It's important to meet them where they have focus, concern and questions. Nevertheless, *everything on the chart is relevant* and has a place in the consultation. The succedent and cadent houses can be explored in the same way if it feels emergent in the session. In fact, a spiritual approach will attract those interested in spiritual concerns (not just immediate matters), so it's appropriate to spend time on the areas which address this development. Whether or not succedent and cadent houses are directly brought in (there is only so much time, and part of the art is what to emphasize, and what to omit), they are grasped by the astrologer, and inform a holistic understanding of the chart.

The planets which aren't a part of the skeleton will vary with every chart. After the discussion of the Sun, they can be brought in and spoken about more directly. My style tends to be improvisational and intuitive, to go with the session's flow. The chart skeleton may reveal issues with Saturnian themes, for instance a Capricorn Moon and a tenth house South Node (let's say in Sagittarius). If Saturn wasn't part of the skeleton, it is a natural planet to emphasize. Another chart may have a Pisces North Node in the eleventh house. Though Neptune was brought in earlier as the dispositor of this Node, it may be instructive to look at the other transpersonal planets to complement the intention.

Ultimately, *everything* will be touched on, so there is no worry. The key is to attain a cohesive understanding of the chart ahead of meeting with the client. A holistic understanding will inform the more compartmentalized discussion within the session.

As discussed earlier, the phasal relationship between Sun and Moon is of major importance. Instead of getting involved with the technicalities (such as explaining what a Balsamic Moon means), I find it better to just have the understanding integrated and speak from that place. Throughout the session, the Sun and Moon are frequently referenced. When talking about how they partner, the phase is a piece which informs the presentation, without direct reference.

Mentioned earlier, I do include Chiron and the four major asteroids, as well as the Black Moon. Similar to the phasal issue, these inform my understanding of the chart instead of being directly referenced. However, if the client has chosen to have a "Large" amount of astrological terminology, then it's appropriate to mention them. In fact, many students or novice astrologers may be especially curious about them.

Conclusion

Since the consultation is recorded, I tend not to spend a lot of time summarizing what has already been discussed. It has been a long journey, and there can be a fatigue factor. There is a lot of information, many new ideas to consider, and it tends to go quite deep into the psyche. I ask the client how they are doing, what's on their mind, and I encourage all questions. They are in charge of how it ends, which is the parallel of how they are in charge of their life. So, the "drying off" segment is a forum for the client to share or ask questions. It usually lasts between five and fifteen minutes. Finally, I ask, "Is there anything else at all before I stop the recording?" They get the last word. It's their consult. I let them know that it was an honor to connect with them at this level of depth and thank them for entrusting me with their soul.

Chapter 12
Counseling Techniques & Strategies

In the next two chapters we'll explore some strategic ways to work with the client—the art of astrological counseling. It has been both a joy and a labor of love to develop these ways of working with people. Many of the techniques and strategies can be challenging to a client. The key is to come from love. Ideally, rapport is established in the beginning stages of a session. Much of what follows works best when this is achieved.

The strategies and techniques discussed in these chapters are not intended to be applied in every session. Like a carpenter who possesses a wide array of tools for every possible job, each session draws from the tool bag. I tailor the consult to address the most significant and pressing issues that the client is working on. In anticipation of the session, I usually get a sense of what I may bring in, but I'm prepared to adjust course to follow the flow of the session.

Timing is crucial. There is no way to teach it because it's largely intuitive. What occurs with me is that I enter "the zone" where it feels like I'm connected to the "intelligence" of the session. I sense when it's a good time to bring in some of the following techniques. There's a delicate balance. Too much focus on presenting chart information turns the consultation into more of a "reading," which is useful, but it's not really *counseling*. Too much discussion and processing away from the chart can be tangential. I find it best to stay with the flow of the session while working along the evolutionary trajectory presented in this book. Another session to go deeper can always be scheduled if needed. Having a timepiece to help keep the session on track is helpful.

The following techniques and strategies are designed to target tendencies which keep a person tethered to their familiar patterns. Much of them have to do with encouraging self-love and acceptance, affirming potential, and addressing the obstacles we often put in the way of our development.

Reinforcing Innocence

As mentioned in the last chapter, a strategy I commonly employ is to reinforce the concept that the themes of the chart are derived from prior states of unconsciousness. We all come from innocence in our spiritual childhood. It is quite common for people to make self-defeating statements when their core issues are exposed. "Yeah, I am terrible at that." When a raw nerve is activated, the energy bound up with it can be released. Negativity can be transformed. Whenever it emerges in a session, it provides an opportunity to assist the client in being more loving to the self.

I might say something like, "I notice that you can be hard on yourself. I don't agree with your self-criticism. To me, any stage of spiritual evolution is totally fine. You are doing the best you can, the best you know how at this point in time. The patterns in your chart form your curriculum and it's totally fine to be a student—that's what we all are. I suspect you are probably very accepting of others, and I invite you to direct that same generosity toward yourself."

Clients frequently make the suggestion that their feelings are not OK, are unjustified, or "shouldn't" be there. I challenge this by stating that emotions naturally emerge as a part of life, they are literally *energy in motion*, and life is simply about engaging with energy. "Anger or fear just happen, right? Does it make sense to you that what Spirit created to happen naturally is "bad"? Or does it make more sense that these emotions have a teaching for us? If we judge them negatively, we are less open to their teaching. Anger might be teaching you to be more assertive in getting your needs met. Fear helps you protect yourself— among other possibilities. These feelings are just the way the human system *survives*. To me, that's totally OK. What do you think?" Much more on the subject of emotions are presented in later sections. As a quick way to reinforce innocence, the client can hear the message that everyone has a Moon, and everyone's Moon is responsible for processing the widest range of emotional material. Astrology can serve as an objective reinforcement of the universality of the human condition, and this can assist a return to innocence.

Challenging Cultural Conditioning

The disparagement of emotion is part of a broader issue of cultural conditioning. In general, we are "trained" to be civil and appropriate, basically "well behaved." The motivation is laudable, to have a smoothly operating society, but it often comes with a cost in terms of the spiritual heath of the individual. The ability to process emotion becomes paused. People can't "let it go" until they actually take measures to release it. It is helpful to discuss how we are "energy processing systems" (as detailed in earlier sections).

The dominant Saturnian paradigm and value system in the Western world is discussed at length in Volume 1 of *The Astrology of Awakening* series. To summarize: there is an emphasis on conformity, being acceptable and appropriate to others, valuing success and material gain, being smart, reasonable and "down to earth," respecting traditions and institutions, and basically giving power away to those highest in the pecking order.

The spirit of this counseling approach is to support growth toward the transpersonal, to claim and embody a person's authenticity. The point is not to champion rebellion from cultural

313

standards, but to have the client question whether they are operating from their own truth, or that of others. In spiritual childhood, it's natural to project parenting dynamics onto culture and society, and Saturn (and also Jupiter to some extent) is the projection screen for this. *Being one's own authority* (Saturn) is part of spiritual maturation—then the gate to the transpersonal becomes more open.

There are many, often subtle, ways in which cultural conditioning can play out. A marker of conditioning is revealed when a client thinks they "should" do something or be a certain way (for instance, raising a family or having a "respectable" job). One strategy is to directly challenge this thinking. "Really? I think you 'should' be yourself. Sure, get married and have children if that is truly what's in your heart. How much have you explored what your truth actually is inside?"

Giving voice to the intentions spelled out in their chart can be quite impactful. However, there's a difference between representing the chart and giving advice. (This is discussed in more detail in a later section.) The condition of Saturn, and the planets which orbit beyond it, provide excellent information for a discussion of conditioning and liberation. In fact, this movement toward liberation and awakening is exactly what many of us are learning to do as we collectively mature in this pivotal time frame.

Usually within the flow of any session, issues of conditioning tend to emerge. Most anyone is still reconciling Saturnian issues in order to move beyond them. We can develop a keen eye to spot these influences and gently point them out to the client. Many times people have little awareness that they are speaking from a very conditioned place, so this can catalyze a lot of insight. Also, clients are able to hear themselves speak from such conditioning when they listen back to the recording of the session. I've been told that this can also be a powerful experience.

Many people do not question the assumptions and ideas which govern their lives. The session is an ideal format to conduct this important assessment. Clients do tend to look at the astrologer with respect, especially if there is rapport and resonance with what is being discussed. Lovingly challenging clients from this position of expertise is a true art which can make an unforgettable impact on their life.

Claiming the Gifts

One of the most enjoyable techniques that I employ is giving expression to the client's possibilities. Much of the first half of the session covers sensitive ground and the tone at times can be serious. Some people have no idea what they are getting into when they seek astrological counsel. To balance any heaviness or seriousness, the flow of the session is supported by giving voice to their potential.

Every chart has gifts for the client to develop and claim. It's actually very easy to identify these gifts, as everything in the chart has a conscious (bright) expression. I frequently quote the maxim, "we teach what we are learning." The main spiritual challenges and issues found in the chart provide fertile ground to search for a client's specific gifts. The most conscious expressions of the Moon and South Node contribute to the realization of spiritual work taken on in the past. The Sun and North Node convey extraordinary potential for further development and blossoming. Also, all of the outer planets relate to potent areas of advanced growth. Jupiter can manifest with a lot of expansion and abundance and Saturn, done consciously, can potentially make a mark on the world. The key is to hone in on the possibilities that would be most striking to reinforce, given the logic of the chart.

For instance, someone with a Gemini Moon and a third house Pluto may historically have a need to feel smart, but also have deep psychological issues around believing they are. Let's say the chart shows Uranus conjunct Mercury. I might create a pregnant pause for a few seconds then ask them, "Do you have any idea how brilliant you are?" This is going to be a provocative moment as it directly challenges their prior struggles and points to their potential. They might say, "I don't feel brilliant, in fact, I had a tough time in school." The reply might be, "Right! I totally get your struggle. It's one of the huge themes in your chart. However, it just so happens that when we follow our spiritual curriculum and grow, the very areas which were initially challenges become our strengths, our special gifts to offer the world. I bet that if you change the story you believe about your innate intelligence, you will be able to access the dormant gift of brilliance waiting for you. In fact, you probably already have, to some degree, as it's the way you're wired. Have you ever just known something, like a lightning bolt of insight? You might disregard these flashes but, if you pay attention, you'll notice you have access to incredible intellectual wizardry. It is your birth right to claim, if you wish."

Slogans

Another technique I love to use is to give clients a slogan—a pithy sentence or phrase which captures the spirit of a major intention in the chart. Slogans can be used for a variety of chart factors, but I have found them to be especially appropriate for the Nodal dynamics. Stating an intention to free oneself from a habitual pattern by promoting the polarity can be helpful. For instance, a slogan for a Cancer North Node would be, "I follow my heart, not society's rules." An example for a Sagittarius North

Node is, "I'm motivated by my calling." Slogans representing the most conscious expression of the South Node are also helpful.

The creation of a masterful slogan can synthesize multiple threads of the chart. Picking out the most central theme and giving voice in a memorable line is a nice take away for the client. Sometimes I share my own when it seems relevant and appropriate for their situation. "I don't need you to love me, that's my job." I invite them to have it as their own if they choose. Here are some other examples:

A client may have a theme of pleasing others, perhaps strong Libra signatures connected to the karmic past. A Taurus Sun may be in the first house suggesting an intention for greater self-alignment and independence. Perhaps there are also strong themes of learning to connect with the transpersonal, such as Uranus or Neptune in aspect to the Sun. A slogan could be, "What other people think of me is none of my business."

Another client might have a theme of hiding, such as a South Node in the twelfth house and a Pisces Moon. The Sun may be in Leo in the 11th house in aspect to industrious Saturn. A fifth house Venus disposits a Libra Ascendant. One possibility is, "I love sharing my creative works!"

Perhaps a chart features a great deal of intensity in the karmic past, such as a Scorpio Moon and a Virgo South Node in the eighth house. Along with the Pisces North Node in the second house, Neptune in Libra is conjunct the Sun. A slogan for this might be, "I'm at peace with myself and the world."

A chart might have the North Node in Aquarius in the sixth house, with Uranus/Sun in Virgo in the first house. A possibility here could be, "I am a master innovator with my work."

There are often multiple possible slogans for any chart. Sharing one, or a few, is completely up to the astrologer in the flow of the session. I have found that people really value, and enjoy, receiving them.

Dismantling Convenient Excuses

This section concerns the inertia of karmic patterns. It is most relevant in discussing the behavioral routines depicted by the South Node. The Moon, Saturn, Pluto and other possible chart factors can also be pertinent. Karmic patterns often have a merry-go-round feel. Certain ways of operating become concretized and life is unconsciously organized around their perpetuation. The maintenance of these patterns is held in place by what I call "convenient excuses," which refers to the reasons given for why further development is not possible. The excuses are the bars on the soul cage. Helping the client see that they are imaginary can be incredibly liberating.

First, it's important to honor what the excuses are, and the mindset that goes into them. Some words that can be used to validate a person's concerns are: "reasonable," "legitimate," or "understandable." However, the patterns depicted by the South Node were developed with some degree of unconsciousness and have played out only within a relative (rather than transpersonal) framework, as the South Node relates directly to the unconsciousness of the Moon. Promoting further growth involves a transpersonal perspective which dismantles the convenient excuses.

The most frequent areas where people find "convenient excuses" are: 1) family responsibility (to children or family of origin), 2) relationship patterns and expectations, 3) money, 4) religious (or educational) standards and obligations, and 5) social acceptance. Below are some ways to work with them.

Family responsibilities run very deep and touch in with core issues of love and attachment. Someone with a Libra South

318

Node in the fourth house may feel that they can't upset the family. I had a client with this placement who was an only child, groomed to follow the family script to become a professional. The tenth house North Node in Aries is a clear intention to do career on one's own terms, while Mars conjunct revolutionary Uranus suggests it will be something new, alternative and likely to be disruptive to the pattern. "I'd love to be an astrologer but I can't. My family would feel so let down. My father and grandfather are lawyers and expect me to be a part of the firm. They are paying for law school too…I can't say 'no'."

A response might be, "Yes, it sounds like they would feel let down. I left a Ph.D. program to be an astrologer and my family thought I was losing my mind! I get it. What it comes down to is whether you are going to let *them* down, or let *yourself* down. Are you willing to be miserable to keep others happy? Do you think that would allow any growth, for *you* or for *them*? My sense is that this is a deep karmic pattern for you, and you have historically let *yourself* down; your family is a projection screen. I'm not saying it's easy, but you are learning courage and self-alignment in this lifetime. You say that you can't say "no," but have you really questioned if that is true? Perhaps this is a test for you to become an astrologer, walking your own chart to get there. I see the resolution of your family expectations as a rite of passage in claiming your authentic self. I bet that they are in on the secret at the soul level too, actually rooting you on. What do you think of that?"

Another example is the parent (usually mother) who feels she should always be there for her children and put her aspirations aside. "I don't want to be a 'bad' mom!" I might say, "Yes, that is completely reasonable and loving—you have a beautiful heart. It's important to be a good mother isn't it? I wouldn't want you to be otherwise. However, let's talk about what a good mother actually is. Would it include acting in service to the children's *spiritual* growth? If so, then I have some helpful news for you. At a soul level, your children knew exactly what they were getting into when they chose you for a mom. There is complete awareness about the spiritual dynamics, the work on the table for all of you. Maybe part of the reason they are your children is to catalyze this issue for you to work through. You agree there is a soul bond right? The learning would go in both directions.

"I got divorced when my son was two years old and worried that I was going to be a 'bad' father. However, I understood his chart and saw that this event fit into his spiritual curriculum. I bet the same thing may be happening in your situation—what you think would be harmful may actually catalyze necessary soul lessons. Providing your children with unconditional love is a profound gift, and loving yourself may also include following the intentions of your own chart. Certainly you would need to work things out on the everyday level and make decisions that are grounded. Many women balance career and family and you can too—in fact, that's the spirit of your chart isn't it?"

Quite frequently, convenient excuses have to do with being a certain way for other people. An analogy I frequently use is that many people are looking for love from the characters on their movie screen. Reorienting them back to the "projector" to find love within is much of the work. Unsatisfying romantic connections can demonstrate this dynamic. An example would be a South Node in Taurus in the seventh house. "I made a vow and I'm a person of my word. She has always been there for me, so how could I leave? She is a good woman, means well. It's not really that bad. I don't want to break her heart."

In response, "Makes a lot of sense to me. Marriage does provide stability and that can serve in many ways. However, the chart suggests the importance of being there for *yourself*, of not abandoning your own heart. Can you give me an example of one relationship in all of history which has been permanent? Or is it true that all connections are temporary, just like life? So, the question is really *when* it ends, not *if*, right? I wonder if 'being there,' and loving your wife now takes deeper spiritual meaning instead of just providing security at the personality level? If so, then who's to say this isn't exactly what she needs to engage lessons on her spiritual path? My concern is that if you are dissatisfied, with underlying resentment, she may turn into your jailor; something I imagine neither one of you wants. I don't think it's your job to protect her from her spiritual curriculum, do you? I'm not suggesting any direction you should go. Rather, a big theme of your chart is to live in connection with your truth and make decisions accordingly."

Another version of relationship responsibility can be found within the realm of "service." Some people's karmic patterns involve helping or assisting others (professionally or personally) and feeling obligated to their welfare. "I can't take care of my own business because other people are depending on me." With the intention in their chart to become autonomous and dedicated to their own aims, we can challenge them to *allow others to support them*. I use the example of growing a "karmic bank account" of helpful capital. In order to balance the energetic books, a shift to being more receptive to receiving help and support from others is appropriate. So, developing their own aims actually opens this up, while staying in a selfless pattern can deepen an unbalanced dynamic. I sometimes mention my own karmic pattern of service (sixth house South Node) and initial struggles of breaking free from it. When I did finally quit my part-time job to do astrology full time, that's when my client load really increased.

Financial concerns are perhaps the most frequent convenient excuse. "I can't do my true work, I have to pay the bills." Again, the concerns are first honored at the personality level as completely legitimate and responsible. Then, a discussion of money and resources from a metaphysical angle is appropriate. I might say, "Does it make sense to you that if you follow through with the intentions outlined in your astrology chart, the universe is *not* going to meet you? Or is it possible that when you do your chart well, the universe will hold up its end of the deal? Einstein says it this way, 'Match the frequency of the reality you want and you cannot help but get that reality. It can be no other way. This is not philosophy. This is physics.' He is basically saying that when we attune with energy, we get a certain result. You have to hold up your end through diligence, confidence and trusting life."

Much of the time, people are of the mindset that material concerns trump spiritual intentions. To turn this inside out, I often mention the metaphysical view that we are just *borrowing* the physical realm for a limited time: our bodies, clothes, shelter, possessions, etc. We can see the spiritual curriculum like a board game, such as *Life* or *Monopoly*—we go through the days and months sometimes gaining money, sometimes spending. I ask clients if they ever remember how much money they won in any board game they've played, or does the *experience* of playing (which is analogous to living life) stay in our memory? When the "game" is over (death), we don't get to keep our bank accounts (the money returns to the box). What remains is the way we lived our life. If we're interested in *spiritually investing* in ourselves, then following the suggestions of the astrology chart turns out to be the most pragmatic choice. Sure, there are immediate concerns, but having a broader perspective can be helpful.

I don't encourage people to be financially irresponsible, but I do suggest they be responsible to their soul intentions. I might ask, "What's the worst that can happen if you take a risk in order to follow a dream?" The answer is usually fear: of accruing debt, of being seen as irresponsible, or of not being able to provide for others. "How much is it *worth* to you to follow the intentions of your chart? Is responsibility defined only in material terms, or could it involve investing in your growth?" I might challenge them to consider that *not* following their heart may, in the long run, be a lot more "costly" than the worst case scenario resulting from "going for it."

This issue comes down to whether or not the person is confident and *trusts life,* and this is what I directly ask them. Trusting life is actually a reflection for trusting the self. I draw the correlation that, in astrology, the same archetype (Venus, Taurus, second house) which involves money is connected with issues of self-worth, confidence and the ability to follow through and handle matters maturely. With trust of self, we can trust our partnership with Spirit. So, gauging the level of self-worth (and issues of self-doubt) frames the discussion. If a client is feeling strong in the self, it's appropriate to assertively champion bold steps. If not, then securing this inner foundation is more appropriate to emphasize.

Another area in which people make excuses is with religious, educational or cultural expectations. For instance, a man who is torn about leaving his church (Sagittarius South Node) to pursue other studies and connections might say, "I'm supposed to stay in the congregation, even strengthen my commitment. Though I'm drawn to many things outside the faith, I have spent my life there, and I shouldn't just leave." In response, "My sense is that you have spent many lives being responsible to your faith and that is very laudable. You certainly are motivated to live what you understand as the 'right' path. The question, though, is whether the continuation of the current path is truly 'right' for who you are now, and what you are becoming. Is it possible that your faith can be seen like your 'roots,' and now you are blossoming and diversifying (Gemini North Node) to *complement* your path? I'm not sure it's a black and white issue, being part of

323

the Church or not. You wouldn't be abandoning the foundation of your experiences, just adding more to it. The fact that you're talking to an astrologer right now indicates a willingness to consider additional information. In my best understanding of your chart, this is not only supported, but very much the intention."

Finally, many people have challenges with living authentically due to fear of social disapproval. They are afraid of deviating from the dominant social norms and paradigms (Saturn), which can block their freedom to truly engage the transpersonal. As mentioned elsewhere in this book, my principle strategy is to discuss how love and acceptance is found within, then played out in how we project our issues onto life. Reorienting them to find love in the "projector" rather than on the "movie screen" is a frequent conversation I initiate. I mention that the way to reconcile the karma of conformity is to live in accordance with one's truth, even if it garners marginalization or disapproval. The inner foundation of love is the springboard to awakening, and letting the chips fall where they may with non-attachment actually resolves the karmic issue. Ultimately, the people who can now connect at a soul level will show up. So the underlying need for connection will be met with people who are more consistent with who the client is becoming.

I am Willing

Building from the section above, the "I am willing" technique is designed to assist the client in accepting the challenges that the chart outlines. Most of the time the ego resists what is most difficult in order to stay safe in what has become familiar. The simple act of being willing to engage the spiritual lessons can loosen habitual contraction and set an entirely new life trajectory.

The chart displays the dynamics already in place on the birthday, stemming from past lives. Our historical patterns tend to replicate in the present life, and allow us the chance to resolve them through more conscious navigation. However, most of us have little knowledge or recollection of our past lives, so we believe what is happening is completely new.

Strategizing how best to approach the complexities of the present landscape is helpful, and certainly a part of counseling. However, the advantage the astrological counselor has is a view into the spiritual context regarding *why* such patterns are present. It can be a most humbling and surprising realization for the client to learn that what they most fear *has already happened*. Some clients may become dispirited by the thought that (in their mind) they have previously "failed" at a particular lesson.

If there is any concern about failure, it is helpful to reframe the good/bad judgments into an understanding of the development from unconsciousness to being more awake. I reinforce that we all start out in our spiritual childhood and it is universal to have lessons on the table. In fact, our work is better able to reach resolution when the past is accepted without judgment. One way to do this is to look at the present iteration of the lesson and be willing to experience *any* outcome, including one that may be overwhelming or construed as "failure."

"I am willing to…." "be wrong," "fail," "lose money," or "get hurt." Whatever underlying issue the ego is strategizing to avoid can be made overt and, thus, accepted. Occasionally I'll mention the issue of rejection in my own chart. I'll state that I'm now willing to have people dislike me, dismiss or reject me, or see me as misguided or crazy. "I'm willing to be a laughingstock!" Clients tend to be softened by this admission and it models the process for them. I explain that when we are willing to have these things happen, *we release the energy involved with their prevention,* and the chances of them actually occurring decrease.

The lessons of the Moon are at the emotional level. Maturation occurs when we are no longer resisting life. If we're unwilling to venture from a contracted place, we may unconsciously bring the issue into our lives (through our solar radiance) so we can face it. Another option is to face it internally. A willingness to face the issue may put an emotional process in motion that helps move the past through, enabling us to create what we want. Thus, we reframe emotional management from something unappealing to something which promotes spiritual evolution.

Having the client agree that they are willing to face whatever occurs is one step. Declaring it is another. If it feels appropriate and the client is willing, I might ask them to state it outright. "I'm willing to fail in order to follow my dreams."

The next step is for the client to follow up with what is actually desired. For instance, "I intend for my new business venture to be successful." The technique actually has two steps: accepting the past, then stating intentions for the present.

Chapter 13
An Elemental Framework for
Astrological Counseling

In this chapter, we'll discuss astrological counseling with the elemental levels (earth-physical, water-emotional, air-mental, fire-soul) as the template. The philosophy is discussed at length in Chapter 1, and this framework can be useful to have in mind while working with clients. We can view every client holistically; to see their evolution in this multi-tiered way. When issues arise in the session, we can hone in on what to emphasize. The following sections are informational, while also providing further techniques and strategies for working with clients.

Earth: Physical

As the foundational level, supporting strength at the earth level is a prerequisite for broader expansion. Most people have some kind of issue with their body, possessions, bank account, self-worth or management of the earth realm. The body is the vessel of the soul. If it's ailing or compromised in some way then it requires attention. Issues of diet, exercise, sleep and all types of self-care are appropriate to discuss. Much of this is common sense, but it can be framed in terms of promoting spiritual health for broader awakening.

Along with a scarcity of self-love, I have also noticed a widespread lack of acceptance of one's body. Any rejection of self is not only abusive, it inhibits our spiritual flowering. One technique I recommend is to spend time solidifying the connection to self by consciously honoring the body. I often suggest an exercise of expressing gratitude to all parts of the body:

"Thank you legs for carrying me around, I appreciate being mobile. Thank you butt for providing me a place to sit. Thank you hands for helping me to feed myself." This can be applied to all parts of the body. These affirmations can be done in the counseling room, or as "homework."

Due to unchallenged cultural conditioning, many women are particularly prone to rejecting their bodies, and I have found this issue is quite prevalent for men as well. A way to frame the discussion is an embrace of naturalness, reminding people that they are essentially animals who need to eat, survive, mate and take care of all bodily functions and systems. Many of us have adopted a belief (often subtle) that the body is sinful, corrupt or "bad" in some way. To counteract this conditioning, we can invite them to *celebrate* their animal nature. Also, we might point out that certain spiritual paths and shamanic traditions involve totem animals, recognizing the divinity of our animal nature. Establishing a more overt and conscious link between the physical and spiritual sets the strongest foundation for development.

Most everyone could bolster their power at the physical level. We can make suggestions for clients to include massage, acupuncture, Reiki, fitness (or other modalities) in their self-care regimen. The session is not an appropriate setting for treatment and diagnosis, unless you have expertise in medical astrology (which has not been my particular focus). It's usually more appropriate to refer clients to those who have deeper expertise in health matters.

Astrology happens at the conceptual air level and speaks in an archetypal language. The more specific (earthy) a client's question, the less astrology can provide an answer. For instance, "Is my small intestine at risk for cancer?" or "Does my chart speak of chronic fatigue syndrome?" Questions of this nature are sometimes asked. To illustrate the symbolic nature of astrology, I might point directly to the chart and say, "That is a great question!

I wish I knew; all I have here is a bunch of symbols on a page. What I can offer is insight into the deeper spiritual issues around health, and also the timing of when matters may be more emphasized. With this big picture understanding, working on the details with a specialist is most appropriate." Chiron, planets in the sixth house and Virgo, tend to be most indicative of health concerns. Also, I have found the second house (earth, physical) to be relevant to matters of the body. The first house (fire) has relevance to issues of action, energy levels and the ability to move freely.

Money tends to come up in many sessions. A spiritual approach is to empower the client to attend to the deeper issues of self-worth which are at the root of being effective and valuing one's skills. Clients may ask, "Does my chart have the ability to make good money?" I might respond with, "Do you believe in yourself? Do you have confidence in your ability to follow through with what is necessary to make good money?" Then, if there is a conscious, empowered response to the chart, the astrological possibilities of manifestation can be discussed. If not, then the potentials are only potentials. It is most empowering to the client to suggest that outcomes are up to *them*. That being said, the condition of Saturn, the tenth house and planets in Capricorn have much to say on this matter, as well as Taurus, Venus and the second house.

Often marginalized, planets in Virgo and the sixth house can also be examined. They play major roles in performing tasks and developing expertise to secure income. Time management and organization are important issues to discuss with clients. Again, quite often people give their power away to what a chart may suggest. A focus on the earth realm reorients them to their own management.

Water: Emotional

The central egoic level is the emotional, and most of us are carrying around unprocessed and unresolved material. Taking efforts to cycle through and release this stuck energy allows for greater embodiment of soul intent.

There are many types of emotional experiences, with many gradations of subtlety and nuance. However, there is consensus in the field of psychology that the following emotions are foundational: love, happiness, sadness, anger, fear, disgust and surprise. Other emotions, such as disappointment, frustration or lust, are secondary and have qualities of the primaries. These seven basic emotions are universal, but do not have the same evolutionary significance. As we've discussed, love is primary and is the foundation of our spiritual condition.

Disgust and surprise tend to be fleeting, most relevant for particular situations. One could be surprised by receiving an unexpected email, or temporarily disgusted by a smell or other noxious stimuli. Happiness is a so-called "positive" emotion and people are universally in accordance with its experience. These three emotions tend to have less evolutionary significance in terms of resolving the past.

Sadness, fear and anger are the "Big Three" to focus on. All three have to do with *expectation*, which typifies ego. When we put requirements on the world, we set ourselves up for anger and/or sadness if they are not met. Then, we may fear that our lack of fulfilment will perpetuate into the future. The Big Three all have to do with time—how we petition the world to bend to our desires, and the subsequent fallout if the world doesn't deliver. The remedy is to be more fully in the present. Then, our expectations diminish, and we are able to be with what is.

If all experience is embraced as a necessary curriculum in the present moment, what's to be angry about? Without expectations, there is no grief—and when we live in the present, we don't fear the future. Though this is an ideal, most of us are still processing through the past, when this broader understanding may have not been in place.

Sadness tends to be private and repressed. Crying is "embarrassing" in cultures which promote strength and accomplishment. There is a tacit agreement to pretend we are happier than we really are, backed by powerful social conditioning which inhibits the cleansing that sadness brings. I have personally found that the expression of sadness is a major step toward being in the present. Without processing it through, we continually strategize to avoid it...and paradoxically, this creates opportunities to get upset!

There are many ways to be with sadness. We can take measures to remove any blockage to it, and it naturally pours through. We can create sacred space for this to unfold through appropriate music, breathing, candles, meditation, or whatever sets a welcoming mood. Through willingness and openness, the unprocessed sadness inside can be contacted. However, many people report very strong barriers. I suggest to be curious about the blockage, have a dialogue and befriend it. The more focus on the internal dynamic the better. Over time, resistance may be softened and the emotion can be released. I do recommend intentionally invoking sadness through particular movies or songs which tend to tug on the heartstrings. Whatever softens and deepens is to be encouraged.

Another emotion to address is fear (and its sidekick, anxiety). Fear is intimately involved with survival concerns, usually an underlying dread or deep concern that something the ego considers "bad" is going to unfold and be devastating. The focus on the future can be completely turned around on a client: What if the fears have *already* happened?

Time and again I listen to clients reveal anxiety and fear. Most of the time they are afraid of the very dynamics that the astrology chart is illustrating. So I explain to them that what they fear has already happened. As discussed in the last chapter, the astrology chart is cast at the birth moment, so the current feelings are actually unfinished work stemming from the past. To find resolution, there is a choice. We can ignore the unprocessed emotion, unconsciously radiate it out, and meet it in some guise in the present. Or we can simply be with it internally. The "I am willing" technique supports this.

Another suggestion is to confront the fear head-on. I encourage the client to do a meditation involving (what is imagined as) the worst case scenario. For instance, someone fearful about not having enough money might imagine getting evicted, being homeless on the streets and begging. Someone anxious about losing a partner can tune into various scenes of the relationship ending and learn to be with what emerges. This inner work is similar to past-life regression or hypnosis which also support *moving into* unresolved dynamics in order to process them through. Though the exercise may be thematically similar to something from a past life, it's completely unnecessary to have biographical information (from prior lives) correct. The *impact* from the past is emotional and that is what's being worked through.

The key is not just imagination, but deepening the heart into the exercise. Fear is like a *wave*—when invited up, it moves through the system. The person may temporarily be in the grips of fear, and the suggestion is to allow the system to do what it naturally does. Fear waves often move through the system like shivers. When fear emerges, we can shake it out. I encourage clients to follow its lead—to make noise, move, dance, or do whatever the energy needs to do to find release. I suggest to *amplify* the energy as a way to partner with it and move it.

332

Amplification may first appear strange or unnecessary because it's stronger than the emotion being felt. However, it creates the space for the unprocessed emotion to move into. The key is to get resistance and judgment out of the way and allow whatever may unfold.

After the systems relaxes, there are two additional steps. First, is to replace the energy just released with love, and second is to send out an intention for a course and outcome that is actually desired.

In discussing the management of anger, it's crucial to emphasize that anger is a physical, visceral, raw energy. Talking or writing about anger is helpful, but it doesn't tend to move it as much as some type of exertion. Women in particular are often conditioned not to express this energy as it's not "ladylike." So, it is helpful to discuss the benefits of pushing beyond the edge of this conditioning; to attempt to get the buried energy out, similar to processing food through the metabolic system and then burning it up through exercise.

One simple technique designed to move anger is to choose something immovable, such as a boulder or house, and suggest trying to push it. Frustration, even anger, tends to emerge in a matter of seconds. Working out, hitting a punching bag or pillow, vigorous dancing, and sexual expression are also quite energetic. The key is not just to exercise, but to be connected to the emotion while doing the expression.

Since anger tends to be raw and intense, I sometimes use a technique to invoke an uninhibited catharsis. I call it "*car*tharsis," as it entails using the container of a car for spontaneous venting. The idea is to get into a car for privacy, roll up the windows, park somewhere remote, and (with or without music playing) take the opportunity to express anger in the most authentic way. I encourage it to be unrestrained, even loud if necessary—often anger can be captured using profanity and I support that expression. Most people never get to just rant and rave. Afterwards, the system tends to feel much lighter. I have done this numerous times myself and have personally seen the benefits.

As mentioned above, when prior energy is released from the system, replacing what has left with love solidifies a more healed foundation. As "energy processing systems," we have an empty "tummy" to feed, and feeding our humanness with love and acceptance is the nourishment we most truly want.

A supportive technique I recommend to help increase the placement on the self-love scale is to go inward and make amends with the prior self for not being as loving. I ask clients at what age they have the most charge around not feeling loved, or the most issues or trouble. I say, "Sounds like s/he could have used some more support." I remind them that it really wasn't someone else's job to provide this love and support as (at the soul level) everybody is a reflection. I tell them, "It was your job all along. And the good news is that everything can be healed in the present moment—the universe did not set it up for us to eternally be prisoners of the past."

This is one place where I sometimes bring in my own experience. I tell the story about one of the most emotional experiences of my life, which happened when I did some therapy sessions which reconnected me with my little boy within, whom I had abandoned. I say, "Around age seven, I was getting information that I wasn't lovable—lots of teasing and being picked on. As a result, I hurt myself by adopting a negative self-image. So, the work I did was to apologize to my seven-year-old and ask his forgiveness for this self-abandonment. Do you know what he said? 'Yes, I forgive you,' and he told me that he wants to be more connected. So, from time to time I check in on him, to see how he is and give him updates on how his life will go. He's continually amazed to hear from me and we have a great time hanging out."

This simple sharing tends to bring more intimacy into the counseling session. It focuses energy on what is truly healing. I find that clients feel safe to be vulnerable when I show depth and humanness, and many have told me that it added substantially to the session. We can spend time cultivating love in any way that feels right. I may say, "Many people would say that they are too busy to spend time just sitting and loving themselves, but everyone goes to sleep. One idea is to simply spend five or ten minutes when getting into bed, hands on heart, circulating heart energy through your system. Also, you can silently feel your heart energy, focus in on it, and raise its vibration at any moment of the day. Breathing into it helps too. The key is that any conscious focus on loving yourself will be helpful. You can't do it 'wrong,' and there are no possible negative side effects!"

Air: Mental

The mind can take us away from Spirit or bring us closer, depending on how it's used. There is a major emphasis on learning and knowledge in our culture and many people are quite identified with their minds. The central issue at this level is the mind's relationship to spiritual awakening. There is both unlearning as well as learning in using the mind in connection with soul.

Much of what we are taught is from perspectives and paradigms at the egoic/relative level. Though completely valid, these perspectives also tend to inhibit the grasping of the transpersonal. In particular, most people instinctively evaluate life in terms of "right" and "wrong," "good" and "bad." This dualistic tendency sets up either/or scenarios for learning, yet truth is seldom black and white. For instance, both science and spirituality have their relative truths and do not have to be competitive. Challenging people to be open to multiple truths, dimensions, and seemingly contradictory understandings, promotes what the Buddhists call "beginner's mind." We can return to a sense of complete wonder about this world.

Learning to question one's thoughts is a helpful exercise. We might ultimately find that our thoughts are resonant and consistent with who we are, but why not do an internal inventory? All of what we've learned occurred prior to this present moment, when we were less mature and conscious. Why should we endlessly perpetuate what we knew then? The issue is not to reject everything which came before, but to verify its current legitimacy and complement it, just as college complements what we learned in high school. Many people have completed their intellectual curriculum at the Saturnian (relative) level, while advanced growth integrates the transpersonal.

Issues around worldly, intellectual and spiritual understandings are not always relevant to discuss within a counseling format. These topics tend to come up if the client mentions them or if the chart emphasizes lessons along the Gemini-Sagittarius (Houses 3-9) axis. The counseling session is not an arena for philosophical debate, but it can highlight issues for a client to reflect upon. Also, worldly issues tend to be secondary to how the mind thinks of the self.

Negative self-talk is rampant. It has been an eye-opener for me to see the extent that it has limited well-being. Virtually no one rates themselves a 10 on the "self-love scale." Debilitating, even abusive, inner dialogue is a main reason for that. I have discovered that most people have a critical inner judge which they are perpetually battling. Astrologically, we can think of the judge as the Saturn function which isn't fully mature. Instead of accepting reality, the less mature Saturn argues with reality and assigns blame for it not being a certain way. Criticism can be directed externally ("the world is going to hell"), or internally ("there is something wrong with me"). The work is for the judge to gain enough maturity to cooperate with the spiritual curriculum that the self is actually co-creating. Saturn can be oblivious to the Uranian level which it orbits within.

It's important to acknowledge the role of the judge, which is mainly to help us improve. It is helpful to look at where we have not made the mark, behaved unprofessionally or irresponsibly. Historically, this tends to be played out with parents, teachers or other authority figures. The issue is that the judge tends to be only focused on immediate results (Saturn), rather than on a broader perspective of spiritual evolution. It holds very high standards, which only those at a highly developed level can meet. As Saturn/Capricorn forms a natural opposition to Moon/Cancer, it is the inner child, doing her best to mature as she goes, that receives the brunt of a critical judge.

It is quite common to hear the client's judge make statements that they *should* be better in some way. In response I might say, "This judge of yours has such a crucial job—to help you do things well. However, this judge seems to not be operating from the perspective of spiritual evolution—it's much more concerned about performance. From a developmental view, we are all operating at a particular stage or level. Our behaviors and performance extend from this level, simply a reflection of where we are in our growth. An acorn goes through a lengthy process in becoming a tree. It doesn't have to be a tree before it's grown, right? And you can be anywhere in your developmental process too. Judgments are completely unnecessary and, frankly, abusive. Here's an idea: instead of judging, how about simply looking at yourself as a work in progress, which is universal? Sure, we can all do certain tasks more adeptly, but our self-talk can be more loving too."

Shifting the workings of the judge may take time as the mental "wiring" can be strongly ingrained. There are several techniques to question the mind and the "stories" we have about ourselves. I have found "The Work" by Byron Katie to be a very effective way to inquire into our thoughts, to see that they are not necessarily true. In fact, the opposite of what we think about ourselves may in fact be as true, or *more* true! The technique can be found in Byron Katie's book, *Loving What Is*, which I frequently recommend.

Sometimes people say they have done "The Work," or another technique to shift the mind, but to no avail. I have found that it may take a lot of repetition, as some patterns and habits have been in place for lifetimes. A person is building new neural connections, which is a mental workout, analogous to building new muscles. I recommend that people do "The Work" on a frequent basis for as long as necessary. Also, writing down your answers to Katie's four questions is much more effective than doing it verbally or silently.

Not only can we shift our thinking to be more loving, we can also learn to loosen our attachments to the mind's workings. We can develop greater non-attachment from our thoughts, to lessen the identification with mind and simply see it as a helpful tool. Most people identify with their mind, they believe that the little voice in their head is who they are. Astrology teaches us otherwise. The Sun is our life energy, who we really are. If the Sun were a boulder, Mercury would be a little tiny pebble next to it, kind of like a sidekick. We can learn to identify as the presence and awareness of our soul connection to life, which is quite an upgrade from the little rational mind. Then, we can see the mind (and all of the planetary functions) as a tool we can use, not so different than a wrench. If you are using a wrench to fix a bike, you are not the wrench, you are just using it to help you accomplish something. Same thing with the mind. It's a really helpful tool for humans to navigate life, but it doesn't have to be our identification.

A common analogy is that the sky is who we are, a vast spaciousness which contains our experience. The thoughts are like clouds—they drift by and continually shift and change. We can learn to just observe our thoughts, as if they were clouds, without attaching, or giving our power away, to them. We can see the mind as endlessly fascinating with non-attachment.

The mind relates to perception and we can learn to view the world differently. One way to promote greater freedom is to suggest to a client to see the "movie" phenomenon being projected from others. "What if you imagined everyone you meet as being like the Sun, radiating out their astrology chart, their energetic attunement, onto all of life? You can then see that they are *creating* their experience of life, including *you*. You can learn to view this as incredibly interesting, without taking any of it personally. You might also learn to see that you are doing the same exact thing yourself." We can receive life as a teacher, pointing us back to the self, instead of getting lost in developments of the personality level on the movie screen.

Fire: Soul

As discussed earlier, supporting the solar curriculum portrayed in the client's chart is a path toward soul realization. Growth at this level involves bringing awareness and presence into active embodiment, to be fully of this world in connection with the soul self. On the way to that promise, it is helpful to develop ways to be more connected with our divinity.

Mindfulness is learning to be aware of what is actually happening in the present moment. There are many ways to be mindful, from savoring each bite of food to paying close attention to nature. Advocating some type of mindfulness practice can only be supportive. In a culture which tends to support "doing," mindfulness involves simply "being." I might ask the client how often they take some time to simplify and just be.

Contemplative practices of all varieties are found at this level. There are dozens of traditions and techniques. Instead of getting into specifics, or advocating a certain spiritual path, a brief and general discussion is more appropriate. The elemental framework (physical, emotional, mental, spiritual) is a basic and easy way to enter a dialogue. When we rest the body, still the heart, and quiet the chatter of the mind, we might connect more strongly with the presence of the soul. The body, heart and mind are not abandoned, but are nourished by presence, just as a flower is supported by sunlight.

The soul operates *intuitively*—providing a sense of alignment with our essential self, and greater connection with the "field" of presence/awareness which envelopes us. Spiritual practice potentially attunes us to the "divine GPS" which can direct our lives. Practitioners may limit the habitual patterns of distraction and entrenchment in the personal story in order to be open to their inner wisdom.

If asked what practice I do myself, or recommend, I suggest a form called *True Meditation* advocated by the teacher Adyashanti (and described in his book of the same title). I explain to clients that it's a non-denominational approach that promotes openness to one's inner experience without judgment or resistance; a practice of learning to allow what is.

There are other ways to use the energy of the present for deeper healing and integration as well. One exercise I suggest is what I call *"spiritual time travel"* –a technique designed to use the awareness of the present to go back and heal the past.

At the transpersonal level, everything happens in the present moment. Through the Sun (presence, awareness) we can access the feelings and qualities of prior moments and bring them

340

into the now. Imagine a veteran who hears an explosion and temporarily has the sensation of being at war again. Similarly, moments from the past can fill our current experience as if they are happening now.

The "spiritual time travel" exercise involves using imagination to enter the most unresolved moments from the past, as if it were a movie. I encourage the client to get into a relaxed meditative state and breathe into these moments, imagining them in the mind's eye. As the scene replays, the "character" in the drama is likely to be scared, upset or angry — the key is to allow whatever emotions are part of the drama to emerge. These emotions can be let out and replaced with love, which is what the person wanted in these moments all along. They might pause the scene at intense moments and have a dialogue with the self about what is occurring, reassuring the "character" that it's going to be ok. They might even tell the "character" why the "future" self is visiting the scene. It can be explained that the moment actually stems from innocence, when the self was less conscious and loving, and that it's totally OK. The next part is to forgive the other characters in the movie for not being so loving, and to thank them for playing their roles so well.

I suggest that clients choose the top five to ten unresolved moments in their biography, whatever intuitively feels right, working their way up to the most difficult. The deeper they are able to go into them, the greater the resolution available. Some clients ask about venturing into past lives through hypnosis or regressive techniques. I tell them that the energetic themes are radiated out in the present lifetime, so that is a great place to start. If they feel compelled to explore past lives, healing is available there too.

Another issue at the soul level is gratitude, which tends to emerge when issues are resolved. Upon successful processing of the past we feel lighter. Instead of thoughts like, "that shouldn't have happened," the opposite emerges: "I accept that it happened." We understand why we co-created the experience as part of our spiritual curriculum.

When a client is unresolved with an issue, it's very difficult to arrive at gratitude for the experience. Processing the emotion needs to come first. Who can genuinely feel the peacefulness of love and acceptance with a fireball of anger in the belly?

To take it a step further, we might even *choose* the experience. What was initially unacceptable is now what we would want to have happen—an amazing turnaround! The ego tends to put an agenda onto the universe and tries to hold on to the past. Operating in connection with the soul involves choosing everything we are currently co-creating, and accepting everything that we created earlier too. Much of the work at the soul level is to completely abide with "what is," and take full responsibility for the entire spiritual journey.

Another facet of arriving in the present is to let go of the coping habits from our past. Whether in the form of eating, smoking, hiding or over-working, we all have certain patterns leftover from the spiritual childhood. The habitual nature of these patterns can unwittingly keep us tethered to a prior state of development, one from which we may be maturing. To complete the growth, two things are necessary. First, we can address these habits through lifestyle change and, second, feel the emotions which the coping mechanisms are defending. Both of these can be challenging, but the rewards are great. Consciously letting them go brings an individual into the present to live who they are now. Renewed health, clarity and alignment with soul intent allows energy to be directed more effectively. It can be a rite of passage to give up particular habits, and give birth to a more awakened self.

Chapter 14
Counseling Issues

In this chapter we'll addresses some additional issues which can emerge during an astrological consultation. I'll give my perspective on some frequently asked questions, and then discuss some of these matters in greater detail. We'll review some helpful counseling tips and further address the role of the astrologer.

Frequently Asked Questions

Recognizing "air" vs. "ground" questions is our first topic. Clients often ask for specifics or predictions, the expectation that astrology reveals details at the mundane level. I tell clients that the chart depicts information at a symbolic level (air), while the chart owner is responsible for how things play out "on the ground." Science now tells us that the "ground" of existence is in constant flux, the "uncertainty principle" underlies our experience. It is common for the ego to want security in this uncertainty, and that is why some people seek counsel. We can answer "air" questions, which involve themes, dynamics and spiritual lessons. "Ground" questions concern details and outcomes—things which an assemblage of symbols cannot possibly address, no matter how strong our desire to know.

Astrology's history with prediction and fortune telling has given the false impression that the purpose of a chart interpretation is to furnish answers. Rather, we're able to provide *questions* for a person to ponder. Clients might ask, "Am I going to get married?" "Do you see me working in a more meaningful career?" "Am I going to move to a new area?" In response to ground questions I might say, "It's completely up to you how the chart manifests. If you're growing and advancing on your spiritual path, it will likely unfold in ways you might enjoy. And if you navigate unconsciously, then you'll simply run into what you need to learn in order to grow. You get to play your hand and sculpt the outcomes."

Still, some do persist. "OK, but how do you see it going?" When there's persistence, I use stronger language to make the point. I might say, "Again, it's really up to you. You're asking me to remove free will from the equation and I can't do that. To me astrology is *co-creative*. It's impossible for me to predict how you will partner with your own energy. In fact, the truth is you know better than anyone! Like the captain of a ship, you have a lot of navigational choices."

"Is that good or bad?" is frequently asked. It's quite easy to understand how astrology developed — to split up the facets of the system in good/bad ways in order to provide an answer. My response is, "In this approach, there is absolutely nothing in astrology that is inherently good or bad. You can look at the energies as if they were colors. Is blue better than brown? Is pink 'bad'? We can judge if we'd like, but to me, everything has a use. Astrological energies are the colors on your palette as you design the artwork of your life. Whether or not the picture comes out 'good' or 'bad' is completely up to you. Now, your personality may not enjoy some of your spiritual lessons and have a negative view on the astrological signatures which correlate. That is true at an ego level, but at the soul level, learning spiritual lessons is not a 'bad' situation, is it? To me, there is nothing to fear in astrology — it's all just energy in partnership with your psyche, to assist your growth."

Another frequent type of question involves the repetition of spiritual patterns. "Are you talking about *past* lives or *this* life?" The opening spiel is the best place to address this. I might say that we are looking at the themes and dynamics coming into the *present* life, which play out in some way for us to integrate the lessons and grow. Nevertheless, many are not accustomed to looking at life in this way, so clarification during the session is sometimes needed.

Clients might recognize the themes being discussed in their present life and ask for specifics about past lives. "Was I a slave in the South?" I address it in this way, "Your chart is an illustration of your energetic composure at the moment of your birth. It builds upon your spiritual past, but does not give details. It's just a bunch of symbols on a page. I have no idea what actually transpired in your past lives, which may number in the thousands, or even millions. What we see is the *impact* of those experiences, how the spiritual history has so far been absorbed and navigated in a more general sense. Your energy becomes radiated out to shape your reality, so the lessons and themes tend to become replicated in the context of your present life. The more you grow, the less the themes and lessons from the past define your life."

Clients sometimes ask if their chart is somehow different than others, for instance more wounded or gifted. I respond that we are all made from the same energies, just in different combinations. Everyone has challenges and potentials. The issue is not what the chart portrays, but how conscious the person is who inhabits it.

"Am I an old soul?" Again, *the person's consciousness is not detected on the chart*, it interacts with the energetic layout that the chart reveals. I might tell a client that a mouse could've been born at the same place and time and have the exact same chart. Putting forth the idea of co-creation with the energies is a very frequent discussion. Many people are looking outside themselves for answers. It is challenging, but also very supportive, to direct them back to the self.

Giving Advice?

It is quite common for clients to ask for advice, which brings up questions about the role of counseling. Is it the job of a counseling astrologer to influence decision making? Yes, and no…complicated! Recall the divide mentioned above between air and ground questions. We can highlight and give focus to what the spiritual dynamics are from the bird's eye perspective, while empowering clients to run the everyday specifics of their lives. I see my job as giving voice to the chart, which doesn't tell a person what to do. However, we can encourage them to follow their heart as they navigate the "ground."

How do we champion the conscious path and not (subtly, or not-so-subtly) tell them what to do? Sometimes the more conscious path is painfully clear given the themes of the chart and the client's life. It might be incredibly difficult not to inject an opinion! Whether a divorce, a move, or a career change, the session can produce moments of realization for the client. It's important not to rush their process.

Many times the spiritually mature path for a client becomes clearer to them and they want to seize a new direction. It is scary to think of making a major shift, so the vulnerability of the personality tends to come forth. "What do you think I should do?" Even in the situations which seem like no-brainers, completely obvious, it's best to have the client arrive at their own conclusions. Then, we can affirm by asking, "Does that feel good in *your* heart?"

There are occasions when a client might strongly petition the astrologer to give advice, "So let's pretend you were in my shoes, what would YOU do?" I might counter with, "This isn't about me. It's not my job to tell you how to engage the possibilities on your path. What is right for me may not be what is right for you. Only you ultimately know your own truth."

However, we can *affirm* the decisions a client makes. When they come to a decision or state an intention we might say, "That choice completely fits the trajectory of growth I see in your chart. Makes sense. Not only is this in line with the intentions, it will likely be successful because you will be living more of who you really are."

There are clients who are not engaging their charts very consciously and are highly invested in their established patterns. The astrologer can lovingly prod the client to imagine new possibilities consistent with the promise of the chart. It can ignite insight or change, or at least have them pause and think. Painting a portrait of the most conscious manifestation of the chart does not constitute "telling people what to do," but there's a deeper dynamic to consider: Sometimes people do arrive at life-altering realizations. It's one of the gems of this work—to be a part of such major turning points. With the gift comes a responsibility. It serves us to check our own process. Do I have an agenda for the client? What is it? Why? Having a solid sense of self-awareness is a foundation to this work.

Self-Awareness

Conventionally, the astrologer is the expert and the client is in a receptive role, a dynamic which is true at the relative level. However, the transpersonal viewpoint reveals that the astrologer is also interacting with *the self* through the client and the session. In fact, we will often draw in clients who reflect our issues and the current activity going on in our charts. What is being said to the client is what we may need to hear for ourselves!

With deep self-awareness and a thorough knowledge of one's own chart, this dynamic is identified for what it is. It doesn't need to be changed, rather worked with consciously. When the curtain is pulled back, we know that our own lessons are being brought forward. Continually checking in with the self is helpful, and here are some questions to keep in mind: Do I have an agenda for this client because I want to resolve the same issues? What part of me is being represented in this client? How do I really feel about this part? Am I over-identified with the client, or have I distanced myself because I'm uncomfortable with this part of me? What are my current lessons? What is the most conscious approach to them?

We can bring self-awareness to the session by striving to conduct it from the most centered place. Taking time to breathe, meditate, or utilize other means to become aware of one's own process can be helpful. Identifying potential triggers ahead of time shows responsibility, and carrying an attitude of non-attachment regarding the client's path is a goal.

On a few rare occasions I have rescheduled with clients because I didn't feel as centered and clear as I knew I could be. It's ok to "call in sick," for physical or emotional reasons. "I want to give you my very best," is received with gratitude from clients. It is good etiquette to reschedule as soon as possible. If you find this happening a lot then consider holding off on taking clients for a while.

Personal Sharing

From the air level, the astrologer has a bird's eye perspective and can see the spiritual landscape a client travels. It is appropriate to be *non-attached* to any outcome, which is very different than *detachment* (being removed and cold). Authenticity and accessibility support the client, connecting in human ways deepens the exchange and impact of the session. It's suitable to share personal information when it *supports the client's process and adds to the session.*

As described earlier, a major focus of my approach is around self-love. I have repeatedly been told by clients that it was helpful for them to hear my story about loving the inner child more deeply. When I share the moment when I apologize to my seven-year-old self and ask for his forgiveness for prior abandonment, the energy with my client tends to deepen. It has the potential to establish a stronger bond, and gives them permission to share more about their own experience of this issue.

Another time that personal sharing is helpful is as a means to establishing rapport, especially at the start of a session. An astrology consultation has a lot of unknowns for people, so some lighter sharing can allow the client to feel more comfortable and relaxed. For instance, "This is your spiritual work, I'm not saying it's easy! In fact, I totally get how much of a struggle relationships are for you, believe me!"

As for sharing from the client, too much or too little both present challenges. I tell clients that the session "is a dialogue, not a presentation," so they are more than welcome to share what comes up. I ask quieter clients questions to draw them in, inviting participation but also not pressuring. Some people want only to be receptive and quiet, and I let them know that it's totally fine.

There also can be too much sharing on the client's end. When this occurs I often stop a long-winded monologue with this, "I can see that this is important for you. My concern is that too much focus on this will take away from doing a thorough job with your chart. I'm noticing how fast time is going by. How about if we continue with this later on if we have time, or we can always schedule another session if you'd like." This is one of the fine arts of counseling: being open to where a client may be going with a long reveal, versus identifying when the information has become completely tangential. It's helpful to interrupt loquacious clients for their own benefit! And often, they thank you for it.

Resistant Clients & Misperceptions

In some cases, clients can be resistant to the consultation. They generally fall into one of two groups. The first are those who are at the consultation not completely by choice. They may have received a gift certificate, a free session, or strong urging from a friend. I always invite them to share whatever is on their mind and honor their skepticism or hesitancy.

The second group are those who resist hearing information as it touches a core truth they may not be ready to explore. Some clients resist (what they feel as) being "analyzed," or told who they are, or who they are supposed to be. They might shut down or sometimes become reactive or argumentative. Maintaining self-confidence is critical. We can tap into our trust in astrology and conduct the session as if the client is a non-skeptic. If an antagonistic client throws the astrologer off center, their negative expectations are more likely to manifest.

In dealing with skepticism, I share that I was a huge skeptic myself in my younger days and know exactly where they are coming from. The most frequent objection to astrology is the belief that it's deterministic. Once again, I emphasize to clients that astrology is co-creative and reveals a partnership with nature. The analogy of the energies being like "paints" is one that tends to work. Instead of getting into more discussion, I say that it will become clearer when we get into the session, and we'll use their chart as the example. So, I basically end the dialogue before it can get too far, and the astrology itself becomes the focus.

Dealing with a broad range of clients' views about astrology is part of the job. Everyone has some sort of bias or expectation. Some do believe it's the work of the devil, and others see it as a gift from God. And everything in between too! Also, there is a broad spectrum within the field of astrology of its understanding and application. It's helpful to keep it simple. Too much discussion on philosophical offshoots does move the focus away from the chart. Engaging questions is appropriate, but keeping the focus on counseling honors the contract for the work.

The most helpful strategy for managing resistant clients is simply to come from heart. There can be a tendency to get defensive or intellectual when a client presents a challenging stance. Showing humility and open-mindedness forges a connection, while an insistence that "I'm right" leads to separation. Arguments seldom win people over, empathy and resonant astrology does. I might say, "My job is to give voice to the themes and dynamics I see in your chart. You determine if the information feels relevant and touches something in you. I don't think you should consider anything which doesn't feel right to your heart. I have no agenda for you whatsoever—only wanting to support your growth. You are welcome to tell me how I can best do that."

Since clients are mostly self-selecting, a very small percentage are resistant. However, it does happen, and it's something which needs a strategy. The best way to manage it is to wow them over!

Darkness & Sexuality Issues

Some people have very dark themes in their biography and side-stepping these can make them feel unseen, as if their experience is not being validated. On the other side of the coin, for the reserved client, too much focus on this is likely to be uncomfortable. Following the cues from the client is necessary— both verbal and non-verbal. It is their session. Meeting them at their level of comfort and disclosure is most supportive.

Counseling is not therapy. I see the role of the counseling astrologer as pointing out and discussing the overarching themes and dynamics that a chart conveys (air focus). Water is about deeper processing, which would be the terrain of a therapist or other specialist. If a client is willing to have a dialogue to attain more awareness about their issues, that would fall within the scope of counseling.

Let's say a client has a Mars/Pluto conjunction in Scorpio in the fourth house. Here's a way to address it: "Your chart portrays some harmful energy in the area relating to family. Lots of force or intensity, which doesn't feel too pleasant. Possible violation or abuse dynamics of some kind. I know this is very personal territory to open up. You don't have to share anything at all, I'm just giving voice to what I see. I get that it was very painful for you." Ending with an empathic statement is most appropriate, instead of asking them for details. The client is empowered to share if, and what, they want. Sometimes they are eager to get into it, other times they might prefer to move on. Usually they ask some additional questions and a dialogue ensues.

If the client is open to a deeper, soulful, discussion of darkness, it is a most challenging and sensitive dialogue. Many people are not mature enough spiritually to fully understand, never mind integrate, the implications. I only recommend the discussion if it absolutely feels supportive and appropriate. As it's been said, "The truth will set you free, but first it will piss you off." The conversation might trigger anger and/or grief. Let's return to the above example. The following is a hypothetical dialogue based on my experience in the counseling room, beginning with the client sharing.

"I was sexually abused by my uncle, beginning when I was around six years old. There was chaos and violence in my home. My mother was angry all of the time and my dad beat her. My brother died in a car accident when I was thirteen. My home life was a nightmare. Why in the world would anyone have to go through that? *Why* does my chart speak of these themes?"

I might reply, "It sounds absolutely horrific and devastating, my heart goes out to you. I can't possibly imagine what you went through and our talk here is not going to change it. All I can do is try to offer some perspective to assist you in making sense of it. Are you interested in exploring that?"

"Yes, that's why I'm here."

"OK. From what I can tell, you have been very interested in passion (Mars/Pluto in Scorpio). Part of you really wants to make deep, intense contact with others, is that right?"

"Of course, who doesn't?"

"Actually some might have a strong need to be a hermit, we're all different. But you are interested in passion. Great. Now, look at all of the intense contact you spoke of in the home? It's a darker or unconscious version of what you are *developing*. You see, we all are moving along a spectrum from dark to bright, waking up. Just like a child doesn't know how to drive a car or run a corporation, you too have been in a process of learning. It looks like your major is in the area of passion."

"Yeah, I want passion, but I don't want to be abused. Why was there so much abuse?"

"Your uncle and parents weren't very mature were they?"

"No, they were like children. At times, I felt more grown up than they were."

"Exactly. We all start out in what I call the 'spiritual childhood,' early in our development. My hunch is that these people are reflections of a part of you which is still resolving buried dynamics (Pluto) in your soul's history around passion."

"What do you mean by 'buried?'"

"If we start out somewhat immature, and we're interested in passion, we're not going to navigate the territory very skillfully at first. We might get hurt, angry or wounded in some way. As children, we don't yet have the psychological and spiritual skills to make sense of it and work through it, so it gets repressed. We

353

all have buried energy in the unconscious, often called the 'shadow.'"

"From past lives?"

"In my view, yes. This is your chart on your birthday, when you took your first breath. This is the area of the home (fourth house), and Pluto and Mars are there, the energies of passion. Do you want to go deeper?"

"Totally."

"This chart indicates what the soul lessons are at your birth. Now, things play out in the present lifetime at the personality level. At the everyday level, your uncle is a child molester and deserves to be in prison. Your parents were abusive, emotionally immature and irresponsible. Everything you feel is completely valid. At the soul level, there is a deeper process going on. Here, *all* of our experiences are a part of our spiritual curriculum, to help *liberate* you from the unconsciousness of your past, when you were less conscious and mature, like everyone else. Liberation involves moving the buried energy through your system. If it doesn't get out, then it can manifest as health problems, depression, suicidal ideation, you name it. Since the energy is understandably unpleasant and easy to avoid, what kind of catalyst do you think is necessary to bring it out?"

"I guess my family!"

"Exactly. The way I understand it, there are soul contracts which catalyze the necessary growth...and our personalities never get the memo; we're in the dark about it."

"You mean my soul *chose* this for me?"

"It's a lot more loving than many people are able to see. Here you are in your 30s now. Have you been with the emotions? Do you think you have grown from your childhood experiences?"

"Absolutely. I have worked through rage like you wouldn't believe. I have gone through years of therapy and I like where I am now. I have a great relationship with my husband, and we plan to raise a family in the most loving way possible."

"Looks like they have helped you move some of that buried emotion! My sense is that the soul intentions have been successful. Can I ask, do you have a lot of passion with your husband?"

"Sure!"

"I thought so. That's what you have been interested in. And the intention to raise a family in a completely transformed (Pluto) way is the conscious version of your chart. Right on!"

"So, my family growing up was teaching me how *not* to be?"

"My view is that they are 'teachers' you 'hired' to resolve what has been left over from your spiritual childhood. They played their roles perfectly to help you grow into who you are now. They helped liberate you from all of this yucky energy which has been inside you. Though things are messy at the personality level, there is actually profound love at the soul level with them—do you feel that?"

"I do. It's just such a shame that so much pain needs to occur."

"I'm not sure it 'needs' to occur. The darker potentials ideally teach us, we get the lessons, and we keep moving forward. For whatever reason, you are especially interested in studying passion as part of your curriculum, and it's easy to get caught up there. But, it's totally fine—just your version of learning. I have been doing this for a while, and let me assure you, everyone has a challenging curriculum. You're not so special."

I always like to normalize the client's experience, to let them know they are in the same boat as everyone else. The most difficult part to discuss with the client is the idea that all experience ultimately stems from within. Some people hear that they are to "blame" for their experiences, an egoic distortion of the spiritual reality. If this comes up, reinforcing the idea of innocence is helpful. Empathy is a major tool—listening to all that a person needs to reveal. Turning painful stories around to a more loving spiritual reality is truly an art. Additionally some clients want more concepts to help them understand spiritual evolution, and astrology itself can be brought in.

We can explain that there are twelve major archetypes in astrology which encapsulate all of life. It is very easy for the ego to judge the darker side of these archetypes and not see anything "spiritual" there. I suggest the reframe from "bad" to "unconscious" in viewing the dark. Also, we can point out how the ego has snuck in, both in our lives, and also in how we view astrology. There is a social bias against the unconscious manifestations of some of the archetypes (for instance, Scorpio's abusiveness, the violence of Aries, or the neuroticism of Virgo), while others are actually reinforced (the placation of Libra, the materialism of Taurus, or the attention-seeking of Leo). It is helpful for clients to see the tyranny of judgment getting in the way of spiritual learning. A brief discussion about the *range* of consciousness interacting with these archetypes can offer some perspective, but returning to support their innocence in this epic journey of awakening brings it home. Conveying a broader understanding of spiritual evolution can certainly be part of effective spiritual counseling.

Professional Boundaries & Ethics

Astrological counseling is a profession and conducting oneself as a professional raises the stature of the field itself. I do suggest the attainment of counseling credentials, and programs tend to address ethics and issues of professional behavior. However, the astrologer/client dynamic is somewhat different than what is found in conventional therapeutic or counseling settings.

The main difference is that astrology consultations are often a single session. Some counseling astrologers do serve as therapists, but we'll address the dynamic of the more singular focus where there is not an ongoing professional relationship. It's more of a big picture discussion and other professionals can be referred for deeper therapeutic exploration. It may be challenging to try to attract many clients to work with, while the gift is having an impact on more people.

Clients come through countless potential avenues. Some are referred by other clients, some are friends of friends, while others may be just choosing a local astrologer out of curiosity, or responding to advertising or a website. There is a great range and diversity of potential clients. I have consulted with teenagers all the way to octogenarians, and with people all over the world. Every client and consultation is unique, so the approach and management of issues tends to vary. We try our best to address the situations which present themselves.

I do not have an age requirement to have a session, but I would not discuss the more serious or adult themes of a chart with an immature sixteen year old. I have agreed to record my thoughts on the charts of newborn babies at the parents' request. Though I prefer to have a consultation, it is not possible to dialogue with the chart owner in this circumstance so it does resemble more of a "reading." The huge challenge is how to present some information to the parents. Many of the same empathic strategies discussed in other sections can be used.

I have chosen not to work with a few people who have come across as inappropriate or even mocking in their initial call. One inquiry went like this: "Are you going to read my palm too? Guess my favorite color? Tell me what planet I should live on?" Another person who called seemed drunk and presented as highly emotional. I had to limit her ramblings and complaints about her life, and asked her to call back at another time to discuss setting up a consult. I take measures to explain the evolutionary, co-creative, focus of this approach to people interested in fortune-telling and prediction. I agree if they say it's not a good match and want to continue their shopping. However, if they choose to work with me after this explanation, I gladly schedule.

Some people only want to trade services and it's OK to refuse if there isn't interest. Trades can be quite demanding. It can actually take several hours to do both ends of the trade, including chart preparation and travel. Some clients might ask a plethora of questions, basically seeking counsel through phone or email. I provide brief answers and explain that a session is where the topic can be explored further.

Another area for setting boundaries is with managing social contexts with clients. Some clients want to turn themselves into friends as a means to talk astrology or receive guidance. Other times it might feel appropriate to be friends. Someone who is referred by a very close mutual friend is a different dynamic compared to a "cold call" client. Another type of social situation involves metaphysically-oriented peers in the community. Networking groups or metaphysical fairs bring like-minded people together. Here, a trade might be quite welcome. Building connections with local practitioners in the community supports everyone.

What about romantic involvement with clients? From my experience in the field, I have heard of many astrologers who've become personally involved with clients. Some people would say that this boundary should never be crossed. Others suggest a waiting period before shifting from a professional role to a personal one. Whether a month, six months, or even a year, waiting allows the professional roles to recede. Yet others see it as no big deal. The theme of this book is that, ultimately, we are all learning to navigate life as the captain of our ship. *Determining our own personal moral compass for this navigation is part of the job.* I am reluctant to propose ethical standards for others to follow, life is simply more complicated than that. I encourage a deep and honest internal inventory of what feels right.

Another consideration is where to conduct sessions. Many astrologers rent office space, which is a terrific option. I have been comfortable seeing clients in a home office. In my case, a very large percentage of my clients are on phone or Skype. It hasn't made sense to rent additional office space, so I haven't. As mentioned earlier, astrological counseling is different than therapy, due to the singular focus. Also, I have had a separate studio area away from the house which creates further boundaries. Again, everyone will have to manage what feels comfortable. There is a wide variety of ways to be an astrological counselor, many potential facets to the job and countless ways to interact with clients. Having your heart serve as the compass is always a good policy.

The Role of Astrologer

Being an astrologer does involve a cosmic or metaphysical orientation not found in many other fields. Whereas the field of counseling is conducted more within a Saturnian framework, astrology brings in other dimensions—conceptually, spiritually, and even personally. Astrology is Uranian, as seen with its inclusion at metaphysical fairs, spiritual ceremonies, or parties.

At this point, astrology is not a part of the mainstream. It has a unique culture and role in society which separates it from more conventional occupations. However, the role of the astrologer may be shifting. Certainly, it is becoming more professional. More and more astrologers have counseling credentials or other qualifications which were not as widespread in times past. How do we strike a balance between the Uranian and Saturnian elements of the field? How can we be cosmic and unconventional, while also contributing positively to the field's professional reputation?

To me, astrologers are currently redefining the field in the 21st Century. It is unknown where it will go, but it does seem to be gaining in acceptance. My sense is that the younger people on this planet are far more progressive and oriented towards the transpersonal than those who are older. As time goes by, they will increasingly inhabit positions of influence. I sense that astrology will become more integrated within culture in more complex ways—quite different than the entertainment and Sun sign focus we have previously seen.

The role of the astrologer is to not only conduct oneself professionally (Saturn), but to represent the collective shift towards the spiritual which is occurring (Uranus). We are *bridging worlds*, in terms of supporting individual growth, as well as being part of a global trend. To me, it is a very unique role, one with great responsibility. A theme of this book is to transform from within. The renewal of astrological counseling is found in the heart. It is my great hope that the focus on self-love put forth here will proliferate—not only in how we approach clients and charts, but ourselves too. The revolution is an "inside job," and the world will reflect this back. The role of the astrologer will shift according to the evolution of consciousness, and it's exciting to be here at this time of history to be able to watch this development.

Chapter 15
Discussion

The final chapter aims to wrap it all up, and provide a discussion of some issues which emerge with this approach. With anything new and unfamiliar, there can initially be some confusion or misperceptions. So, the first part of this chapter is to address some of the misperceptions I have heard. Most people do not perceive or receive the world from a transpersonal viewpoint. For instance, try asking somebody if they understand the entire world as their own consciousness. It is a process to integrate this perspective—after all, it's a big shift!

After clarifying what this approach is <u>not</u>, the next part of the chapter is to summarize what it actually is. My vision of this work will be offered in a concise way. I realize there has been a fair amount of repetition of some of the key points—it was intentional. The same is true of this summation chapter. Just as we learn a new language by practice, new neural pathways of understanding and perception are strengthened through repetition.

Finally I would like to offer some words about my personal process. It has been an incredible journey for me to arrive at this culmination point in my work. Some biographical information is included, as well as my chart. You will see that I, too, am teaching exactly what I am learning.

Misperceptions

I joke with myself that I have become an "egologist," someone who studies how the ego has injected itself into life. The first volume of this series is a discussion of the ego's projection into astrology itself. Suffice it to say, it hasn't always been the most popular message! It has been a challenge for me to present and clarify the transpersonal perspective. I have experienced some misperceptions of the message, various ways in which the more frequent egoic perspective hears and interprets what is being offered.

The first and most obvious egoic distortion I've had to address is seeing the ego itself as negative. The point has been made numerous times in this book, but to restate, the ego is simply the organization and maintenance of the separate self. It is beautiful, necessary, and part of our humanness. *The issue is the over-identification with ego at the exclusion of what is beyond.* The overarching view is that nature (and its parts) is not positive or negative—the consciousness which interacts with nature can either distort and mismanage, or partner in more awake ways.

We are not "leaving the Moon to become the Sun." That would be impossible. How could we leave our physical, biological, human system? Again, the issue is identification (and attachment). When we are 50 years old, we no longer *identify* as a five-year-old, but the inner child remains. A butterfly no longer identifies as a caterpillar, but the same organism is now able to fly. We can learn to identify as an energy body (Sun); awareness and presence itself. We maintain a connection with the physical (Moon), but not as our sole identity. As we exist in physical form, we are bridging worlds, so there is no "leaving." In fact, we are creating "heaven" on "earth," so the point is to be completely grounded on the earth plane to create tangible expressions of evolution. *The interaction with the relative realm is where lessons reach completion.*

I have also heard the misperception that, in this approach, "The Moon is bad and the Sun is good," or "There is a preference for light over shadow." Again, there is nothing wrong with being human—the issue is the misuse of our lunar defense mechanisms which contract us and limit our growth. There isn't a preference for light; rather we are becoming more conscious as we advance through the liberating channel. Darkness is where we begin—it has tremendous evolutionary value as we find our true self within it. It's not to be avoided, rather explored fully and loved so we can blossom. Also, the Sun has been misused, distorted, and reduced to personality and ego, what I call the *egoic takeover*. None of this makes it "bad" either. Any value judgments are completely unnecessary and certainly not the point of this approach.

We exist within separation consciousness, where dualisms are part of life. Some people insist that a transpersonal perspective is suggesting that "good" and "bad" are being negated and bypassed, or "the transpersonal is not operating in the real world." The Saturnian realm is not only completely honored and valued, it is actually where the focus is! Saturn orbits within the organizational matrix of Uranus, the dreaming process of Neptune and the evolutionary urgency of Pluto. The transpersonal *informs* what happens in the relative realm. *Positive and negative are brought to a broader context*, not eliminated. In contrast, the dominant paradigms on this planet (including what is found in conventional astrology) tend to negate the transpersonal.

Another criticism is that the approach focuses on awakening and liberation while excluding manifestation and being. I can see where this is coming from. The scope of this approach addresses the geocentric chart, which is geared towards the reconciliation of egoic issues as consciousness evolves (liberation). The heliocentric chart relates to manifestation and being, which are equally important. A thorough analysis of heliocentric astrology will be addressed in a future volume. As for enrollment in the liberating channel—we do have to effectively maintain and strengthen our biological system (Moon) to be clear vessels for spiritual creativity. Again, there is no "leaving," the issue is resolving attachments and identifications which preclude awakening.

I have also heard that this approach is "taking the masculine and feminine out of the Sun & Moon." Once again, *the transpersonal perspective does not eliminate the relative, but adds to it.* From the relative vantage point of the Earth's surface, the Sun and Moon appear equal, a complementary pair which correlate with yang and yin, masculine and feminine.

Another criticism is that the transpersonal is "overly optimistic about the realism of the human condition," a frequent critique of "new age" thinking, often called "spiritual bypass." I believe it is very clear in this book that this is not the spirit of the *Awakening* approach—quite the opposite. I suggest the attainment of counseling credentials and experience in the field. I have personally spent my entire adult life being a counselor in the trenches of the realism of the human struggle. I worked for twenty years in the mental health field, including twelve years on a psychiatric unit dealing with the most severe pathologies on the planet. Again, the addition of a transpersonal perspective does not negate our humanness, but adds broader spiritual meaning to our experiences.

I have heard that this approach "is not rooted in the tradition." The intention is to *build* on the tradition, similar to the progress and advancement found in every field. All of the planets, signs, houses, aspects, etc. are exactly the same. This criticism would have to be extended to all versions of modern astrology which have a person-centered or humanistic focus.

I have heard the argument that "not using the system of essential dignities disregards the realism of planetary placements." The thinking is that there are definite challenges (and benefits) to some placements which cannot be ignored. Yes, life within the Saturnian realm is valid. If we're to flatten the variable of consciousness and look at the system in terms of what is advantageous for self-gain, these designations are relevant. As discussed at length in *Volume 1*, I believe the exaltations seamlessly reflect the Patriarchal Value System which has been dominant on the planet for centuries. If the motivation of astrological counsel is to maximize gain within this framework, then it's appropriate to use the system of essential dignities. If we want to support spiritual growth, then it's appropriate to move from Saturn to the transpersonal where we level judgments and bring in the variable of consciousness.

Judgments and rankings disregard the chart owner's consciousness as the co-creative variable. When we fully implement the spectrum of consciousness (dark to bright), it becomes clear that all chart factors manifest in challenging or advantageous ways, *depending on the consciousness of the chart owner*. Astrology "works" with animals, which is a different form of consciousness animating the chart. A dog with Mercury in Virgo is not going to write the *Declaration of Independence* better than Thomas Jefferson, who had Mercury in Pisces. *There is a conscious side to everything in astrology*, and all judgments about astrological factors potentially undermines this reality. In this approach, everything has evolutionary value. We all have the perfect charts for our growth—there's nothing "bad" about having a particular energetic attunement to learn certain spiritual lessons.

Though it was addressed in earlier chapters, it bears repeating, because I have heard the criticism that, in this approach, "the Ascendant isn't important." The issue is the identification with the mask, believing who we pretend to be. The Ascendant is one of the four directions on the chart, showing how planetary energy is dispersed into the world. It is a house cusp, not a planet; *planets are about consciousness*. My view is that we need to be more careful about conflating the Ascendant with how we understand planets. The Ascendant (and the first house) correlates with Mars and Aries, which concern behavior choices, action and personal assertion. I don't believe this archetypal grouping is more important than any of the other eleven. It has been seen as more important due to the "me-first" orientation we are waking up from, the folly of only identifying in our separateness. All of the house cusps are important and relevant within their scope.

A Vision for 21ˢᵗ Century Astrology

The collective consciousness is evolving. All of our paradigms, methods and ways to navigate life are gradually going to reflect it. We can look at history and see how consciousness has progressed through the various Levels in the evolutionary trajectory in which we are living.

Change is constant. To me, the question is not if something *should* change, but *how*? Astrology has the potential to not only keep up with the times, but to actually lead us forward. There is a palpable hunger for deep spiritual meaning and experience in the collective right now. The next frontier for astrology is how to further meet that desire. The aim of this approach is to clarify how astrology can be understood and utilized at a transpersonal level (Level 7), which does shift from more "ground" uses (prediction, wanting certainty, self-gain, reliance on left-brain, dualism, relative orientation, mainstream value system, seeing the world as separate), to more fully incorporating "air" (archetypal focus, uncertainty, spiritual evolution, dreaming processes, Oneness, transpersonal orientation, beyond consensus reality, seeing the world as the self).

We are gradually entering the "Age of Aquarius," though there is debate as to when it actually starts—and some perspectives vary by hundreds of years! Nevertheless, the astrology of the 21ˢᵗ Century certainly emphasizes the

Uranus/Aquarius archetype. The planet Uranus recently entered Aries which is a signal of renewal. The current square to Pluto is highlighting the friction between past and future. In 2020 we begin to see further cementing of Aquarian principles in our collective milieu with the Jupiter/Saturn conjunction initiating a 20-year cycle. Pluto empowers whatever it touches, while also revealing the darker components. It will enter Aquarius in 2023 and will be there until 2044. Immediately following, Pluto enters another transpersonal sign (Pisces) and will be in opposition to Uranus for several years, the half-way point of their epic cycle which began in the 1960s.

At this point (2015), our task is to address the inclusion of the transpersonal. The spirit of Aquarius is to have *universal principles* as our guide. That has been motivating the *Astrology of Awakening* approach, and a review of some key points follows.

Aldous Huxley writes, "Rudiments of the Perennial Philosophy may be found among the traditionary lore of primitive peoples in every region of the world, and in its fully developed forms it has a place in every one of the higher religions. A version of this Highest Common Factor in all preceding and subsequent theologies was first committed to writing more than twenty-five centuries ago, and since that time the inexhaustible theme has been treated again and again, from the standpoint of every religious tradition and in all the principal languages of Asia and Europe."

The basic idea is that Oneness is found within separation and is gradually discovered and integrated consciously. The gradual discovery involves the evolution of consciousness, which advances through increasingly less egoically-focused stages. Huxley points out the principle issue is to resolve the "me-first" focus which typifies earlier stages. He writes, "It is only when we have renounced our preoccupation with 'I,' 'me,' 'mine,' that we can truly possess the world in which we live.....provided that we regard nothing as property. And not only is everything ours; it is also everybody else's."

There have been numerous philosophers, scholars and theorists who have put forth ideas about how consciousness advances and matures. From Meister Eckhart, to Sri Aurobindo, to 20th Century psychologists, to some astrologers, many have attempted to clarify this motion. I don't believe there is one right answer, but some kind of schema is necessary to go by. I choose to use the model put forth by transpersonal philosopher Ken Wilber, as his cross-cultural, historical breadth of world knowledge is matched by his depth of spiritual understanding and personal experience. The Nine Levels discussed throughout this book have proven to be a solid and reliable guide for the journey.

Astrology is not included in most evolutionary models of consciousness. The elemental levels I put forth (earth, water, air, fire) fit seamlessly into the evolutionary ascension of a liberating channel towards spiritual realization. All of this occurs in the relative world, in linear time, as we spiritually mature. Also, there is the accompanying manifesting channel which is the reverse; how Oneness divides to occupy denser levels in states of separation. Understanding life in terms of the four elements (physical, emotional, mental, spiritual) is found universally, from Jungian psychology, to yogic practices, to astrology, to countless other models and applications. The integration of the Perennial Philosophy to this astrological model fits easily.

The liberating and manifesting channels respectively correlate with the relative and transpersonal. The former begins with the physical, while the latter, the metaphysical. We exist within both of these channels and we're composed of both matter and energy. As portrayed in nature, the Sun is energy while the Moon is physical. Seeing the Moon as our connection to the relative realm (separation) and the Sun to the transpersonal (awakening) is a natural correlation.

And this brings us to the big issue: The transpersonal has not historically been a part of astrology. As a result, the Sun has usually been seen in egoic ways (personality, Sun sign astrology). In fact, many see it as the ego itself! Consciousness is rightfully focused on egoic development in the earlier stages, just like a child. However, the big step on our path towards "adulthood" is to follow what Huxley (and countless others) suggests. We need to relax the preoccupation with the personal self to realize that we are *borrowing* energy. The life force is a flame which connects with all energy—indicative of how the Sun connects us to Oneness. Releasing the *egoic takeover* (identification only in separation) is the determining issue of whether we advance to Level 7.

Modern astrology has largely been organized and applied from Level 5. Here, the Sun and Moon are only seen from the relative perspective (same size, yin/yang pair), which has its appropriate scope and application in terms of psychological dynamics. What is largely absent is a broader spiritual framework. Robert Hand says, "Modern astrology has had one really tragic flaw in addition to its inarticulate language: its complete lack of a philosophical foundation rooted in any coherent philosophical or spiritual tradition of the world."

It is my hope that the *Awakening* approach satisfies this criticism, as it incorporates the broadest consensus of philosophical and spiritual traditions throughout history. As for inarticulate language, that is part of the price of accepting the uncertainty principle. We release the stranglehold on astrology as being predictive about matters on the ground, and allow it to breathe in the air. Astrology then matures from its role of fortune-telling into clarifying our co-creative partnership. What we are really dealing with here is giving people back their free will. If that means that language is more expansive about possibilities, then that is OK with me.

I find it most interesting that the broad philosophy being put forth here does connect with forms of traditional astrology. It is simply a modern spin on the same idea. Hand has lectured on "The Ascent of the Soul," based on Greek philosophy, which follows the same basic idea of liberation and manifestation. As Huxley points out, it is found everywhere. The issue is that the astrological approach and methods we have inherited are based on the understandings and orientation of consciousness from earlier times, when the world was very different.

Saturn was understood as the farthest orbiting planet and life was generally only understood in relative (separation) ways accordingly. The emphasis is on earthy pragmatics, self-gain, and a Patriarchal Value System dominated. The Sun and Moon were understood as equal size "lights" orbiting around the Earth, and yes, people thought the Earth was flat. The parallel is a "flatland" approach which levels the depth of consciousness. The ego evaluates everything as being "good" or "bad" for one's self-interests from this leveled perspective. Here, we add the vertical dimension of the evolution of consciousness.

Too often there is competition with ideas and paradigms. Some people think in either/or terms as if traditional or modern astrology is valid. When we move outwards to fully integrate with Uranus, we don't discredit Saturn, but place it in a broader framework. *Astrology at Level 7 does not negate its relevance at the other levels.* In fact, it builds upon them, so there is reverence and appreciation. A transpersonal astrology includes the relative perspective completely, but an astrology which only understands life at the relative level excludes the transpersonal. The concentric circles of the planetary orbits is helpful in portraying this.

At the Uranian level, we understand that everything is essentially energy. Energy may temporarily take the form of matter, but all matter eventually returns to the eternal, interconnected energetic "field" which envelops all of life. The recycling of energy is consistent with the idea of reincarnation which is assumed in this approach. Reincarnation is not accepted universally, but a majority of people on the planet do agree with it. Therefore, its inclusion does bring astrology into broader congruence with the consciousness currently on the planet. In years past, our identification was more on the physical and "provable" ideas—most versions of mainstream astrology do not assume reincarnation. Therefore, the evolutionary view is undercut—the chart is not approached with this trajectory in mind. The Moon is not seen as a window into the past. Depth is leveled, and the Moon is projected outwards.

Today we know how entangled the Earth's energy is with the Moon. Instead of seeing it as a "planet" which orbits "out there," it actually forms a dyad relationship with Earth, an energetic *system* which travels together. We are surrounded by lunar energy, our initial orientation is an emotional, biological being maturing from unconsciousness. We start out completely enmeshed in ego and evaluate the entire world from this perspective. We gradually develop to understand and exist in the world from other perspectives. We learned of the heliocentric reality in the 16th Century, and ascended from the Earth's surface through air and space travel in the 20th. Many branches of science have now informed us that the world is quite different than what we previously thought (particularly quantum physics).

Throughout astrology, parallels are made between astronomical reality and deeper psycho-spiritual meaning. For instance, Jupiter is the big planet and relates to expansion, Mercury is quick like the mind, and Mars is red which correlates to passion. If we are to make these parallels with the other planets, why not with (what we now understand about) the Sun and Moon? If astrologers of yesteryear knew that 64 million Moons fit into the Sun, and the Moon reflects the Sun's light while orbiting around it, wouldn't that have been included in their approach and practice? The *Awakening* approach incorporates this broader viewpoint (transpersonal), while also preserving the relative (Earth's surface). Should we ignore what we now know about reality?

There is abundant love for the innocence and understandable perspectives from our spiritual childhood. In fact, another theme which runs through this book is unconditional self-love, particularly for the unconsciousness of our past. A central part of the vision is to have love as the foundation of our astrology. It is a sensitive topic and one easily ignored. Part of our collective development might be the courage to include it.

As we venture inward and embrace ourselves fully, this foundation of love sets the conditions for our spiritual blossoming. We become aware that we are the dreamer, projecting our consciousness through our solar radiance onto all of life. We learn that we are interacting with the self through the world, each of us the writer, director and lead actor of our dramas. Instead of jockeying for positive experiences, we learn to take full responsibility for experiencing loving bonds and greater unity with life. When it's found within, it becomes reflected back, just like the Moon (ego, relative realm) reflects the light of the Sun (soul, transpersonal).

And this is what it all comes down to: healing the amnesia of separation. We are all whole, there is nothing that we lack, and our hearts are connected to an endless supply of love. The more we feel and experience this, the more we will trust life. Instead of having astrology cater to the underlying insecurity or fear which can result from feeling disconnected, it can support the conscious realization of our wholeness. Instead of trying to make the best of the dream we are projecting onto life, we can realize that we are creating it, and wake up into a more conscious and co-creative navigation. I believe the astrological approach spelled out in these pages reveals each person's unique path of spiritual awakening, a significant advancement, and I sincerely hope it's considered.

I now see human behavior much differently than before. It occurs to me that almost all behavior can be construed as requests for love. It is almost entirely unconscious, and much of the time in reaction to not feeling it within. We are motivated by the most pure and innocent of all human needs. It is the way we are built, and there is absolutely nothing wrong with it. In fact, it's to be celebrated. Even more, we can make it the centerpiece of a 21st Century astrology.

Spiritual Child and Adult

The overarching theme of this book is maturation. We all develop from our spiritual childhood to adulthood, like a seed growing into a flower. The Moon naturally has a relationship with Saturn as noted in the polarity of Cancer/Capricorn. We all start out most oriented to the relative world and learn to adapt to the structures which organize life.

Today, we know that Saturn orbits within the outer planets, which have much to do with the further reaches of spiritual evolution. Saturn now assumes the role of the gateway. It brings the transpersonal energies into manifestation for us to shape evolution accordingly. Today, the spiritual adult is also such a bridge. We not only develop the inner and social planet functions to be functional humans, we also bring in the spiritual scope of the transpersonal.

Let's explore this process of spiritual maturation by contrasting the spiritual child living only within the Saturnian realm, with the adult who is able to bridge worlds.

*The spiritual child tends to want only positive experiences. The adult learns to be with what is, knowing that both "positive" and "negative" experiences serve growth.

*The child sees life outside the self as separate, the adult learns to see the world as the self.

*The child tends to be caught up in the everyday (Saturnian) world, trying to fit in and excel within established social and cultural frameworks. The adult understands that all other people, traditions, paradigms and cultural norms are in a process of evolution. The adult does not give power away to these things, but strives to make them more conscious.

*Seeing the world and others as separate, the child is prone to be competitive, trying to get ahead in the world to be viable. The adult sees others as sacred reflections; supporting and loving them benefits the self.

*The child uses the logical mind (Mercury) to evaluate life; everything is split into dualistic pairings (good/bad, male/female, right/wrong). The adult is also able to employ the lens of Uranus, which includes paradox and multiple perspectives, and sees everything as spiritually useful and part of the One.

*The child projects an early developmental view onto nature. The Moon and Sun are seen as "mommy" and "daddy" and the planets are seen as angels (benefic) or devils (malefic) who grant reward or deliver punishment. The adult retracts these projections and understands that nature is a reflection of self. The world is seen in progressively more nuanced ways.

*The child sees life as finite and death as something threatening—the aim is to survive. The adult sees life as infinite and death as a transition. The aim is to mature and grow in order to move to another adventure.

*The child takes everything quite seriously, while the adult is able to be non-attached, "in the world, but not of it." The child tends to be only identified with personality, while the adult is aware of the soul.

*The child easily falls back on defense or coping mechanisms in order to survive, maintain equilibrium or find pleasure. The adult learns to be with what is, accepting all experiences as the spiritual curriculum that the self is co-creating.

*The child blames others for triggering difficult emotions. The adult has gratitude for others for bringing up necessary emotional material to work through.

*The child has little awareness that the past is being projected onto the context of the present moment. The adult realizes that the present is a canvas to heal the past.

*The child looks to others and the world to provide love. The adult finds it within.

*The child is taught to trust authority. The adult trusts her own authority.

*The child feels he should be a certain way. The adult feels he can be completely himself.

*The child is sensitive to group pressures and wants to find inclusion. The adult is non-attached as to whether others include or not, the issue is connection to self.

*The child sees matter as the foundation of reality and finds security in a seemingly objective word. The adult understands that we're enveloped within a field of energy, matter is temporary, and one creates a subjective experience of reality.

*The child may feel a sense of existential crisis or loss with the knowledge that the world is illusory or dreamlike. The adult accepts this and sees it as a welcome challenge to continue the awakening process.

Ideally, astrology can help each person understand their path towards spiritual adulthood and the astrologer can promote its realization. I believe we are at the critical time in history when we are collectively ready to make this movement. I am not an expert on 2012, the Mayan Calendar, or other systems which put an emphasis on this time frame. However, my sense is that this period of evolution requires us to mature in order for us to survive. It is my deepest hope that astrology can be a useful tool in this regard.

About My Process

In one way or another, I have been writing this book for many lifetimes. Counseling has been the path of my soul, and this work comes at a most pivotal moment of my unfolding. It represents a culmination point, the blossoming of what began in the whispers of a dream a very long time ago. I invite you into a piece of my story.

As a youngster in school, I always wanted to help. I was drawn to the children with special needs, eager to see what I could do. I began my counseling career as a teenager, working with children with disabilities. Through college and into adulthood, I went on to work in a variety of settings in the mental health field. At my Saturn return, I graduated from Naropa University in Boulder, Colorado, with a master's degree in Transpersonal Counseling Psychology. I wrote my thesis on using astrology as a tool for counseling. I continued to work in mental health settings as I developed my own practice as an astrological counselor. Today my dream has been fully realized. I now have a busy practice and have counseled thousands of clients with the approach outlined in this work.

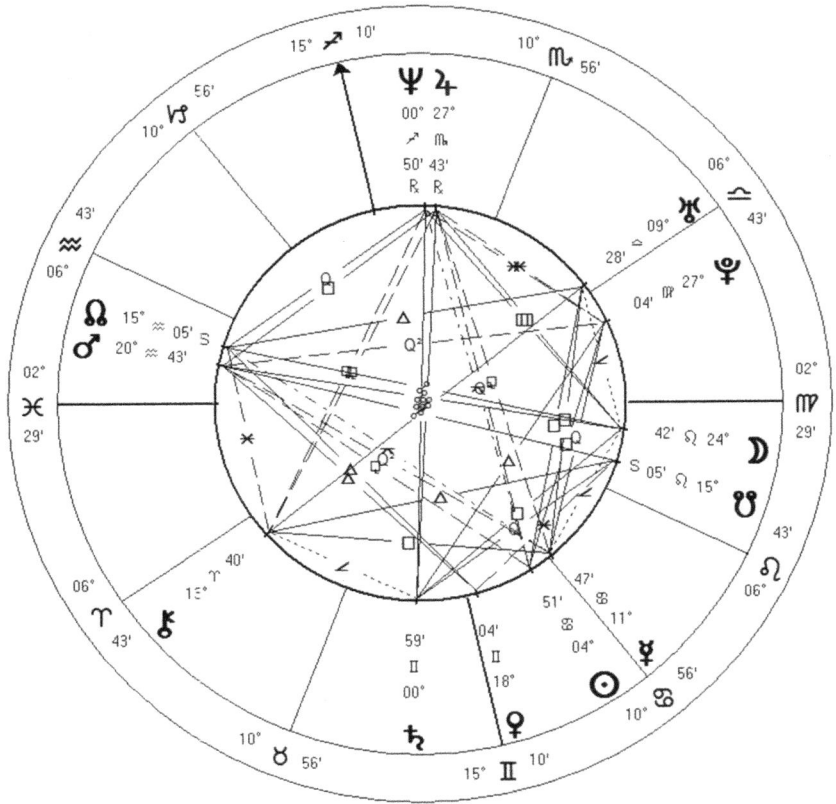

I was initially supporting peoples' needs for comfort and acceptance—basically helping people feel better. Now I lovingly but fiercely catalyze spiritual development. This is precisely the work that my own chart conveys. I have a sixth house South Node, which has to do with assisting others. It is in the sign of Leo, which pertains to the needs of the personality in its earlier development. The Leo Moon next to the South Node has a strategy of being helpful in order to be liked. The Cancer Sun (emotional support, counseling) serves as the dispositor of the South Node. I have been a counselor trying to be the good guy:

377

"What can I do to make you happy?" I would tirelessly try to help; the sixth house can be indefatigable! I became exhausted working night shifts on a psychiatric unit, helping those in very dire and devastating life situations feel a bit more comfortable. And then I began to wake up and "graduated" from it all...

My Cancer Sun is square Uranus, and the transpersonal planet serves as the dispositor of my twelfth house North Node in Aquarius. The other constant of my life has been a deep immersion in spirituality. As you have seen, I have developed an awareness of the metaphysical. From a variety of spiritual-seeking experiences to intensive study, I have been open, receptive and most hungry for Spirit. The passionate planet Mars is in Aquarius in my chart, right next to the North Node. I have wanted the freedom to dive into this terrain, and I have done so. What I discovered has been somewhat shocking. The world as we commonly experience it is simply not what it appears!

When we understand the transpersonal, we are better able to live freely. You see, I used to live in a soul cage of needing people to like (and love) me, and trying to earn that love through being helpful. This was the unconscious motivation of my early years and counseling career. When I came to realize that love is found inside of me, I released the petition that others should provide it. The freedom I am increasingly experiencing has been exquisite, and this is what motivates me now.

My path has ventured from the satisfaction of egoic/personality needs to a dedication to spiritual development. When I first became interested in astrology, it quickly became clear to me that the field seemed to mirror this trajectory. As discussed in Volume 1 of this series, much of the astrology we've inherited is blatantly and obviously about the maintenance and promotion of egoic concerns. The field could not have been otherwise, as it reflects the development of our collective consciousness. And now our evolution is at a crossroads.

We have reached the threshold of the transpersonal—primed and ready to venture beyond, no longer just trying to make the best of our imprisonment. We are entering a whole new epoch of astrology. The egoic emphasis of what we've inherited operates within another perspective entirely. To claim and integrate the transpersonal perspective, I am thrilled to have shared my thoughts in this book—a true labor of love. However, the shift does not occur through debate, fancy arguments or chart examples, but through a quantum shift in perception. It happens when you realize (at One level) that I am you. Namaste y'all. ☺

Acknowledgements

First and foremost I have gratitude for my clients, who've helped shape this approach as well as supporting me. I am blessed to have worked with so many incredible people, a great sacred honor. I also give thanks to my students and readers who have been instrumental in my astrological, teaching and writing development.

Appreciation for Amy Edwards, my editor and friend. Like an angel, you came into my life at the perfect time and were the ideal person to help see this project through. Additional editing support came from Phoebe Brown, thank you so much. As always, my good friend Bill Streett served as graphic designer for the cover and interior figures, as well as creating my new website. Your steadfast support over the years has been exceptionally valuable. Thanks to Lloyd Raleigh for many sessions as writing buddies—we're done! The back cover photograph was taken by Kathy Brodie, and given a professional touch by Clif Edwards—thank you both. Thanks to NASA for the amazing cover image, it's wonderful for the public to have access to such pictures.

Adam Gainsburg, Jessica Murray and Heather McCloskey Beck contributed endorsements for the back cover. Those words touch my heart deeply and I am grateful beyond measure to be seen as you have written. I have tremendous gratitude for all of my astrology colleagues, friends, allies and associates. Here's to the perpetuation of our beloved craft in the 21st Century, may it continue to grow and serve humanity. Thanks to Steven Forrest for being an excellent mentor and providing a solid foundation of astrological knowledge.

Finally, deep gratitude for Spirit—what a glorious, meaningful and intelligent existence. I am humbled and refreshed as I engage my process of awakening. Thank you for this opportunity, these abilities, these challenges, and all of this life.

Glossary

Awareness: An all-enveloping field, which is the context that holds all the content of the manifest world, including every aspect of our experience.

Charged: The elemental energy that aligns with the right brain, primarily involves various degrees of quality.

Consciousness: The result of the mixture of awareness with the unconscious of the separate self.

Dreambody: The connection between soul and body, (Sun and Moon), which bridges the transpersonal with the relative.

Duality: Oneness as it appears in multiple forms in the relative, manifest world.

Ego: The apparent separate self that is preoccupied with its survival and personal preferences. It correlates to the astrological Moon.

Ego dream: The experience of being caught in relative reality, unaware that the external world is a projection of the psyche. What most people simply call "my life."

Egoic takeover: The individual claiming ownership of transpersonal phenomena for personal reasons.

Enlightenment: The abiding state of complete awakening into Spirit.

Evolution: A process of incremental growth towards a more advanced stage of being. Human evolution includes healing as well as growth.

Evolutionary Astrology: A branch of astrology that asserts reincarnation and spiritual growth as the overarching human story.

Integration: The result of having processed necessary lessons sufficiently such that noticeable and consistent changes occur in perceptions, belief, and behavior.

Karma: The law of cause and effect; the natural consequences of our actions; the collection of prior behavioral tendencies that will eventually need to be addressed and integrated.

Left brain: The left hemisphere of the brain, which pertains to content, order, rationality, precision, reason, logic, temporal distinctions.

Liberation: The evolutionary channel from the physical and personal to the nonphysical and transpersonal in the sequence of earth, water, air, fire. This channel involves the evolution of consciousness in the direction of spiritual awakening.

Manifestation: The evolutionary channel that moves in the reverse direction from the liberation channel. It's most dramatic event occurs when a soul incarnates into an individual human.

Neutral: The elemental energy that aligns with the left brain, involving various degrees of quantity but not quality.

Nondual: The foundational level of reality. The Oneness that exists outside of time and space and yet also gives rise to both of them.

Patriarchal Value System: The dominant paradigm on the planet for the last several millennia. Found in many facets of culture and society across the globe, this value system is based on aggression, accumulation of material resources, traditional values, and obedience to authority.

Personal story: The narrative each of us carries about our separate self. It is usually rife with interpretations and preferences which derive from the ego.

Presence: The capacity for focusing consciousness on whatever is unfolding in the moment.

Progressive evolution: The development of consciousness through elemental levels in the process of spiritual growth.

Relative reality: The common, everyday world filled with separation, value judgments, and egoic attachments.

Right brain: The right hemisphere of the brain, which relates to process, creativity, intuition, emotion, inspiration.

Samsara: The cycle of birth, death, and rebirth.

Shadow: Any part of ourself that we'd prefer not to see and that we typically repress, deny, and project onto others.

Soul: A part of Spirit which separates to fulfill evolutionary work.

Soul cage: Staying limited in separation consciousness and orbiting around ego. The inability to move beyond creates confinement in the relative realm.

Spirit: One of many words used to describe the all-encompassing context of Existence. Other names include God, Goddess, Allah, the Creator, Brahman, the Tao, Oneness, or the Absolute.

Spiritual awakening: Loosening the identification with ego and connecting with *and identifying as* the broader field of awareness. Also referred to as "awakening."

Spiritual giveback: The reverse of the egoic takeover. The individual releases the claim of the transpersonal back to Spirit.

Transpersonal: Pertaining to phenomena beyond the personal, including soul and Spirit.

Unconscious: The deep well of accumulated experiences absorbed by the separate self.

Wholeness: The state of accepting and connecting with all of who we are, not just what meets ego preferences.

Note: The charts of famous people used in this book are consistent with Astrodatabank (and chart details are easily found on their website). All charts are cast using Porphyry house system, True Node and Parallax Moon.

Bibliography & Recommended Further Reading

Adyashanti. *The End of Your World*. Sounds True. Boulder, CO. 2008.

-----. *True Meditation*. Sounds True. Boulder, CO. 2006.

Alli, Antero. *Astrologik: The Oracular Art of Astrology*. Vertical Pool. Berkeley, CA. 1990.

Arroyo, Stephen. *Astrology Karma & Transformation*, 2nd Edition. CRCS Publications. Sebastopol, CA. 1992.

-----. *Astrology, Psychology and the Four Elements*. CRCS Publications. Sebastopol, CA. 1975.

Bogart, Gregory. *Astrology and Spiritual Awakening*. Dawn Mountain Press. Berkeley, CA. 1994.

Diaz, Armand. *Integral Astrology: Understanding the Ancient Discipline in the Contemporary World.* Integral Transformation, LLC. New York, NY. 2012.

Fernandez, Maurice. *Astrology and the Evolution of Consciousness: Volume 1*. Evolutionary Astrology, Inc. Land O' Lakes, FL. 2009.

Forrest, Steven. *Yesterday's Sky*. Seven Paws Press. Borrego Springs, CA. 2008.

-----. *The Book of Pluto*. ACS Publications. San Diego, CA. 1994.

-----. *The Inner Sky*. Bantam. New York, NY. 1984.

Foundation for Inner Peace. *A Course in Miracles*. Mill Valley, CA. 1976.

George, Demetra. *Asteroid Goddesses*. ACS Publications. San Diego, CA. 1986.

Godman, David, ed. *Be As You Are: The Teachings of Sri Ramana Maharshi*. Penguin. 1992.

Grasse, Ray. *The Waking Dream*. Quest Books. Wheaton, IL. 1996.

Green, Jeffrey Wolf. *Pluto: The Evolutionary Journey of the Soul, Volume 1*. Llewellyn Publications. St. Paul, MN. 1985.

Greene, Liz & Howard Sasportas. *The Luminaries*. Weiser. York Beach, ME. 1992.

Guttman, Arielle. *Venus Star Rising*. Sophia Venus Productions. Santa Fe, NM. 2010.

Hand, Robert. *Horoscope Symbols*. Schiffer Publishing. Atglen, PA. 1981.

Hawking, S. *A Brief History of Time*. Bantam. New York, NY. 1988.

Huxley, Aldous. *The Perennial Philosophy*. Harper & Row. New York, NY. 1945.

Judith, A. *Eastern Body, Western Mind*. Berkeley, CA. Celestial Arts. 1996.

Katie, Byron. *A Thousand Names for Joy*. Harmony Books. New York, NY. 2007.

-----. *Loving What Is*. Harmony Books. New York, NY. 2002.

Katz, Jerry. *One, Essential Writings on Nonduality*. Sentient Publications. Boulder, CO. 2007.

Le Grice, Keiron. *The Archetypal Cosmos*. Floris Books. Great Britain. 2010.

Levine, Rick. *Quantum Astrology*. Levine & Associates. Redmond, WA. 1994.

Marks, Tracey. *The Astrology of Self-Discovery*. CRCS Publications. Sebastopol, CA. 1985.

McDermott, Robert, ed. *The Essential Aurobindo: Writings of Sri Aurobindo*, 2nd Edition. Lindisfarne Books. Great Barrington, MA. 2001.

McKenna, Jed. *Spiritual Enlightenment: The Damnedst Thing*. Wisefool Press. Fairfield, IA. 2002.

Merriman, Ray. *Evolutionary Astrology: The Journey of the Soul Through States of Consciousness*. Seek-It Publications. W. Bloomfield, MI. 1991.

Meyers, Eric. *The Astrology of Awakening Volume 1: Eclipse of the Ego*. Astrology Sight. Asheville, NC. 2012.

-----. *Elements & Evolution: The Spiritual Landscape of Astrology*. Astrology Sight. Asheville, NC. 2010.

-----. *Uranus: The Constant of Change*. Astrology Sight. Longmont, CO. 2008.

-----. *Between Past & Presence: A Spiritual View of the Moon & Sun*. Astrology Sight. Longmont, CO. 2006.

Mindell, Arnold. *Quantum Mind*. Lao Tse Press. Portland, OR. 2000.

Rudhyar, Dane. *The Astrology of Personality*. Aurora Press. Santa Fe, NM. 1991.

-----. *The Planetary and Lunar Nodes*. CSA Press. Lakemont, GA. 1971.

-----. *The Lunation Cycle*. Aurora Press. Santa Fe, NM. 1967.

Sedgwick, Philip. *The Sun at the Center*. Llewellyn Publications. St. Paul, MN. 1990.

Schulman, Martin. *Karmic Astrology*. Weiser. York Beach, ME. 1979.

Tarnas, Richard. *Cosmos & Psyche*. Penguin. New York, NY. 2006.

Tolle, Eckhart. *The Power of Now*. New World Library. Lovato, CA. 1999.

Wilber, Ken. *Integral Psychology*. Shambhala. Boston, MA. 2000.

-----. *The Marriage of Sense and Soul*. Random House. New York, NY. 1998.

-----. *A Brief History of Everything*. Shambhala. Boston, MA. 1996.

Yogananda, Paramahansa. *Man's Eternal Quest*. Self-Realization Fellowship. Los Angeles, CA. 1975.

Zukav, Gary. *The Seat of the Soul*. Simon and Schuster. New York, NY. 1989.

-----. *The Dancing Wu Li Masters*. Morrow Quill. New York, NY. 1979.

CPSIA information can be obtained
at www.ICGtesting.com
Printed in the USA
LVHW020723041021
699444LV00008B/452